Kubeflow for Machine Learning
From Lab to Production

Trevor Grant, Holden Karau, Boris Lublinsky,
Richard Liu, and Ilan Filonenko

Beijing · Boston · Farnham · Sebastopol · Tokyo

Kubeflow for Machine Learning

by Trevor Grant, Holden Karau, Boris Lublinsky, Richard Liu, and Ilan Filonenko

Published by O'Reilly Media, Inc., 1005 Gravenstein Highway North, Sebastopol, CA 95472.

O'Reilly books may be purchased for educational, business, or sales promotional use. Online editions are also available for most titles (*http://oreilly.com*). For more information, contact our corporate/institutional sales department: 800-998-9938 or *corporate@oreilly.com*.

Acquisitions Editor: Jonathan Hassell	**Indexer:** Sue Klefstad
Development Editor: Amelia Blevins	**Interior Designer:** David Futato
Production Editor: Deborah Baker	**Cover Designer:** Karen Montgomery
Copyeditor: JM Olejarz	**Illustrator:** Kate Dullea
Proofreader: Justin Billing	

November 2020:   First Edition

Revision History for the First Edition
2020-10-12:   First Release

See *http://oreilly.com/catalog/errata.csp?isbn=9781492050124* for release details.

978-1-492-05012-4

[LSI]

Table of Contents

Foreword

Occasionally over the years people will ask me what skills are most in demand in tech. Ten years ago I would tell them to study machine learning, which can scale automated decision making in ways previously impossible. However, these days I have a different answer: machine learning engineering.

Even just a few years ago if you knew machine learning and started at an organization, you would likely walk in the door as the only person with that skill set, allowing you to have an outsized impact. However, a side effect of the proliferation of books, tutorials, e-courses, and boot camps (some of which I have written myself) teaching an entire generation of technologists the skills required is that now machine learning is being used across tens of thousands of companies and organizations.

These days a more likely scenario is that, walking into your new job, you find an organization using machine learning locally but unable to deploy it to production or able to deploy models but unable to manage them effectively. In this setting, the most valuable skill is not being able to train a model, but rather to manage all those models and deploy them in ways that maximize their impact.

In this volume, Trevor Grant, Holden Karau, Boris Lublinsky, Richard Liu, and Ilan Filonenko have put together what I believe is an important cornerstone in the education of data scientists and machine learning engineers. For the foreseeable future the open source Kubeflow project will be a common tool in an organization's toolkit for training, management, and deployment of machine learning models. This book represents the codification of a lot of knowledge that previously existed scattered around internal documentation, conference presentations, and blog posts.

If you believe, as I do, that machine learning is only as powerful as how we use it, then this book is for you.

— Chris Albon
Director of Machine Learning,
The Wikimedia Foundation
https://chrisalbon.com

Preface

We wrote this book for data engineers and data scientists who are building machine learning systems/models they want to move to production. If you've ever had the experience of training an excellent model only to ask yourself how to deploy it into production or keep it up to date once it gets there, this is the book for you. We hope this gives you the tools to replace `Untitled_5.ipynb` with something that works relatively reliably in production.

This book is not intended to serve as your first introduction to machine learning. The next section points to some resources that may be useful if you are just getting started on your machine learning journey.

Our Assumption About You

This book assumes that you either understand how to train models locally, or are working with someone who does. If neither is true, there are many excellent introductory books on machine learning to get you started, including *Hands-On Machine Learning with Scikit-Learn, Keras, and TensorFlow*, 2nd Edition, by Aurélien Géron (O'Reilly).

Our goal is to teach you how to do machine learning in a repeatable way, and how to automate the training and deployment of your models. A serious problem here is that this goal includes a wide range of topics, and it is more than reasonable that you may not be intimately familiar with all of them.

Since we can't delve deeply into every topic, we would like to provide you a short list of our favorite primers on several of the topics you will see covered here:

- *Python for Data Analysis*, 2nd Edition, by Wes McKinney (O'Reilly)
- *Data Science from Scratch*, 2nd Edition, by Joel Grus (O'Reilly)
- *Introduction to Machine Learning with Python* by Andreas C. Müller and Sarah Guido (O'Reilly)

- *Hands-On Machine Learning with Scikit-Learn, Keras, and TensorFlow*, 2nd Edition, by Aurélien Géron (O'Reilly)
- *Kubernetes: Up and Running* by Brendan Burns et al. (O'Reilly)
- *Learning Spark* by Holden Karau et al. (O'Reilly)
- *Feature Engineering for Machine Learning* by Alice Zheng and Amanda Casari (O'Reilly)
- *Building Machine Learning Pipelines* by Hannes Hapke and Catherine Nelson (O'Reilly)
- *Apache Mahout: Beyond MapReduce* by Dmitriy Lyubimov and Andrew Palumbo (CreateSpace)
- *R Cookbook*, 2nd Edition, by J. D. Long and Paul Teetor (O'Reilly)
- *Serving Machine Learning Models* by Boris Lublinsky (O'Reilly)
- "Continuous Delivery for Machine Learning" (*https://oreil.ly/y59_n*) by Danilo Sato et al.
- *Interpretable Machine Learning* (*https://oreil.ly/hBiw1*) by Christoph Molnar (self-published)
- "A Gentle Introduction to Concept Drift in Machine Learning" (*https://oreil.ly/KnJL0*) by Jason Brownlee
- "Model Drift and Ensuring a Healthy Machine Learning Lifecycle" (*https://oreil.ly/q9o6P*) by A. Besir Kurtulmus
- "The Rise of the Model Servers" (*https://oreil.ly/zvIyU*) by Alex Vikati
- "An Overview of Model Explainability in Modern Machine Learning" (*https://oreil.ly/lo36s*) by Rui Aguiar
- *Machine Learning with Python Cookbook* by Chris Albon (O'Reilly)
- Machine Learning Flashcards (*https://machinelearningflashcards.com*) by Chris Albon

Of course, there are many others, but those should get you started. Please don't be overwhelmed by this list—you certainly don't need to be an expert in each of these topics to effectively deploy and manage Kubeflow. In fact, Kubeflow exists to streamline many of these tasks. However, there may be some topic into which you wish to delve deeper—and so this should be thought of as a "getting started" list.

Containers and Kubernetes are a wide, rapidly evolving area of practice. If you want to deepen your knowledge of Kubernetes we recommend looking at the following:

- *Cloud Native Infrastructure* by Justin Garrison and Kris Nova (O'Reilly)
- *Kubernetes: Up and Running* by Brendan Burns et al. (O'Reilly)

Your Responsibility as a Practitioner

This book helps you put your machine learning models into production to solve real-world problems. Solving real-world problems with machine learning is great, but as you go forth and apply your skills, remember to think about the impact.

First, it's important to make sure your models are sufficiently accurate, and there are great tools for this in Kubeflow, covered in "Training and Deploying a Model" on page 19. Even the best tools will not save you from all mistakes—for example, hyper-parameter tuning on the same dataset to report final cross-validation results.

Even models with significant predictive power can have unintended effects and biases that may not show up during the regular training-evaluation phase. Unintended biases can be hard to discover, but there are many stories (e.g., the Amazon machine learning–based recruiting engine that turned out to have intense biases and decided to hire only men (*https://oreil.ly/VekPG*)) that demonstrate the profound potential implications of our work. Failing to address these issues early on can lead to having to abandon your entire work, as demonstrated by IBM's decision to stop its facial recognition program (*https://oreil.ly/WKUXl*) and similar pauses across the industry after the implications of racial bias in facial recognition in the hands of law enforcement became clear.

Even seemingly unbiased data, like raw purchase records, can turn out to have intense biases resulting in incorrect recommendations or worse. Just because a dataset is public and widely available does not mean it is unbiased. The well-known practice of word embeddings (*https://oreil.ly/1dmOV*) has been shown to have many types of bias, including sexism, anti-LGBTQ, and anti-immigrant. When looking at a new dataset it is crucial to look for examples of bias in your data and attempt to mitigate it as much as possible. With the most popular public datasets, various techniques are often discussed in the research, and you can use these to guide your own work.

While this book does not have the tools to solve bias, we encourage you to think critically about potential biases in your system and explore solutions *before going into production*. If you don't know where to start, check out Katharine Jarmul's excellent introductory talk (*https://oreil.ly/fiVYL*). IBM has a collection of tools and examples in its AI Fairness 360 open source toolkit (*http://aif360.mybluemix.net*) that can be a great place to start your exploration. A critical step to reducing bias in your models is to have a diverse team to notice potential issues early. As Jeff Dean (*https://oreil.ly/PJNsF*) said: "AI is full of promise, with the potential to revolutionize so many different areas of modern society. In order to realize its true potential, our field needs to be welcoming to all people. As it stands today, it is definitely not. Our field has a problem with inclusiveness."

It's important to note that removing biases or validating accuracy in your results is not a "one and done"; model performance can degrade and biases can be introduced over time—even if you don't personally change anything.[1]

Conventions Used in This Book

The following typographical conventions are used in this book:

Italic
> Indicates new terms, URLs, email addresses, filenames, and file extensions.

`Constant width`
> Used for program listings, as well as within paragraphs to refer to program elements such as variable or function names, databases, data types, environment variables, statements, and keywords.

`Constant width bold`
> Shows commands or other text that should be typed literally by the user.

`Constant width italic`
> Shows text that should be replaced with user-supplied values or by values determined by context.

 This element signifies a tip or suggestion.

 This element signifies a general note.

 This element indicates a warning or caution.

---

1 Remember the Twitter bot that through reinforcement learning became a neo-Nazi in less than a weekend?

We will use warnings to indicate any situations where the resulting pipeline is likely to be nonportable and call out portable alternatives that you can use.

Code Examples

Supplemental material (code examples, etc.) is available for download at *https://oreil.ly/Kubeflow_for_ML*. These code examples are available under an Apache 2 license, or as described in the next section.

There are additional examples under their own respective licenses that you may find useful. The Kubeflow project has an example repo (*https://oreil.ly/yslNT*), which at the time of writing is available under an Apache 2 license. Canonical also has a set of resources (*https://oreil.ly/TOt_E*) that may be of special interest to MicroK8s users.

Using Code Examples

If you have a technical question or a problem using the code examples, please send email to *bookquestions@oreilly.com*.

This book is here to help you get your job done. In general, if example code is offered with this book, you may use it in your programs and documentation. You do not need to contact us for permission unless you're reproducing a significant portion of the code. For example, writing a program that uses several chunks of code from this book does not require permission. Selling or distributing examples from O'Reilly books does require permission. Answering a question by citing this book and quoting example code does not require permission. Incorporating a significant amount of example code from this book into your product's documentation does require permission.

Additional details on license can be found in the repos.

We appreciate, but generally do not require, attribution. An attribution usually includes the title, author, publisher, and ISBN. For example: "*Kubeflow for Machine Learning* by Holden Karau, Trevor Grant, Boris Lublinsky, Richard Liu, and Ilan Filonenko (O'Reilly). Copyright 2021 Holden Karau, Trevor Grant, Boris Lublinsky, Richard Liu, and Ilan Filonenko, 978-1-492-05012-4."

If you feel your use of code examples falls outside fair use or the permission given above, feel free to contact us at *permissions@oreilly.com*.

O'Reilly Online Learning

O'REILLY® For more than 40 years, *O'Reilly Media* has provided technology and business training, knowledge, and insight to help companies succeed.

Our unique network of experts and innovators share their knowledge and expertise through books, articles, and our online learning platform. O'Reilly's online learning platform gives you on-demand access to live training courses, in-depth learning paths, interactive coding environments, and a vast collection of text and video from O'Reilly and 200+ other publishers. For more information, visit *http://oreilly.com*.

How to Contact the Authors

For feedback, email us at *intro-to-ml-kubeflow@googlegroups.com*. For random ramblings, occasionally about Kubeflow, follow us online:

Trevor
- Twitter (*https://twitter.com/rawkintrevo*)
- Blog (*https://rawkintrevo.org*)
- GitHub (*https://github.com/rawkintrevo*)
- Myspace (*https://myspace.com/rawkintrevo*)

Holden
- Twitter (*http://twitter.com/holdenkarau*)
- YouTube (*https://www.youtube.com/user/holdenkarau*)
- Twitch (*https://www.twitch.tv/holdenkarau*)
- LinkedIn (*https://www.linkedin.com/in/holdenkarau*)
- Blog (*http://blog.holdenkarau.com*)
- GitHub (*https://github.com/holdenk*)
- Facebook (*https://www.facebook.com/hkarau*)

Boris
- LinkedIn (*https://www.linkedin.com/in/boris-lublinsky-b6a4a/*)
- GitHub (*https://github.com/blublinsky*)

Richard
- GitHub (*https://github.com/richardsliu*)

Ilan

- LinkedIn (*https://www.linkedin.com/in/ifilonenko*)
- GitHub (*https://github.com/ifilonenko*)

How to Contact Us

Please address comments and questions concerning this book to the publisher:

O'Reilly Media, Inc.
1005 Gravenstein Highway North
Sebastopol, CA 95472
800-998-9938 (in the United States or Canada)
707-829-0515 (international or local)
707-829-0104 (fax)

You can access the web page for this book, where we list errata, examples, and any additional information, at *https://oreil.ly/Kubeflow_for_Machine_Learning*.

Email *bookquestions@oreilly.com* to comment or ask technical questions about this book.

For news and information about our books and courses, visit *http://oreilly.com*.

Find us on Facebook: *http://facebook.com/oreilly*

Follow us on Twitter: *http://twitter.com/oreillymedia*

Watch us on YouTube: *http://www.youtube.com/oreillymedia*

Acknowledgments

The authors would like to thank everyone at O'Reilly Media, especially our editors Amelia Blevins and Deborah Baker, as well as the Kubeflow community for making this book possible. Clive Cox and Alejandro Saucedo from Seldon (*https://www.seldon.io*) made amazing contributions to Chapter 8, without which this book would be missing key parts. We'd like to thank Google Cloud Platform for resources that allowed us to ensure examples worked on GCP. Perhaps most importantly, we'd like to thank our reviewers, without whom this book would not exist in its current form. This includes Taka Shinagawa, Pete MacKinnon, Kevin Haas, Chris Albon, Hannes Hapke, and more. To all early readers and reviewers of books, thank you for your contributions.

Holden

Would like to thank her girlfriend Kris Nóva for her help debugging her first Kubeflow PR, as well as the entire Kubeflow community for being so welcoming. She would also like to thank her wife Carolyn DeSimone, her puppy Timbit DeSimone-Karau (pictured in Figure P-1), and her stuffed animals for the support needed to write. She would like to thank the doctors at SF General and UCSF for fixing up her hands so she could finish writing this book (although she does wish the hands did not hurt anymore) and everyone who came to visit her in the hospital and nursing home. A special thank you to Ann Spencer, the first editor who showed her how to have fun writing. Finally, she would like to thank her datefriend Els van Vessem for their support in recovering after her accident, especially reading stories and reminding her of her love of writing.

Figure P-1. Timbit the dog

Ilan

Would like to thank all his colleagues at Bloomberg who took the time to review, mentor, and encourage him to write and contribute to open source. The list includes but is not limited to: Kimberly Stoddard, Dan Sun, Keith Laban, Steven Bower, and Sudarshan Kadambi. He would also like to thank his family—Galia, Yuriy, and Stan—for their unconditional love and support.

Richard

Would like to thank the Google Kubeflow team, including but not limited to: Jeremy Lewi, Abhishek Gupta, Thea Lamkin, Zhenghui Wang, Kunming Qu, Gabriel Wen, Michelle Casbon, and Sarah Maddox—without whose support none of this would have been possible. He would also like to thank his cat Tina (see Figure P-2) for her support and understanding during COVID-19.

Figure P-2. Tina the cat

Boris

Would like to thank his colleagues at Lightbend, especially Karl Wehden, for their support in writing the book, their suggestions and proofreads of the early versions of the text, and his wife Marina for putting up with his long hours and feeding him during these hours.

Trevor

Trevor would like to thank his office mates Apache and Meowska (see Figure P-3) for reminding him of the importance of naps, and everyone who listened to him give a talk on Kubeflow last year (especially the people who listened to the bad versions, and especially especially people who listened to the bad versions but still are reading this book now—you're the best). He'd also like to thank his mom, sister, and brother for tolerating his various shenanigans over the years.

Figure P-3. Apache and Meowska

Grievances

The authors would also like to acknowledge the struggles of API changes, which made writing this book so frustrating. If you ever struggle with API changes, know that you are not alone; they are annoying to almost everyone.

Holden would also like to acknowledge the times Timbit DeSimone-Karau was a little sh*t and dug up the yard while she was working. We have a special grievance to vent with the person who hit Holden with their car, slowing down the release of this book.

Trevor has a grievance to air with his girlfriend, who has been badgering him (with increasing persistence) to propose to her throughout this entire project, and while he has been "working on it"—if he hasn't asked her to marry him by the time this book comes out: **Katie, will you marry me?**

# CHAPTER 1

Kubeflow: What It Is and Who It Is For

If you are a data scientist trying to get your models into production, or a data engineer trying to make your models scalable and reliable, Kubeflow provides tools to help. Kubeflow solves the problem of how to take machine learning from research to production. Despite common misconceptions, Kubeflow is more than just Kubernetes and TensorFlow—you can use it for all sorts of machine learning tasks. We hope Kubeflow is the right tool for you, as long as your organization is using Kubernetes. "Alternatives to Kubeflow" on page 9 introduces some options you may wish to explore.

This chapter aims to help you decide if Kubeflow is the right tool for your use case. We'll cover the benefits you can expect from Kubeflow, some of the costs associated with it, and some of the alternatives. After this chapter, we'll dive into setting up Kubeflow and building an end-to-end solution to familiarize you with the basics.

Model Development Life Cycle

Machine learning or model development essentially follows the path: data → information → knowledge → insight. This path of generating insight from data can be graphically described with Figure 1-1.

Model development life cycle (MDLC) is a term commonly used to describe the flow between training and inference. Figure 1-1 is a visual representation of this continuous interaction, where upon triggering a model update the whole cycle kicks off yet again.

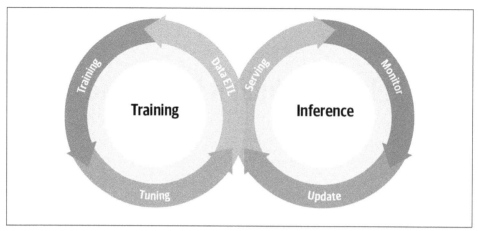

Figure 1-1. Model development life cycle

Where Does Kubeflow Fit In?

Kubeflow is a collection of cloud native tools for all of the stages of MDLC (data exploration, feature preparation, model training/tuning, model serving, model testing, and model versioning). Kubeflow also has tooling that allows these traditionally separate tools to work seamlessly together. An important part of this tooling is the pipeline system, which allows users to build integrated end-to-end pipelines that connect all components of their MDLC.

Kubeflow is for both data scientists and data engineers looking to build production-grade machine learning implementations. Kubeflow can be run either locally in your development environment or on a production cluster. Often pipelines will be developed locally and migrated once the pipelines are ready. Kubeflow provides a unified system—leveraging Kubernetes for containerization and scalability, for the portability and repeatability of its pipelines.

Why Containerize?

The isolation provided by containers allows machine learning stages to be portable and reproducible. Containerized applications are isolated from the rest of your machine and have all their requirements included (from the operating system up).[1] Containerization means no more conversations that include "It worked on my machine" or "Oh yeah, we forgot about just one, you need this extra package."

---

1 For more on containers, see this Google cloud resource (*https://oreil.ly/wqetc*). In situations with GPUs or TPUs, the details of isolation become more complicated.

Containers are built in composable layers, allowing you to use another container as a base. For example, if you have a new natural language processing (NLP) library you want to use, you can add it on top of the existing container—you don't have to start from scratch each time. The composability allows you to reuse a common base; for example, the R and Python containers we use both share a base Debian container.

A common worry about using containers is the overhead. The overhead of containers depends on your implementation, but a paper from IBM[2] found the overhead to be quite low, and generally faster than virtualization. With Kubeflow, there is some additional overhead of having operators installed that you may not use. This overhead is negligible on a production cluster but may be noticeable on a laptop.

 Data scientists with Python experience can think of containers as a heavy-duty virtual environment. In addition to what you're used to in a virtual environment, containers also include the operating system, the packages, and everything in between.

Why Kubernetes?

Kubernetes (*https://kubernetes.io*) is an open source system for automating the deployment, scaling, and management of containerized applications. It allows our pipelines to be scalable without sacrificing portability, enabling us to avoid becoming locked into a specific cloud provider.[3] In addition to being able to switch from a single machine to a distributed cluster, different stages of your machine learning pipeline can request different amounts or types of resources. For example, your data preparation step may benefit more from running on multiple machines, while your model training may benefit more from computing on top of GPUs or tensor processing units (TPUs). This flexibility is especially useful in cloud environments, where you can reduce your costs by using expensive resources only when required.

You can, of course, build your own containerized machine learning pipelines on Kubernetes without using Kubeflow; however the goal of Kubeflow is to standardize this process and make it substantially easier and more efficient.[4] Kubeflow provides a common interface over the tools you would likely use for your machine learning

---

2 W. Felter et al., "An Updated Performance Comparison of Virtual Machines and Linux Containers," 2015 IEEE International Symposium on Performance Analysis of Systems and Software (ISPASS), March 29-31, 2015, doi: 10.1109/ISPASS.2015.7095802.

3 Kubernetes does this by providing a container orchestration layer. For more information about Kubernetes, check out its documentation (*https://oreil.ly/h2ami*).

4 Spotify was able to increase the rate of experiments ~7x; see this Spotify Engineering blog post (*https://oreil.ly/EoxeS*).

implementations. It also makes it easier to configure your implementations to use hardware accelerators like TPUs without changing your code.

Kubeflow's Design and Core Components

In the machine learning landscape, there exists a diverse selection of libraries, tool sets, and frameworks. Kubeflow does not seek to reinvent the wheel or provide a "one size fits all" solution—instead, it allows machine learning practitioners to compose and customize their own stacks based on specific needs. It is designed to simplify the process of building and deploying machine learning systems at scale. This allows data scientists to focus their energies on model development instead of infrastructure.

Kubeflow seeks to tackle the problem of simplifying machine learning through three features: composability, portability, and scalability.

Composability

> The core components of Kubeflow come from data science tools that are already familiar to machine learning practitioners. They can be used independently to facilitate specific stages of machine learning, or composed together to form end-to-end pipelines.

Portability

> By having a container-based design and taking advantage of Kubernetes and its cloud native architecture, Kubeflow does not require you to anchor to any particular developer environment. You can experiment and prototype on your laptop, and deploy to production effortlessly.

Scalability

> By using Kubernetes, Kubeflow can dynamically scale according to the demand on your cluster, by changing the number and size of the underlying containers and machines.[5]

These features are critical for different parts of MDLC. Scalability is important as your dataset grows. Portability is important to avoid vendor lock-in. Composability gives you the freedom to mix and match the best tools for the job.

Let's take a quick look at some of Kubeflow's components and how they support these features.

---

5 Local clusters like Minikube are limited to one machine, but most cloud clusters can dynamically change the kind and number of machines as needed.

Data Exploration with Notebooks

MDLC always begins with data exploration—plotting, segmenting, and manipulating your data to understand where possible insight might exist. One powerful tool that provides the tools and environment for such data exploration is Jupyter. Jupyter is an open source web application that allows users to create and share data, code snippets, and experiments. Jupyter is popular among machine learning practitioners due to its simplicity and portability.

In Kubeflow, you can spin up instances of Jupyter that directly interact with your cluster and its other components, as shown in Figure 1-2. For example, you can write snippets of TensorFlow distributed training code on your laptop, and bring up a training cluster with just a few clicks.

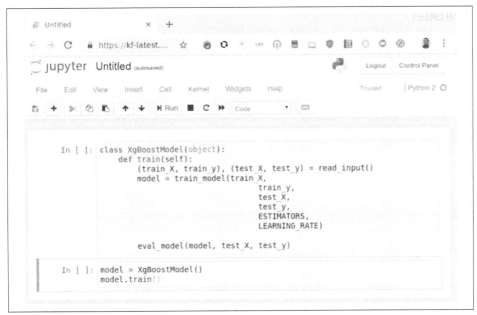

Figure 1-2. Jupyter notebook running in Kubeflow

Data/Feature Preparation

Machine learning algorithms require good data to be effective, and often special tools are needed to effectively extract, transform, and load data. One typically filters, normalizes, and prepares one's input data in order to extract insightful features from otherwise unstructured, noisy data. Kubeflow supports a few different tools for this:

- Apache Spark (one of the most popular big data tools)
- TensorFlow Transform (integrated with TensorFlow Serving for easier inference)

These distinct data preparation components can handle a variety of formats and data sizes and are designed to play nicely with your data exploration environment.[6]

 Support for Apache Beam with Apache Flink in Kubeflow Pipelines is an area of active development.

Training

Once your features are prepped, you are ready to build and train your model. Kubeflow supports a variety of distributed training frameworks. As of the time of writing, Kubeflow has support for:

- TensorFlow (*https://www.tensorflow.org*)
- PyTorch (*https://pytorch.org*)
- Apache MXNet (*https://mxnet.apache.org*)
- XGBoost (*https://github.com/dmlc/xgboost*)
- Chainer (*https://chainer.org*)
- Caffe2 (*https://caffe2.ai*)
- Message passing interface (MPI) (*https://oreil.ly/0zln4*)

In Chapter 7 we will examine how Kubeflow trains a TensorFlow model in greater detail and Chapter 9 will explore other options.

Hyperparameter Tuning

How do you optimize your model architecture and training? In machine learning, hyperparameters are variables that govern the training process. For example, what should the model's learning rate be? How many hidden layers and neurons should be in the neural network? These parameters are not part of the training data, but they can have a significant effect on the performance of the training models.

With Kubeflow, users can begin with a training model that they are unsure about, define the hyperparameter search space, and Kubeflow will take care of the rest—spin up training jobs using different hyperparameters, collect the metrics, and save the results to a model database so their performance can be compared.

---

6 There is still some setup work to make this function, which we cover in Chapter 5.

Model Validation

Before you put your model into production, it's important to know how it's likely to perform. The same tool used for hyperparameter tuning can perform cross-validation for model validation. When you're updating existing models, techniques like A/B testing and multi-armed bandit can be used in model inference to validate your model online.

Inference/Prediction

After training your model, the next step is to serve the model in your cluster so it can handle prediction requests. Kubeflow makes it easy for data scientists to deploy machine learning models in production environments at scale. Currently Kubeflow provides a multiframework component for model serving (KFServing), in addition to existing solutions like TensorFlow Serving and Seldon Core.

Serving many types of models on Kubeflow is fairly straightforward. In most situations, there is no need to build or customize a container yourself—simply point Kubeflow to where your model is stored, and a server will be ready to service requests.

Once the model is served, it needs to be monitored for performance and possibly updated. This monitoring and updating is possible via the cloud native design of Kubeflow and will be further expanded upon in Chapter 8.

Pipelines

Now that we have completed all aspects of MDLC, we wish to enable reusability and governance of these experiments. To do this, Kubeflow treats MDLC as a machine learning pipeline and implements it as a graph, where each node is a stage in a workflow, as seen in Figure 1-3. Kubeflow Pipelines is a component that allows users to compose reusable workflows at ease. Its features include:

- An orchestration engine for multistep workflows
- An SDK to interact with pipeline components
- A user interface that allows users to visualize and track experiments, and to share results with collaborators

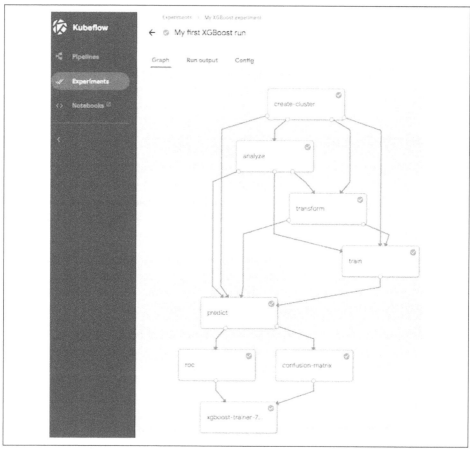

Figure 1-3. A Kubeflow pipeline

Component Overview

As you can see, Kubeflow has built-in components for all parts of MDLC: data preparation, feature preparation, model training, data exploration, hyperparameter tuning, and model inference, as well as pipelines to coordinate everything. However, you are not limited to just the components shipped as part of Kubeflow. You can build on top of the components or even replace them. This can be OK for occasional components, but if you find yourself wanting to replace many parts of Kubeflow, you may want to explore some of the alternatives available.

Alternatives to Kubeflow

Within the research community, various alternatives exist that provide uniquely different functionality to that of Kubeflow. Most recent research has focused around model development and training, with large improvements being made in infrastructure, theory, and systems.

Prediction and model serving, on the other hand, have received relatively less attention. As such, data science practitioners often end up hacking together an amalgam of critical systems components that are integrated to support serving and inference across various workloads and continuously evolving frameworks.

Given the demand for constant availability and horizontal scalability, solutions like Kubeflow and various others are gaining traction throughout the industry, as powerful architectural abstraction tools, and as convincing research scopes.

Clipper (RiseLabs)

One interesting alternative to Kubeflow is Clipper, a general-purpose low-latency prediction serving system developed by RiseLabs. In an attempt to simplify deployment, optimization, and inference, Clipper has a layered architecture system. Through various optimizations and its modular design, Clipper, achieves low latency and high-throughput predictions at levels comparable to TensorFlow Serving, on three TensorFlow models of varying inference costs.

Clipper is divided across two abstractions, aptly named *model selection* and *model abstraction* layers. The model selection layer is quite sophisticated in that it uses an adaptive online model selection policy and various ensemble techniques. Since the model is continuously learning from feedback throughout the lifetime of the application, the model selection layer self-calibrates failed models without needing to interact directly with the policy layer.

Clipper's modular architecture and focus on containerization, similar to Kubeflow, enables caching and batching mechanisms to be shared across frameworks while also reaping the benefits of scalability, concurrency, and flexibility in adding new model frameworks.

Graduating from theory into a functional end-to-end system, Clipper has gained traction within the scientific community and has had various parts of its architectural designs incorporated into recently introduced machine learning systems. Nonetheless, we have yet to see if it will be adopted in the industry at scale.

MLflow (Databricks)

MLflow was developed by Databricks as an open source machine learning develop-ment platform. The architecture of MLflow leverages a lot of the same architectural paradigms as Clipper, including its framework-agnostic nature, while focusing on three major components that it calls Tracking, Projects, and Models.

MLflow Tracking functions as an API with a complementing UI for logging parame-ters, code versions, metrics, and output files. This is quite powerful in machine learn-ing as tracking parameters, metrics, and artifacts is of paramount importance.

MLflow Projects provides a standard format for packaging reusable data science code, defined by a YAML file that can leverage source-controlled code and dependency management via Anaconda. The project format makes it easy to share reproducible data science code, as reproducibility is critical for machine learning practitioners.

MLflow Models are a convention for packaging machine learning models in multiple formats. Each MLflow Model is saved as a directory containing arbitrary files and an MLmodel descriptor file. MLflow also provides the model's registry, showing lineage between deployed models and their creation metadata.

Like Kubeflow, MLflow is still in active development, and has an active community.

Others

Because of the challenges presented in machine learning development, many organi-zations have started to build internal platforms to manage their machine learning life cycle. For example: Bloomberg, Facebook, Google, Uber, and IBM have built, respec-tively, the Data Science Platform, FBLearner Flow, TensorFlow Extended, Michelan-gelo, and Watson Studio to manage data preparation, model training, and deployment.[7]

With the machine learning infrastructure landscape always evolving and maturing, we are excited to see how open source projects, like Kubeflow, will bring much-needed simplicity and abstraction to machine learning development.

Introducing Our Case Studies

Machine learning can use many different types of data, and the approaches and tools you use may vary. In order to showcase Kubeflow's capabilities, we've chosen case studies with very different data and best practices. When possible, we will use data from these case studies to explore Kubeflow and some of its components.

---

7 If you want to explore more of these tools, two good overviews are Ian Hellstrom's 2020 blog post (*https:// oreil.ly/doROU*) and this 2019 article by Austin Kodra (*https://oreil.ly/bbI3_*).

Modified National Institute of Standards and Technology

In ML, Modified National Institute of Standards and Technology (MNIST) commonly refers to the dataset of handwritten digits for classification. The relatively small data size of digits, as well as its common use as an example, allows us to explore a variety of tools. In some ways, MNIST has become one of the standard "hello world" examples for machine learning. We use MNIST as our first example in Chapter 2 to illustrate Kubeflow end-to-end.

Mailing List Data

Knowing how to ask good questions is something of an art. Have you ever posted a message to a mailing list, asking for help, only for no one to respond? What are the different types of questions? We'll look at some of the public Apache Software Foundation mailing list data and try to create a model that predicts if a message will be answered. This example is scaled up and down by choosing which projects and what time period we want to look at, so we can use a variety of tools to solve it.

Product Recommender

Recommendation systems are one of the most common and easily understood applications of machine learning, with many examples from Amazon's product recommender to Netflix's movie suggestions. The majority of recommender implementations are based on collaborative filtering—an assumption that if person A has the same opinion as person B on a set of issues, A would be more likely to share B's opinion on other issues than would a randomly chosen third person. This approach is built on a well-developed algorithm with quite a few implementations, including TensorFlow/Keras implementation.[8]

One of the problems with rating-based models is that they can't be standardized easily for data with nonscaled target values, such as the purchase or frequency data. This excellent Medium post (*https://oreil.ly/LncEo*) shows how to convert such data into a rating matrix that can be used for collaborative filtering. Our example leverages data and code from Data Driven Investor (*https://oreil.ly/LncEo*) and code described on Piyushdharkar's GitHub (*https://oreil.ly/p3TB_*). We'll use this example to explore how to build an initial model in Jupyter and move on to building a production pipeline.

---

8 For example, see the Piyushdharkar's GitHub (*https://oreil.ly/LFxR9*).

CT Scans

As we were writing this book, the world was going through the COVID-19 pandemic. AI researchers were being called on to apply methods and techniques to assist medical providers with understanding the disease. Some research showed that CT scans were more effective at early detection than RT-PCR tests (the traditional COVID test). However, diagnostic CT scans use low dosages of radiation and are therefore "noisy"—that is to say, CT scans are more clear when more radiation is used.

A new paper proposes (*https://oreil.ly/OXrFs*) an open source solution for denoising CT scans with off-the-shelf methods available entirely from open source projects (as opposed to proprietary FDA-approved solutions). We implement this approach to illustrate how one might go from academic article to real-world solution, to show the value of Kubeflow for creating reproducible and sharable research, and to provide a starting off point for any reader who might want to contribute to the fight against COVID-19.

Conclusion

We are so glad you've decided to use this book to start your adventures into Kubeflow. This introduction should have given you a feel for Kubeflow and its capabilities. However, like all adventures, there may come a point when your guidebook isn't enough to carry you through. Thankfully, there is a collection of community resources where you can interact with others on similar paths. We encourage you to sign up for the Kubeflow Slack workspace (*http://kubeflow.slack.com*), one of the more active areas of discussion. There is also a Kubeflow discussion mailing list (*https://oreil.ly/Ca6R3*). There is a Kubeflow project page (*https://www.kubeflow.org*) as well.

 If you want to quickly explore Kubeflow end-to-end, there are some Google codelabs (*https://oreil.ly/YRfkm*) that can help you.

In Chapter 2, we'll install Kubeflow and use it to train and serve a relatively simple machine learning model to give you an idea of the basics.

Hello Kubeflow

Welcome to your first steps into the exciting world of Kubeflow!

First off, we'll set up Kubeflow on your machine, or on a cloud provider. Then we'll dive into a comprehensive example. The goal of this example is to get a model trained and start serving as quickly as possible. In some parts of the first section, it may seem like we are instructing you to mindlessly enter commands. While we want you to follow along, we strongly encourage you to revisit this chapter after you've finished the book to reflect on the commands you entered, and consider how much your understanding has grown while reading.

We'll provide instructions for setting up and testing our example on a local machine and a link to instructions for performing the same on real clusters. While we will point you to the config files and OCI containers that are driving all of this, they are not the focus of this chapter; they will be covered in detail in subsequent chapters. The focus of this chapter is an end-to-end example that you can follow along with at home.

In future chapters we will dig into the "why" of everything we're doing, we promise.

For now, just enjoy the ride.

Getting Set Up with Kubeflow

One of the great things about Kubeflow being built with Kubernetes is the ability to do our initial development and exploration locally, moving into more powerful and distributed tools later on. Your same pipeline can be developed locally and moved into a cluster.

Though you could get started with Kubeflow locally, you don't have to. You can just as easily do your initial work with one of the cloud providers or on-premises Kubernetes clusters.

One of the faster ways to get started with Kubeflow is using the click-to-deploy app on Google Cloud Platform (GCP). If you're in a rush to get started, go ahead and check out this Kubeflow documentation page (*https://oreil.ly/GBbsc*).

Installing Kubeflow and Its Dependencies

Before we approach the biggest requirement for Kubeflow, access to a Kubernetes cluster, let's get the tools set up. Kubeflow is fairly self-contained but does require kubectl. The rest of the dependencies are inside containers, so you don't have to worry about installing them.

Whether you use a local or a remote Kubernetes cluster, having the development tools installed locally will simplify your life.

Regardless of your cluster, you need to install Kubeflow's core dependency kubectl, for communicating with Kubernetes. kubectl is widely packaged, with the different installation options covered in the Kubernetes documentation (*https://oreil.ly/tUpe0*). If you want to use a package manager to install kubectl, Ubuntu users can use snap (see Example 2-1) and Mac users can use Homebrew (see Example 2-2); other installation options are covered in the Kubernetes documentation (*https://oreil.ly/vQPYQ*). kubectl can also be installed as a local binary from this Kubernetes documentation page (*https://oreil.ly/iT5Pv*).

Example 2-1. Install kubectl with snap

```
sudo snap install kubectl --classic
```

Example 2-2. Install kubectl with Homebrew

```
brew install kubernetes-cli
```

Once you have the minimum dependencies installed, you can now install Kubeflow from this GitHub repo (*https://oreil.ly/WTHLZ*), as in Example 2-3.

Example 2-3. Install Kubeflow

```
PLATFORM=$(uname) # Either Linux or Darwin
export PLATFORM
mkdir -p ~/bin
#Configuration
export KUBEFLOW_TAG=1.0.1
# ^ You can also point this to a different version if you want to try
KUBEFLOW_BASE="https://api.github.com/repos/kubeflow/kfctl/releases"
# Or just go to https://github.com/kubeflow/kfctl/releases
KFCTL_URL=$(curl -s ${KUBEFLOW_BASE} |\
              grep http |\
              grep "${KUBEFLOW_TAG}" |\
              grep -i "${PLATFORM}" |\
              cut -d : -f 2,3 |\
              tr -d '\" ' )
wget "${KFCTL_URL}"
KFCTL_FILE=${KFCTL_URL##*/}
tar -xvf "${KFCTL_FILE}"
mv ./kfctl ~/bin/
rm "${KFCTL_FILE}"
# It's recommended that you add the scripts directory to your path
export PATH=$PATH:~/bin
```

You should now have Kubeflow installed on your machine. To make sure it's installed, run `kfctl version` and check that it returns the expected version. Now let's cover some optional tools that you can install to ease your future Kubeflowing.

Setting Up Local Kubernetes

Being able to have the same software running locally and in production is one of the great advantages of Kubeflow. To support this, you will need a local version of Kubernetes installed. While there are several options, we find Minikube the simplest. Minikube is a local version of Kubernetes that allows you to use your local computer to simulate a cluster. Two other common options for a local version of Kubeflow are `microk8s`, supported on many Linux platforms, and `MiniKF`, which uses Vagrant to launch a VM to run Kubernetes with Kubeflow.

> A local Kubernetes cluster is not strictly required, but many data scientists and developers find it helpful to have a local cluster to test with.

Minikube

Minikube is a local version of Kubernetes that can run Kubeflow. There are installation guides for Minikube on the main Kubernetes documentation page (*https://oreil.ly/lNeon*) as well as the Kubeflow-specific page (*https://oreil.ly/B17Wp*).

The most common failure in the automatic setup of Minikube is missing a hypervisor or Docker. Regardless of your OS, you should be able to use VirtualBox (*https://oreil.ly/h1uoS*); however, other options like KVM2 on Linux, Hyper-V on Windows, and HyperKit on macOS all work as well.

 When starting Minikube make sure to give it plenty of memory and disk space, e.g., `minikube start --cpus 16 --memory 12g --disk-size 15g`. Note: you don't need 16 CPU cores to run this; this is just the number of virtual CPUs Minikube will use.

Setting Up Your Kubeflow Development Environment

Kubeflow's pipeline system is built in Python, and having the SDK installed locally will allow you to build pipelines faster. However, if you can't install software locally, you can still use Kubeflow's Jupyter environment to build your pipelines.

Setting up the Pipeline SDK

To begin setting up the Pipeline SDK you will need to have Python (*https://oreil.ly/IbfY2*) installed. Many people find it useful to create isolated virtual environments for their different projects; see how in Example 2-4.

Example 2-4. Create a virtual environment

```
virtualenv kfvenv --python python3
source kfvenv/bin/activate
```

Now you can use the pip command to install the Kubeflow Pipelines package and its requirements, as in Example 2-5.

Example 2-5. Install Kubeflow Pipeline SDK

```
URL=https://storage.googleapis.com/ml-pipeline/release/latest/kfp.tar.gz
pip install "${URL}" --upgrade
```

If you use a virtual environment you will need to activate it whenever you want to use the Pipeline SDK.

In addition to the SDK, Kubeflow ships a number of components. Checking out a fixed version of the standard components, as in Example 2-6, allows us to create more reliable pipelines.

Example 2-6. Clone the Kubeflow Pipelines repo

```
git clone --single-branch --branch 0.3.0 https://github.com/kubeflow/pipelines.git
```

Setting up Docker

Docker (*https://www.docker.com*) is an important part of the minimum requirements, allowing you to customize and add libraries and other functionality to your own custom containers. We'll cover more on Docker in Chapter 3. Docker can be installed from the standard package managers in Linux or with Homebrew on macOS.

In addition to installing Docker, you will want a place to store the container images, called a container registry. The container registry will be accessed by your Kubeflow cluster. The company behind Docker offers Docker Hub (*https://hub.docker.com*) and RedHat offers Quay (*https://quay.io*), a cloud neutral platform you can use. Alternatively, you can also use your cloud provider's container registry.[1] A cloud vendor's specific container registry often offers greater security on images stored there and can configure your Kubernetes cluster automatically with the permissions required to fetch those images. In our examples, we'll assume that you've set your container registry via an environment variable $CONTAINER_REGISTRY, in your shell.

 If you use a registry that isn't on the Google Cloud Platform, you will need to configure Kubeflow Pipelines container builder to have access to your registry by following the Kaniko configuration guide (*https://oreil.ly/88Ep-*).

To make sure your Docker installation is properly configured, you can write a one-line Dc and push it to your registry. For the Dockerfile we'll use the FROM command to indicate we are based on top of Kubeflow's TensorFlow notebook container image, as in Example 2-7 (we'll talk more about this in Chapter 9). When you push a container, you need to specify the tag, which determines the image name, version, and where it is stored—as shown in Example 2-8.

Example 2-7. Specify the new container is built on top of Kubeflow's container

```
FROM gcr.io/kubeflow-images-public/tensorflow-2.1.0-notebook-cpu:1.0.0
```

Example 2-8. Build the new container and push to a registry for use

```
IMAGE="${CONTAINER_REGISTRY}/kubeflow/test:v1"
docker build  -t "${IMAGE}" -f Dockerfile .
docker push "${IMAGE}"
```

With this setup, you're now ready to start customizing the containers and components in Kubeflow to meet your needs. We'll do a deeper dive into building containers

---

1 Just search "cloudname" plus the container registry name for documentation.

from scratch in Chapter 9. As we move forward in future chapters we'll use this pattern to add tools when needed.

Editing YAML

While Kubeflow abstracts the details of Kubernetes away from us to a large degree, there are still times when looking at or modifying the configuration is useful. Most of Kubernetes configuration is represented in YAML, so having tools set up to easily look at and edit YAMLs will be beneficial. Most integrated development environments (IDEs) offer some sort of tooling for editing YAML, but you may have to install these separately.

For IntelliJ there is a YAML plugin (*https://oreil.ly/Awmeq*). For emacs there are many modes available for YAML editing, including yaml-mode (*https://oreil.ly/lWZE5*) (which is installable from Milkypostman's Emacs Lisp Package Archive (MELPA) (*https://melpa.org*)). Atom has syntax highlighting available as a package YAML (*https://oreil.ly/z47Sa*). If you use a different IDE, don't throw it away just for better YAML editing before you explore the plugin available. Regardless of IDE you can also use the YAMLlint website (*http://www.yamllint.com*) to check your YAML.

Creating Our First Kubeflow Project

First, we need to make a Kubeflow project to work in. To create a Kubeflow deployment we use the `kfctl` program.[2] When using Kubeflow you need to specify a manifest file that configures what is built and how there are various manifests for different cloud providers.

We'll start with an example project using a vanilla configuration, as seen in Example 2-9. In this project we'll build a simple end-to-end pipeline for our MNIST example. We chose this example because it's the standard "hello world" of machine learning.

Example 2-9. Create first example project

```
# Pick the correct config file for your platform from
# https://github.com/kubeflow/manifests/tree/[version]/kfdef
# You can download and edit the configuration at this point if you need to.
# For generic Kubernetes with Istio:
MANIFEST_BRANCH=${MANIFEST_BRANCH:-v1.0-branch}
export MANIFEST_BRANCH
MANIFEST_VERSION=${MANIFEST_VERSION:-v1.0.1}
```

---

2 Not to be confused with the legacy `kfctl.sh` script.

```
export MANIFEST_VERSION

KF_PROJECT_NAME=${KF_PROJECT_NAME:-hello-kf-${PLATFORM}}
export KF_PROJECT_NAME
mkdir "${KF_PROJECT_NAME}"
pushd "${KF_PROJECT_NAME}"

manifest_root=https://raw.githubusercontent.com/kubeflow/manifests/
# On most environments this will create a "vanilla" Kubeflow install using Istio.
FILE_NAME=kfctl_k8s_istio.${MANIFEST_VERSION}.yaml
KFDEF=${manifest_root}${MANIFEST_BRANCH}/kfdef/${FILE_NAME}
kfctl apply -f $KFDEF -V
echo $?

popd
```

Example 2-9 assumes you're using an existing Kubernetes cluster (like local Mini-kube). While your running `kfctl apply` you will see lots of status messages and maybe even some error messages. Provided it prints out a 0 at the end you can safely ignore most errors as they are automatically retried.

> This deployment process can take up to *30 minutes*.

If you've decided to go straight ahead with a cloud provider, the Kubeflow installation guide (*https://oreil.ly/EMRVV*) has information on how to get started.

> The Kubeflow user interface can come up before Kubeflow is fully deployed, and accessing it then can mean you won't have a proper namespace. To make sure Kubeflow is ready, run `kubectl get pods --all-namespaces -w` and wait for all of the pods to become RUNNING or COMPLETED. If you see pods being preempted, make sure you launched a cluster with enough RAM and disk space. If you can't launch a large enough cluster locally, consider a cloud provider. (Ilan and Holden are currently working on a blog post on this topic.)

Training and Deploying a Model

In traditional machine learning texts, the training phase is the one that is given the most attention, with a few simple examples on deployment, and very little treatment of model management. Throughout this book, we assume that you are a data scientist who knows how to select the correct model/algorithm or work with someone who does. We focus on the deployment and model management more than traditional ML texts.

Training and Monitoring Progress

The next step is to train the model using a Kubeflow Pipeline. We will use a precreated training container[3] that downloads the training data and trains the model. For Example 2-10, we have a prebuilt workflow in `train_pipeline.py` that trains a `Ran domForestClassifier` in the ch2 folder on this book's GitHub example repo (*https:// oreil.ly/Kubeflow_for_ML*).

Example 2-10. Create training workflow example

```
dsl-compile --py train_pipeline.py --output job.yaml
```

If you run into problems here, you should check out the Kubeflow troubleshooting guide (*https://oreil.ly/nvNnC*).

The Kubeflow UI, as seen in Figure 2-1, is accessed in a few different ways. For local deployments a quick port forward is the simplest way to get started: just run `kubectl port-forward svc/istio-ingressgateway -n istio-system 7777:80` and then go to `localhost:7777`. If you have deployed on GCP you should go to `https://<deploy ment_name>.endpoints.<project_name>.cloud.goog`. Otherwise, you can get the address of the gateway service by running `kubectl get ingress -n istio-system`.

Figure 2-1. Kubeflow web UI

---

3 The container is from this GitHub repo (*https://oreil.ly/f-bO3*).

Click pipelines, or add _/pipeline/ to the root URL and you should see the Pipelines web UI, as in Figure 2-2.

Figure 2-2. Pipelines web UI

From here we can upload our pipeline. Once we've uploaded the pipeline we can use the same web UI to create a run of the pipeline. After you click the uploaded pipeline you'll be able to create a run, as shown in Figure 2-3.

Figure 2-3. Pipeline detail page

Test Query

Finally, let's query our model and monitor the results. A "sanity check" is a simple test to ensure our model is making predictions that are theoretically reasonable. For example—we're attempting to guess what digit was written. If our model comes back with answers like 77, orange Kool-Aid, or ERROR, those would all fail the sanity check. We expect to see digits between 0 and 9. Sanity checking models before putting them into production is always a wise choice.

The web UI and model serving are exposed through the same Istio gateway. So, the model will be available at *http://<WEBUI_URL>/seldon<mnist-classifier/api<v0.1/predictions*. If you're using Google IAP, you may find the iap_curl project helpful for making requests.

There is a Python script available (*https://oreil.ly/Kubeflow_for_MLch02*) for pulling an image from the MNIST dataset, turning it into a vector, displaying the image, and sending it to the model. Turning the image into a vector is normally part of the pre-prediction transformation; we'll cover more of this in Chapter 8. Example 2-11 is a fairly clear Python example of how one can query the model. The model returns a JSON of the 10 digits and the probability of whether the submitted vector represents a specific digit. Specifically, we need an image of a handwritten digit that we can turn into an array of values.

Example 2-11. Model query example

```
import requests
import numpy as np

from tensorflow.examples.tutorials.mnist import input_data
from matplotlib import pyplot as plt

def download_mnist():
    return input_data.read_data_sets("MNIST_data/", one_hot=True)


def gen_image(arr):
    two_d = (np.reshape(arr, (28, 28)) * 255).astype(np.uint8)
    plt.imshow(two_d, cmap=plt.cm.gray_r, interpolation='nearest')
    return plt
mnist = download_mnist()
batch_xs, batch_ys = mnist.train.next_batch(1)
chosen = 0
gen_image(batch_xs[chosen]).show()
data = batch_xs[chosen].reshape((1, 784))
features = ["X" + str(i + 1) for i in range(0, 784)]
request = {"data": {"names": features, "ndarray": data.tolist()}}
deploymentName = "mnist-classifier"
uri = "http://" + AMBASSADOR_API_IP + "/seldon/" + \
    deploymentName + "/api/v0.1/predictions"

response = requests.post(uri, json=request)
```

For example, see the handwritten 3 in Figure 2-4.

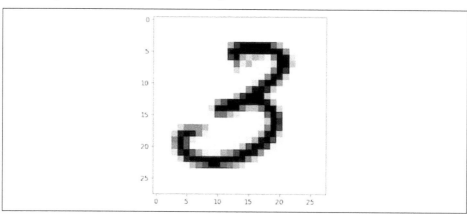

Figure 2-4. Handwritten 3

This returns the following:

```
{'data': {'names': ['class:0',
                    'class:1',
                    'class:2',
                    'class:3',
                    'class:4',
                    'class:5',
                    'class:6',
                    'class:7',
                    'class:8',
                    'class:9'],
          'ndarray':[[0.03333333333333333,
                      0.26666666666666666,
                      0.03333333333333333,
                      0.13333333333333333, ## It was actually this
                      0.1,
                      0.06666666666666667,
                      0.1,
                      0.26666666666666666,
                      0.0,
                      0.0]]},
 'meta': {'puid': 'tb02ff58vcinl82jmkkoe80u4r', 'routing': {}, 'tags': {}}}
```

We can see that even though we wrote a pretty clear *3*, the model's best guess was a tie between *1* and *7*. That being said, `RandomForestClassifier` is a bad model for handwriting recognition—so this isn't a surprising result. We used `RandomForestClassifier` for two reasons: first, to illustrate model explainability in Chapter 8, and second, so you can experiment with a more reasonable model and compare performance.

> While we've deployed our end-to-end example here without any real validation, you should always validate before real production.

Going Beyond a Local Deployment

Some of you have been trying this out on a local Kubernetes deployment. One of the powers of Kubeflow is the ability to scale using Kubernetes. Kubernetes can run on a single machine or many computers, and some environments can dynamically add more resources as needed. While Kubernetes is an industry standard, there are variations in Kubeflow's setup steps required depending on your provider. Kubeflow's getting started guide (*https://oreil.ly/eq6rC*) has installation instructions for GCP, AWS, Azure, IBM Cloud, and OpenShift. Once Kubeflow is installed on your Kubernetes cluster, you can try this same example again and see how the same code can run, or take our word for it and move on to more interesting problems.

When deploying on cloud providers, Kubeflow can create more than just Kubernetes resources that should be deleted too. For example, on Google you can delete the ancillary services by going to the deployment manager.

Conclusion

In this chapter, you got your first real taste of Kubeflow. You now have your development environment properly configured and a Kubeflow deployment you can use throughout the rest of this book. We covered a simple end-to-end example with the standard MNIST, allowing you to see the different core components of Kubeflow in action. We introduced the pipeline, which ties all of Kubeflow together, and you used it to train your model. In Chapter 3 we will explore Kubeflow's design and set up some optional components. Understanding the design will help you choose the right components.

Kubeflow Design: Beyond the Basics

You made it through two chapters. Well done. So far you have decided to learn Kube-flow and worked through a simple example. Now we want to take a step back and look at each component in detail. Figure 3-1 shows the main Kubeflow components and the role they play in the overall architecture.

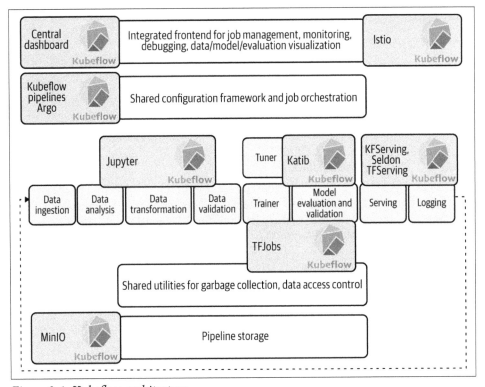

Figure 3-1. Kubeflow architecture

Essentially, we'll look at the core elements that make up our example deployment as well as the supporting pieces. In the chapters that follow, we will dig into each of these sections in greater depth.

That said, let's get started.

Getting Around the Central Dashboard

Your main interface to Kubeflow is the central dashboard (see Figure 3-2), which allows you to access the majority of Kubeflow components. Depending on your Kubernetes provider, it might take up to half an hour to have your ingress become available.

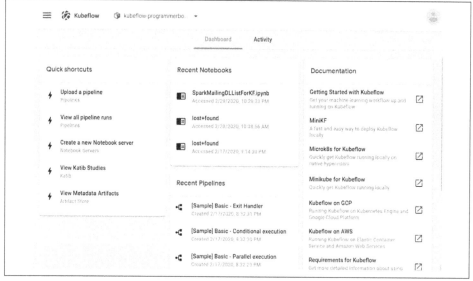

Figure 3-2. The central dashboard

> While it is meant to be automatic, if you don't have a namespace created for your work, follow Kubeflow's "Manual profile creation" instructions (*https://oreil.ly/_6iC5*).

From the home page of the central dashboard you can access Kubeflow's Pipelines, Notebooks, Katib (hyperparameter tuning), and the artifact store. We will cover the design of these components and how to use them next.

Notebooks (JupyterHub)

The first step of most projects is some form of prototyping and experimentation. Kubeflow's tool for this purpose is JupyterHub (*https://jupyter.org/hub*)—a multiuser hub that spawns, manages, and proxies multiple instances of a single-user Jupyter notebook (*https://oreil.ly/C4dtQ*). Jupyter notebooks support the whole computation process: developing, documenting, and executing code, as well as communicating the results.

To access JupyterHub, go to the main Kubeflow page and click the notebook button. On the notebook page, you can connect to existing servers or create a new one.

To create a new server, you need to specify the server name and namespace, pick an image (from CPU optimized, GPU optimized, or a custom image that you can create), and specify resource requirements—CPU/memory, workspace, data volumes, custom configuration, and so on. Once the server is created, you can connect to it and start creating and editing notebooks.

In order to allow data scientists to do cluster operations without leaving the notebook's environment, Kubeflow adds kubectl (*https://oreil.ly/i-PFC*) to the provided notebook images, which allows developers to use notebooks to create and manage Kubernetes resources. The Jupyter notebook pods run under a special service account `default-editor`, which has namespace-scoped permissions to the following Kubernetes resources:

- Pods
- Deployments
- Services
- Jobs
- TFJobs
- PyTorchJobs

You can bind this account to a custom role, in order to limit/extend permissions of the notebook server. This allows notebook developers to execute all of the (allowed by role) Kubernetes commands without leaving the notebook environment. For example, the creation of a new Kubernetes resource can be done by running the following command directly in a Jupyter notebook:

```
!kubectl create -f myspec.yaml
```

The contents of your `yaml` file will determine what resource is created. If you're not used to making Kubernetes resources, don't worry—Kubeflow's pipelines include tools to make them for you.

To further increase Jupyter capabilities, Kubeflow also provides support in the note-books for such important Kubeflow components as Pipelines and metadata management (described later in "Metadata" on page 32). Jupyter notebooks can also directly launch distributed training jobs.

Training Operators

JupyterHub is a great tool for initial experimentation with the data and prototyping ML jobs. However, when moving to train in production, Kubeflow provides several training components to automate the execution of machine learning algorithms, including:

- Chainer training (*https://oreil.ly/AjfwS*)
- MPI training (*https://oreil.ly/SK19W*)
- Apache MXNet training (*https://oreil.ly/FvDdQ*)
- PyTorch training (*https://oreil.ly/0z4j6*)
- TensorFlow training (*https://oreil.ly/YMGKx*)

In Kubeflow, distributed training jobs are managed by application-specific control-lers, known as operators. These operators extend the Kubernetes APIs to create, manage, and manipulate the state of resources. For example, to run a distributed TensorFlow training job, the user just needs to provide a specification that describes the desired state (number of workers and parameter servers, etc.), and the Tensor-Flow operator component will take care of the rest and manage the life cycle of the training job.

These operators allow the automation of important deployment concepts such as scalability, observability, and failover. They can also be used by pipelines to chain their execution with the execution of other components of the system.

Kubeflow Pipelines

In addition to providing specialized parameters implementing specific functionality, Kubeflow has Pipelines (*https://oreil.ly/QZjNV*), which allows you to orchestrate the execution of machine learning applications. This implementation is based on Argo Workflows (*https://oreil.ly/6PsLK*), an open source, container-native workflow engine for Kubernetes. Kubeflow installs all of the Argo components.

At a high level, the execution of a pipeline contains the following components (*https://oreil.ly/QZjNV*):

Python SDK

You create components or specify a pipeline using the Kubeflow Pipelines domain-specific language (*https://oreil.ly/c2DRj*) (DSL).

DSL compiler

The DSL compiler (*https://oreil.ly/5o2Yw*) transforms your pipeline's Python code into a static configuration (YAML).

Pipeline Service

The Pipeline Service creates a pipeline run from the static configuration.

Kubernetes resources

The Pipeline Service calls the Kubernetes API server to create the necessary Kubernetes custom resource definitions (*https://oreil.ly/5wPjy*) (CRDs) to run the pipeline.

Orchestration controllers

A set of orchestration controllers execute the containers needed to complete the pipeline execution specified by the Kubernetes resources (CRDs). The containers execute within Kubernetes Pods on virtual machines. An example controller is the Argo Workflow (*https://oreil.ly/leX50*) controller, which orchestrates task-driven workflows.

Artifact storage

The Kubernetes Pods store two kinds of data:

Metadata

Experiments, jobs, runs, single scalar metrics (generally aggregated for the purposes of sorting and filtering), etc. Kubeflow Pipelines stores the metadata in a MySQL database.

Artifacts

Pipeline packages, views, large-scale metrics like time series (usually used for investigating an individual run's performance and for debugging), etc. Kubeflow Pipelines stores the artifacts in an artifact store like MinIO server (*https://docs.minio.io*), Google Cloud Storage (GCS) (*https://oreil.ly/k1bQz*), or Amazon S3 (*https://aws.amazon.com/s3*).

Kubeflow Pipelines gives you the ability to make your machine learning jobs repeatable and handle new data. It provides an intuitive DSL in Python to write your pipelines with. Your pipelines are then compiled down to an existing Kubernetes workflow engine (currently Argo Workflows). Kubeflow's pipeline components make it easy to use and coordinate the different tools required to build an end-to-end machine learning project. On top of that, Kubeflow can track both data and metadata, improving how we can understand our jobs. For example, in Chapter 5 we use these artifacts to understand the schema. Pipelines can expose the parameters of the under-lying machine learning algorithms, allowing Kubeflow to perform tuning.

Hyperparameter Tuning

Finding the right set of hyperparameters for your training model can be a challenging task. Traditional methodologies such as grid search can be time-consuming and quite tedious. Most existing hyperparameter systems are tied to one machine learning framework and have only a few options for searching the parameter space.

Kubeflow provides a component (called Katib) that allows users to perform hyper-parameter optimizations easily on Kubernetes clusters. Katib is inspired by Google Vizier (*https://oreil.ly/UInbP*), a black-box optimization framework. It leverages advanced searching algorithms such as Bayesian optimization to find optimal hyper-parameter configurations.

Katib supports hyperparameter tuning (*https://oreil.ly/O5mC9*) and can run with any deep learning framework, including TensorFlow, MXNet, and PyTorch.

As in Google Vizier, Katib is based on four main concepts:

Experiment
    A single optimization run over a feasible space. Each experiment contains a con-figuration describing the feasible space, as well as a set of trials. It is assumed that objective function $f(x)$ does not change in the course of the experiment.

Trial
    A list of parameter values, x, that will lead to a single evaluation of $f(x)$. A trial can be "completed," which means that it has been evaluated and the objective value $f(x)$ has been assigned to it, otherwise it is "pending." One trial corresponds to one job.

Job
    A process responsible for evaluating a pending trial and calculating its objective value.

Suggestion
    An algorithm to construct a parameter set. Currently, Katib supports the follow-ing exploration algorithms:

    - Random
    - Grid
    - Hyperband (*https://oreil.ly/LlCKw*)
    - Bayesian optimization (*https://oreil.ly/Pa83u*)

Using these core concepts, you can increase your model's performance. Since Katib is not tied to one machine learning library, you can explore new algorithms and tools with minimal modifications.

Model Inference

Kubeflow makes it easy to deploy machine learning models in production environments at scale. It provides several model serving options, including TFServing (*https://oreil.ly/Hp2sb*), Seldon serving (*https://oreil.ly/sWc71*), PyTorch serving (*https://oreil.ly/bLJxg*), and TensorRT (*https://oreil.ly/fuv-7*). It also provides an umbrella implementation, KFServing (*https://oreil.ly/qEvqq*), which generalizes the model inference concerns of autoscaling, networking, health checking, and server configuration.

The overall implementation is based on leveraging Istio (*https://istio.io*) (covered later) and Knative serving (*https://knative.dev*)—serverless containers on Kubernetes. As defined in the Knative documentation (*https://oreil.ly/h6O1E*), the Knative serving project provides middleware primitives that enable:

- Rapid deployment of serverless containers
- Automatic scaling up and down to zero
- Routing and network programming for Istio components

Since model serving is inherently spiky, rapid scaling up and down is important. Knative serving simplifies the support for continuous model updates, by automatically routing requests to newer model deployments. This requires scaling down to zero (minimizing resource utilization) for unused models while keeping them available for rollbacks. Since Knative is cloud native it benefits from its underlying infrastructure stack and therefore provides all the monitoring capabilities that exist within Kubernetes, such as logging, tracing, and monitoring. KFServing also makes use of Knative eventing (*https://oreil.ly/fpLrH*) to give optional support for pluggable event sources.

Similar to Seldon, every KFServing deployment is an orchestrator, wiring together the following components:

Preprocessor
   An optional component responsible for the transformation of the input data into content/format required for model serving

Predictor
   A mandatory component responsible for an actual model serving

Postprocessor
   An optional component responsible for the transformation/enriching of the model serving result into content/format required for output

Additional components can enhance one's overall model serving implementation, but are outside of the main execution pipeline. Tools like outlier detection and model explainability can run in this environment without slowing down the overall system.

While all of these individual components and techniques have existed for a long time, having them integrated into the serving system of Kubeflow reduces the complexity involved in bringing new models into production.

In addition to the components directly supporting ML operations, Kubeflow also provides several supporting components.

Metadata

An important component of Kubeflow is metadata management, providing capabilities to capture and track information about a model's creation. Many organizations build hundreds of models a day, but it's very hard to manage all of a model's related information. ML Metadata is both the infrastructure and a library for recording and retrieving metadata associated with an ML developer's and data scientist's workflow. The information, which can be registered in the metadata component includes:

- Data sources used for the model's creation
- The artifacts generated through the components/steps of the pipeline
- The executions of these components/steps
- The pipeline and associated lineage information

ML Metadata tracks the inputs and outputs of all components and steps in an ML workflow and their lineage. This data powers several important features listed in Table 3-1 and shown in Figure 3-3.

Table 3-1. Examples of ML Metadata operations

Operation	Example
List all artifacts of a specific type.	All models that have been trained.
Compare two artifacts of the same type.	Compare results from two experiments.
Show a DAG of all related executions and their input and output artifacts.	Visualize the workflow of an experiment for debugging and discovery.
Display how an artifact was created.	See what data went into a model; enforce data retention plans.
Identify all artifacts that were created using a given artifact.	Mark all models trained from a specific dataset with bad data.
Determine if an execution has been run on the same inputs before.	Determine whether a component/step has already completed the same work and the previous output can just be reused.
Record and query context of workflow runs.	Track the owner and changes used for a workflow run; group the lineage by experiments; manage artifacts by projects.

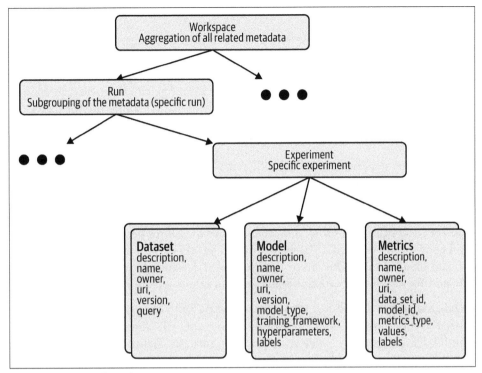

Figure 3-3. Metadata diagram

Component Summary

The magic of Kubeflow is making all of these traditionally distinct components work together. While Kubeflow is certainly not the only system to bring together different parts of the machine learning landscape, it is unique in its flexibility in supporting a wide range of components. In addition to that, since it runs on standard Kubernetes, you can add your own components as desired. Much of this magic of tool integration happens inside of Kubeflow's pipelines, but some of the support components are essential to allowing these tools to interact.

Support Components

While these components aren't explicitly exposed by Kubeflow, they play an important role in the overall Kubeflow ecosystem. Let's briefly discuss each of them. We also encourage you to research them more on your own.

MinIO

The foundation of the pipeline architecture is shared storage. A common practice today is to keep data in external storage. Different cloud providers have different solutions, like Amazon S3, Azure Data Storage, Google Cloud Storage, etc. The variety of solutions makes it complex to port solutions from one cloud provider to another. To minimize this dependency, Kubeflow ships with MinIO, a high-performance distributed object storage server, designed for large-scale private cloud infrastructure. Not just for private clouds, MinIO can also act as a consistent gateway to public APIs.

MinIO can be deployed in several different configurations. The default with Kubeflow is as a single container mode when MinIO runs using the Kubernetes built-in persistent storage on one container. Distributed MinIO lets you pool multiple volumes into a single object storage service.[1] It can also withstand multiple node failures and yet ensure full data protection (the number of failures depends on your replication configuration). MinIO Gateway provides S3 APIs on top of Azure Blob storage, Google Cloud storage, Gluster, or NAS storage. The gateway option is the most flexible, and allows you to create cloud independent implementation without scale limits.

While Kubeflow's default MinIO setup works, you will likely want to configure it further. Kubeflow installs both the MinIO server and UI. You can get access to the MinIO UI and explore what is stored, as seen in Figure 3-4, by using port-forwarding, as in Example 3-1, or exposing an ingress. You can log in using Kubeflow's default minio/minio123 user.

Example 3-1. Setting up port-forwarding

```
kubectl port-forward -n kubeflow svc/minio-service 9000:9000 &
```

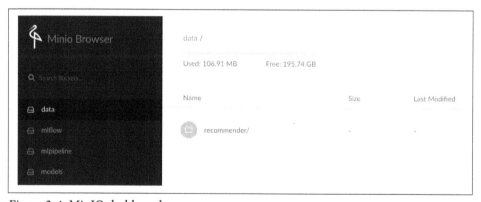

Figure 3-4. MinIO dashboard

---

1 This can run on multiple servers while exposing a consistent endpoint.

In addition, you can also install the MinIO CLI (mc) (*https://oreil.ly/_AAEv*) to access your MinIO installation using commands from your workstation. For macOS, use Homebrew, as in Example 3-2. For Linux Ubuntu, use snap, as in Example 3-3.

Example 3-2. Install MinIO on Mac

```
brew install minio/stable/minio
```

Example 3-3. Install MinIO on Linux

```
pushd ~/bin
wget https://dl.min.io/client/mc/release/linux-amd64/mc
chmod a+x mc
```

You need to configure MinIO to talk to the correct endpoint, as in Example 3-4.

Example 3-4. Configure MinIO client to talk to Kubeflow's MinIO

```
mc config host add minio http://localhost:9000 minio minio123
```

Once you've configured the command line you can make new buckets, as in Example 3-5, or change your setup.

Example 3-5. Create a bucket with MinIO

```
mc mb minio/kf-book-examples
```

MinIO exposes both native and S3-compatible APIs. The S3-compatible APIs are most important since most of our software can talk to S3, like TensorFlow and Spark.

Using MinIO with systems built on top of Hadoop (mostly Java-based) requires Hadoop 2.8 or higher.

Kubeflow installation hardcodes MinIO credentials—minio/minio123, which you can use directly in your applications—but it's generally a better practice to use a secret, especially if you might switch to regular S3. Kubernetes secrets provide you with a way to store credentials on the cluster separate from your application.[2] To set one up for MinIO or S3, create a secret file like in Example 3-6. In Kubernetes secret values

---

2 Storing credentials inside your application can lead to security breaches.

for the ID and key have to be base64 encoded. To encode a value, run the command
`echo -n xxx | base64`.

Example 3-6. Sample MinIO secret

```
apiVersion: v1
kind: Secret
metadata:
  name: minioaccess
  namespace: mynamespace
data:
  AWS_ACCESS_KEY_ID: xxxxxxxxxx
  AWS_SECRET_ACCESS_KEY: xxxxxxxxxxxxxxxxxxxx
```

Save this YAML to the file *minioaccess.yaml*, and deploy the secret using the command `kubectl apply -f minioaccess.yaml`. Now that we understand data communication between pipeline stages, let's work to understand network communication between components.

Istio

Another supporting component of Kubeflow is Istio (*https://istio.io*)—a service mesh providing such vital features as service discovery, load balancing, failure recovery, metrics, monitoring, rate limiting, access control, and end-to-end authentication. Istio, as a service mesh, layers transparently onto a Kubernetes cluster. It integrates into any logging platform, or telemetry or policy system and promotes a uniform way to secure, connect, and monitor microservices. Istio implementation co-locates each service instance with a sidecar network proxy. All network traffic (HTTP, REST, gRPC, etc.) from an individual service instance flows via its local sidecar proxy to the appropriate destination. Thus, the service instance is not aware of the network at large and only knows about its local proxy. In effect, the distributed system network has been abstracted away from the service programmer.

Istio implementation is logically split into a data plane and control plane. The data plane is composed of a set of intelligent proxies. These proxies mediate and control all network communication between pods. The control plane manages and configures the proxies to route traffic.

The main components of Istio are:

Envoy (https://oreil.ly/7i49v)
Istio data plane is based on Envoy proxy, which provides features like failure handling (for example, health checks and bounded retries), dynamic service discovery, and load balancing. Envoy has many built-in features, including:

- Dynamic service discovery
- Load balancing
- TLS termination
- HTTP/2 and gRPC proxies
- Circuit breakers
- Health checks
- Staged rollouts with percent-based traffic splitting
- Fault injection
- Rich metrics

Mixer (https://oreil.ly/NV5xk)
Mixer enforces access control and usage policies across the service mesh, and collects telemetry data from the Envoy proxy and other services. The proxy extracts request-level attributes, and sends them to Mixer for evaluation.

Pilot (https://oreil.ly/lIAq_)
Pilot provides service discovery for the Envoy sidecars and traffic management capabilities for intelligent routing (e.g., A/B tests, canary rollouts) and resiliency (timeouts, retries, circuit breakers, etc.). This is done by converting high-level routing rules that control traffic behavior into Envoy-specific configurations, and propagating them to the sidecars at runtime. Pilot abstracts platform-specific service discovery mechanisms and synthesizes them into a standard format that any sidecar conforming with the Envoy data plane APIs can consume.

Galley (https://oreil.ly/gZdIY)
Galley is Istio's configuration validation, ingestion, processing, and distribution component. It is responsible for insulating the rest of the Istio components from the details of obtaining user configuration from the underlying platform.

Citadel (https://oreil.ly/sLh70)
Citadel enables strong service-to-service and end-user authentication by providing identity and credential management. It allows for upgrading unencrypted traffic in the service mesh. Using Citadel, operators can enforce policies based on service identity rather than on relatively unstable layer 3 or layer 4 network identifiers.

Istio's overall architecture is illustrated in Figure 3-5.

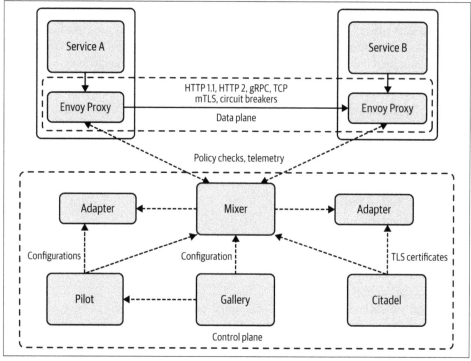

Figure 3-5. Istio architecture

Kubeflow uses Istio to provide a proxy to the Kubeflow UI and to route requests appropriately and securely. Kubeflow's KFServing leverages Knative, which requires a service mesh, like Istio.

Knative

Another unseen support component used by Kubeflow is Knative. We will begin by describing the most important part: Knative Serving. Built on Kubernetes and Istio, Knative Serving (*https://oreil.ly/fcndQ*) supports the deploying and serving of server‐less applications. The Knative Serving project provides middleware primitives that enable:

- Rapid deployment of serverless containers
- Automatic scaling up and down to zero
- Routing and network programming for Istio components
- Point-in-time snapshots of deployed code and configurations

Knative Serving is implemented as a set of Kubernetes CRDs. These objects are used to define and control behavior of a serverless workload:

Service (https://oreil.ly/EbQRg)

The `service.serving.knative.dev` resource manages the workload as a whole. It orchestrates the creation and execution of other objects to ensure that an app has a configuration, a route, and a new revision for each update of the service. Service can be defined to always route traffic to the latest revision or to a specified revision.

Route (https://oreil.ly/FH50y)

The `route.serving.knative.dev` resource maps a network endpoint to one or more revisions. This allows for multiple traffic management approaches, including fractional traffic and named routes.

Configuration (https://oreil.ly/cNsj3)

The `configuration.serving.knative.dev` resource maintains the desired state for deployment. It provides a clean separation between code and configuration and follows the Twelve-Factor App methodology. Modifying a configuration creates a new revision.

Revision (https://oreil.ly/jxpW1)

The `revision.serving.knative.dev` resource is a point-in-time snapshot of the code and configuration for each modification made to the workload. Revisions are immutable objects and can be retained for as long as is useful. Knative Serving Revisions can be automatically scaled up and down according to incoming traffic.

Knative's overall architecture is illustrated in Figure 3-6.

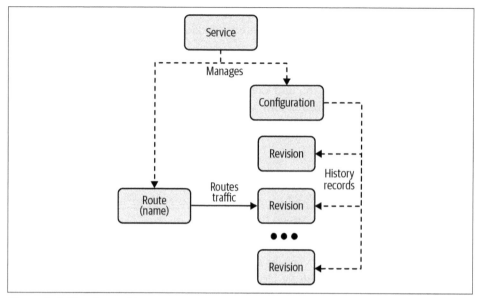

Figure 3-6. Knative architecture

Apache Spark

A more visible supporting component in Kubeflow is Apache Spark. Starting in Kubeflow 1.0, Kubeflow has a built-in Spark operator for running Spark jobs. In addition to the Spark operator, Kubeflow provides integration for using Google's Dataproc and Amazon's Elastic Map Reduce (EMR), two managed cloud services for running Spark. The components and the operator are focused on production use and are not well suited to exploration. For exploration, you can use Spark inside of your Jupyter notebook.

Apache Spark allows you to handle larger datasets and scale problems that cannot fit on a single machine. While Spark does have its own machine learning libraries, it is more commonly used as part of a machine learning pipeline for data or feature preparation. We cover Spark in more detail in Chapter 5.

Kubeflow Multiuser Isolation

The latest version of Kubeflow introduced multiuser isolation, which allows sharing the same pool of resources across different teams and users. Multiuser isolation provides users with a reliable way to isolate and protect their own resources, without accidentally viewing or changing each other's resources. The key concepts of such isolation are:

Administrator

An administrator is someone who creates and maintains the Kubeflow cluster. This person has permission to grant access permissions to others.

User

A user is someone who has access to some set of resources in the cluster. A user needs to be granted access permissions by the administrator.

Profile

A profile is a grouping of all Kubernetes namespaces and resources owned by a user.

As of version 1.0, Kubeflow's Jupyter notebook service is the first application to be fully integrated with multiuser isolation. Notebooks and their creation are controlled by the profile access policies set by the administrator or the owners of the profiles. Resources created by the notebooks (e.g., training jobs and deployments) will also inherit the same access. By default, Kubeflow provides automatic profile creation for authenticated users on first login,[3] which creates a new namespace. Alternatively, profiles for users can be created manually (*https://oreil.ly/6aklV*). This means that every user can work independently in their own namespace and use their own Jupyter server and notebooks. To share access to your server/notebooks with others, go to the manage contributors page and add your collaborators' emails.

Kubeflow's Repositories

As you've seen, Kubeflow is comprised of a number of different components. These components are hosted under the Kubeflow GitHub organization (*https://oreil.ly/LxSB5*). The most important repositories to be familiar with are `kfctl`, which is hosted in the kfctl repo (*https://oreil.ly/aGAsV*), and Kubeflow Pipelines, in the pipelines repo (*https://oreil.ly/SXu1d*). The pipelines repo is especially important as its prebuilt components can save you time. Using the other components does not require explicit installation, but looking at the components issues, like in Katib (*https://oreil.ly/OGJYQ*), can be useful to check for known workarounds for any problems you encounter.

---

3 To enable users to log in, they should be given minimal permission scope that allows them to connect to the Kubernetes cluster. For example, for GCP users, they can be granted IAM roles: Kubernetes Engine Cluster Viewer and IAP-secured Web App User.

Conclusion

You now know the different components of Kubeflow and how they fit together. Kubeflow's central dashboard gives you access to its web components. You've seen that JupyterHub facilitates the explorative phase of model development. We've covered the different built-in training operators for Kubeflow. We revisited Kubeflow pipelines to discuss how they tie together all of Kubeflow's other components. We introduced Katib, Kubeflow's tool for hyperparameter tuning that works on pipelines. We talked about the different options for serving your models with Kubeflow (including KF Serving and Seldon). We discussed Kubeflow's system for tracking your machine learning metadata and artifacts. Then we wrapped it up with some of Kubeflow's supporting components that enable the rest, Knative and Istio. By understanding the different parts of Kubeflow, as well as the overall design, you should now be able to start seeing how your machine learning tasks and workflow translate to Kubeflow.

The next few chapters will help you gain insights into these components and how to apply them to your use cases.

# CHAPTER 4

Kubeflow Pipelines

In the previous chapter we described Kubeflow Pipelines (*https://oreil.ly/387tH*), the component of Kubeflow that orchestrates machine learning applications. Orchestration is necessary because a typical machine learning implementation uses a combination of tools to prepare data, train the model, evaluate performance, and deploy. By formalizing the steps and their sequencing in code, pipelines allow users to formally capture all of the data processing steps, ensuring their reproducibility and auditability, and training and deployment steps.

We will start this chapter by taking a look at the Pipelines UI and showing how to start writing simple pipelines in Python. We'll explore how to transfer data between stages, then continue by getting into ways of leveraging existing applications as part of a pipeline. We will also look at the underlying workflow engine—Argo Workflows, a standard Kubernetes pipeline tool—that Kubeflow uses to run pipelines. Understanding the basics of Argo Workflows allows you to gain a deeper understanding of Kubeflow Pipelines and will aid in debugging. We will then show what Kubeflow Pipelines adds to Argo.

We'll wrap up Kubeflow Pipelines by showing how to implement conditional execution in pipelines and how to run pipelines execution on schedule. Task-specific components of pipelines will be covered in their respective chapters.

Getting Started with Pipelines

The Kubeflow Pipelines platform consists of:

- A UI for managing and tracking pipelines and their execution
- An engine for scheduling a pipeline's execution
- An SDK for defining, building, and deploying pipelines in Python
- Notebook support for using the SDK and pipeline execution

The easiest way to familiarize yourself with pipelines is to take a look at prepackaged examples.

Exploring the Prepackaged Sample Pipelines

To help users understand pipelines, Kubeflow installs with a few sample pipelines. You can find these prepackaged in the Pipeline web UI, as seen in Figure 4-1. Note that at the time of writing, only the Basic to Conditional execution pipelines are generic, while the rest of them will run only on Google Kubernetes Engine (GKE). If you try to run them on non-GKE environments, they will fail.

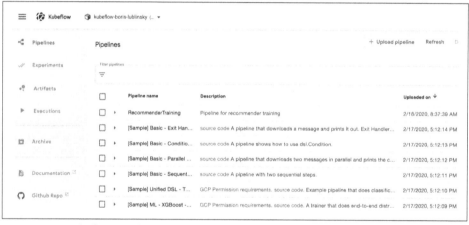

Figure 4-1. Kubeflow pipelines UI: prepackaged pipelines

Clicking a specific pipeline will show its execution graph or source, as seen in Figure 4-2.

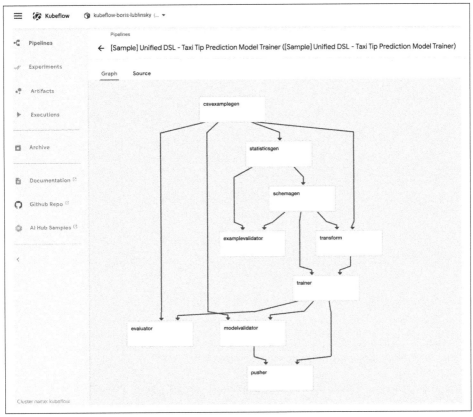

Figure 4-2. Kubeflow pipelines UI: pipeline graph view

Clicking the source tab will show the pipeline's compiled code, which is an Argo YAML file (this is covered in more detail in "Argo: the Foundation of Pipelines" on page 54).

In this area you are welcome to experiment with running pipelines to get a better feel for their execution and the capabilities of the Pipelines UI.

To invoke a specific pipeline, simply click it; this will bring up Pipeline's view as presented in Figure 4-3.

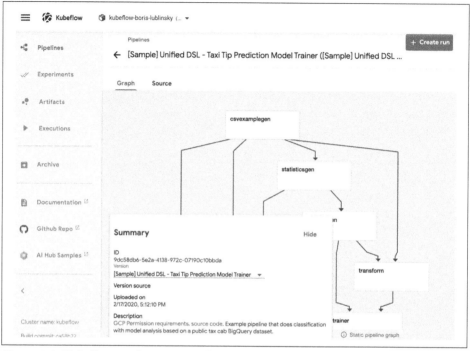

Figure 4-3. Kubeflow pipelines UI: pipeline view

To run the pipeline, click the "Create Run" button and follow the instructions on the screen.

 When running a pipeline you must choose an experiment. Experiment here is just a convenience grouping for pipeline executions (runs). You can always use the "Default" experiment created by Kubeflow's installation. Also, pick "One-off" for the Run type to execute the pipeline once. We will talk about recurring execution in "Running Pipelines on Schedule" on page 65.

Building a Simple Pipeline in Python

We have seen how to execute precompiled Kubeflow Pipelines, now let's investigate how to author our own new pipelines. Kubeflow Pipelines are stored as YAML files executed by a program called Argo (see "Argo: the Foundation of Pipelines" on page 54). Thankfully, Kubeflow exposes a Python domain-specific language (DSL) (*https://oreil.ly/7LdzK*) for authoring pipelines. The DSL is a Pythonic representation of the operations performed in the ML workflow and built with ML workloads specifically in mind. The DSL also allows for some simple Python functions to be used as pipeline stages without you having to explicitly build a container.

The Chapter 4 examples can be found in the notebooks in this book's GitHub repository (*https://oreil.ly/Kubeflow_for_ML_ch04*).

A pipeline is, in its essence, a graph of container execution. In addition to specifying which containers should run in which order, it also allows the user to pass arguments to the entire pipeline and between participating containers.

For each container (when using the Python SDK), we must:

- Create the container—either as a simple Python function, or with any Docker container (read more in Chapter 9).
- Create an operation that references that container as well as the command line arguments, data mounts, and variable to pass the container.
- Sequence the operations, defining which may happen in parallel and which must complete before moving on to a further step.[1]
- Compile this pipeline, defined in Python, into a YAML file that Kubeflow Pipelines can consume.

Pipelines are a key feature of Kubeflow and you will see them again throughout the book. In this chapter we are going to show the simplest examples possible to illustrate the basic principles of Pipelines. This won't feel like "machine learning" and that is by design.

For our first Kubeflow operation, we are going to use a technique known as *lightweight Python functions*. We should not, however, let the word *lightweight* deceive us. In a lightweight Python function, we define a Python function and then let Kubeflow take care of packaging that function into a container and creating an operation.

For the sake of simplicity, let's declare the simplest of functions an echo. That is a function that takes a single input, an integer, and returns that input.

Let's start by importing `kfp` and defining our function:

```
import kfp
def simple_echo(i: int) -> int:
    return i
```

---

1 This can often be automatically inferred when passing the result of one pipeline stage as the input to others. You can also specify additional dependencies manually.

Note that we use `snake_case`, not `camelCase`, for our function names. At the time of writing there exists a bug (feature?) such that camel case names (for example: naming our function `simpleEcho`) will produce errors.

Next, we want to wrap our function `simple_echo` into a Kubeflow Pipeline operation. There's a nice little method to do this: `kfp.components.func_to_container_op`. This method returns a factory function with a strongly typed signature:

```
simpleStronglyTypedFunction =
   kfp.components.func_to_container_op(deadSimpleIntEchoFn)
```

When we create a pipeline in the next step, the factory function will construct a ContainerOp, which will run the original function (echo_fn) in a container:

```
foo = simpleStronglyTypedFunction(1)
type(foo)
Out[5]: kfp.dsl._container_op.ContainerOp
```

If your code can be accelerated by a GPU it is easy to mark a stage as using GPU resources; simply add `.set_gpu_limit(NUM_GPUS)` to your `ContainerOp`.

Now let's sequence the ContainerOp(s) (there is only one) into a pipeline. This pipeline will take one parameter (the number we will echo). The pipeline also has a bit of metadata associated with it. While echoing numbers may be a trivial use of parameters, in real-world use cases you would include variables you might want to tune later such as hyperparameters for machine learning algorithms.

Finally, we compile our pipeline into a zipped YAML file, which we can then upload to the Pipelines UI.

```
@kfp.dsl.pipeline(
  name='Simple Echo',
  description='This is an echo pipeline. It echoes numbers.'
)
def echo_pipeline(param_1: kfp.dsl.PipelineParam):
  my_step = simpleStronglyTypedFunction(i= param_1)

kfp.compiler.Compiler().compile(echo_pipeline,
  'echo-pipeline.zip')
```

It is also possible to run the pipeline directly from the notebook, which we'll do in the next example.

A pipeline with only one component is not very interesting. For our next example, we will customize the containers of our lightweight Python functions. We'll create a new pipeline that installs and imports additional Python libraries, builds from a specified base image, and passes output between containers.

We are going to create a pipeline that divides a number by another number, and then adds a third number. First let's create our simple add function, as shown in Example 4-1.

Example 4-1. A simple Python function

```
def add(a: float, b: float) -> float:
   '''Calculates sum of two arguments'''
   return a + b

add_op = comp.func_to_container_op(add)
```

Next, let's create a slightly more complex function. Additionally, let's have this function require and import from a nonstandard Python library, numpy. This must be done within the function. That is because global imports from the notebook will not be packaged into the containers we create. Of course, it is also important to make sure that our container has the libraries we are importing installed.

To do that we'll pass the specific container we want to use as our base image to .func_to_container(, as in Example 4-2.

Example 4-2. A less-simple Python function

```
from typing import NamedTuple
def my_divmod(dividend: float, divisor:float) -> \
      NamedTuple('MyDivmodOutput', [('quotient', float), ('remainder', float)]):
   '''Divides two numbers and calculate  the quotient and remainder'''
   #Imports inside a component function:
   import numpy as np ❶

   #This function demonstrates how to use nested functions inside a
   # component function:
   def divmod_helper(dividend, divisor): ❷
       return np.divmod(dividend, divisor)

   (quotient, remainder) = divmod_helper(dividend, divisor)

   from collections import namedtuple
   divmod_output = namedtuple('MyDivmodOutput', ['quotient', 'remainder'])
   return divmod_output(quotient, remainder)

divmod_op = comp.func_to_container_op(
              my_divmod, base_image='tensorflow/tensorflow:1.14.0-py3') ❸
```

❶ Importing libraries inside the function.

❷ Nested functions inside lightweight Python functions are also OK.

❸ Calling for a specific base container.

Now we will build a pipeline. The pipeline in Example 4-3 uses the functions defined previously, my_divmod and add, as stages.

Example 4-3. A simple pipeline

```
@dsl.pipeline(
    name='Calculation pipeline',
    description='A toy pipeline that performs arithmetic calculations.'
)
def calc_pipeline(
    a='a',
    b='7',
    c='17',
):
    #Passing pipeline parameter and a constant value as operation arguments
    add_task = add_op(a, 4) #Returns a dsl.ContainerOp class instance.

    #Passing a task output reference as operation arguments
    #For an operation with a single return value, the output
    # reference can be accessed using `task.output`
    # or `task.outputs['output_name']` syntax
    divmod_task = divmod_op(add_task.output, b) ❶

    #For an operation with multiple return values, the output references
    # can be accessed using `task.outputs['output_name']` syntax
    result_task = add_op(divmod_task.outputs['quotient'], c) ❶
```

❶ Values being passed between containers. Order of operations is inferred from this.

Finally, we use the client to submit the pipeline for execution, which returns the links to execution and experiment. Experiments group the executions together. You can also use kfp.compiler.Compiler().compile and upload the zip file as in the first example if you prefer:

```
client = kfp.Client()
#Specify pipeline argument values
# arguments = {'a': '7', 'b': '8'} #whatever makes sense for new version
#Submit a pipeline run
client.create_run_from_pipeline_func(calc_pipeline, arguments=arguments)
```

Following the link returned by create_run_from_pipeline_func, we can get to the execution web UI, which shows the pipeline itself and intermediate results, as seen in Figure 4-4.

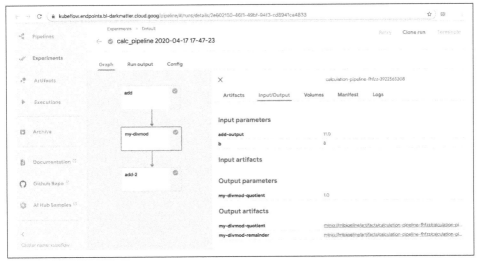

Figure 4-4. Pipeline execution

As we've seen, the *lightweight* in *lightweight Python functions* refers to the ease of making these steps in our process and not the power of the functions themselves. We can use custom imports, base images, and how to hand off small results between containers.

In the next section, we'll show how to hand larger data files between containers by mounting volumes to the containers.

Using Annotations to Simplify Our Pipeline

As you may have noticed, directly calling `comp.func_to_container_op` all the time can get kind of repetitive. To avoid this, you can create a function that returns a `kfp.dsl.ContainerOp`. Since people don't always like creating absurdly large and fat functions to do everything in real life, we'll leave this here as an aside in case the reader is interested in it. It's also worth noting that adding the `@kfp.dsl.component` annotation instructs the Kubeflow compiler to turn on static type checking:

```
@kfp.dsl.component
def my_component(my_param):
  ...
  return kfp.dsl.ContainerOp(
    name='My component name',
    image='gcr.io/path/to/container/image'
  )
```

Finally, when it comes to incorporating these components into pipelines, you would do something like this:

```
@kfp.dsl.pipeline(
  name='My pipeline',
```

```
        description='My machine learning pipeline'
    )
    def my_pipeline(param_1: PipelineParam, param_2: PipelineParam):
        my_step = my_component(my_param='a')
```

Storing Data Between Steps

In the previous example, the data passed between containers was small and of primitive types (such as numeric, string, list, and arrays). In practice however, we will likely be passing much larger data (for instance, entire datasets). In Kubeflow, there are two primary methods for doing this—persistent volumes inside the Kubernetes cluster, and cloud storage options (such as S3), though each method has inherent problems.

Persistent volumes abstract the storage layer. Depending on the vendor, persistent volumes can be slow with provisioning and have IO limits. Check to see if your vendor supports read-write-many storage classes, allowing for storage access by multiple pods, which is required for some types of parallelism. Storage classes can be one of the following.[2]

ReadWriteOnce
> The volume can be mounted as read-write by a single node.

ReadOnlyMany
> The volume can be mounted read-only by many nodes.

ReadWriteMany
> The volume can be mounted as read-write by many nodes.

Your system/cluster administrator may be able to add read-write-many support.[3] Additionally, many cloud providers include their proprietary read-write-many implementations, see for example dynamic provisioning (*https://oreil.ly/je18X*) on GKE. but make sure to ask if there is a single node bottleneck.

Kubeflow Pipelines' `VolumeOp` allows you to create an automatically managed persistent volume, as shown in Example 4-4. To add the volume to your operation you can just call `add_pvolumes` with a dictionary of mount points to volumes, e.g., `download_data_op(year).add_pvolumes({"/data_processing": dvop.volume})`.

---

2 Kubernetes persistent volumes can provide different access modes (*https://oreil.ly/KbGrQ*).

3 Generic read-write-many implementation is NFS server (*https://oreil.ly/QXEBX*).

Example 4-4. Mailing list data prep

```
dvop = dsl.VolumeOp(name="create_pvc",
                    resource_name="my-pvc-2",
                    size="5Gi",
                    modes=dsl.VOLUME_MODE_RWO)
```

While less common in the Kubeflow examples, using an object storage solution, in some cases, may be more suitable. MinIO provides cloud native object storage by working either as a gateway to an existing object storage engine or on its own.[4] We covered how to configure MinIO back in Chapter 3.

Kubeflow's built-in `file_output` mechanism automatically transfers the specified local file into MinIO between pipeline steps for you. To use `file_output`, write your files locally in your container and specify the parameter in your `ContainerOp`, as shown in Example 4-5.

Example 4-5. File output example

```
    fetch = kfp.dsl.ContainerOp(name='download',
                                image='busybox',
                                command=['sh', '-c'],
                                arguments=[
                                    'sleep 1;'
                                    'mkdir -p /tmp/data;'
                                    'wget ' + data_url +
                                    ' -O /tmp/data/results.csv'
                                ],
                                file_outputs={'downloaded': '/tmp/data'})
    # This expects a directory of inputs not just a single file
```

If you don't want to use MinIO, you can also directly use your provider's object storage, but this may compromise some portability.

The ability to mount data locally is an essential task in any machine learning pipeline. Here we have briefly outlined multiple methods and provided examples for each.

Introduction to Kubeflow Pipelines Components

Kubeflow Pipelines builds on Argo Workflows (*https://oreil.ly/S2GuQ*), an open source, container-native workflow engine for Kubernetes. In this section we will describe how Argo works, what it does, and how Kubeflow Pipeline supplements Argo to make it easier to use by data scientists.

---

4 Usage of the cloud native access storage can be handy if you need to ensure portability of your solution across multiple cloud providers.

Argo: the Foundation of Pipelines

Kubeflow installs all of the Argo components. Though having Argo installed on your computer is not necessary to use Kubeflow Pipelines, having the Argo command-line tool makes it easier to understand and debug your pipelines.

 By default, Kubeflow configures Argo to use the Docker executor. If your platform does not support the Docker APIs, you need to switch your executor to a compatible one. This is done by changing the containerRuntimeExecutor value in the Argo *params* file. See Appendix A for details on the trade-offs. The majority of the examples in this book use the Docker executor but can be adapted to other executors.

On macOS, you can install Argo with Homebrew, as shown in Example 4-6.[5]

Example 4-6. Argo installation

```
#!/bin/bash
# Download the binary
curl -sLO https://github.com/argoproj/argo/releases/download/v2.8.1/argo-linux-amd64

# Make binary executable
chmod +x argo-linux-amd64

# Move binary to path
mv ./argo-linux-amd64 ~/bin/argo
```

You can verify your Argo installation by running the Argo examples with the command-line tool in the Kubeflow namespace: follow these Argo instructions (*https://oreil.ly/QFxv2*). When you run the Argo examples the pipelines are visible with the argo command, as in Example 4-7.

Example 4-7. Listing Argo executions

```
$ argo list -n kubeflow
NAME              STATUS      AGE   DURATION
loops-maps-4mxp5  Succeeded   30m   12s
hello-world-wsxbr Succeeded   39m   15s
```

Since pipelines are implemented with Argo, you can use the same technique to check on them as well. You can also get information about specific workflow execution, as shown in Example 4-8.

---

5 For installation of Argo Workflow on another OS, refer to these Argo instructions (*https://oreil.ly/s9CZM*).

Example 4-8. Getting Argo execution details

```
$ argo get hello-world-wsxbr -n kubeflow    ❶
Name:              hello-world-wsxbr
Namespace:         kubeflow
ServiceAccount:    default
Status:            Succeeded
Created:           Tue Feb 12 10:05:04 -0600 (2 minutes ago)
Started:           Tue Feb 12 10:05:04 -0600 (2 minutes ago)
Finished:          Tue Feb 12 10:05:23 -0600 (1 minute ago)
Duration:          19 seconds

STEP                    PODNAME              DURATION  MESSAGE
 ✓ hello-world-wsxbr    hello-world-wsxbr    18s
```

❶ `hello-world-wsxbr` is the name that we got using `argo list -n kubeflow` above. In your case the name will be different.

We can also view the execution logs by using the command in Example 4-9.

Example 4-9. Getting the log of Argo execution

```
$ argo logs hello-world-wsxbr -n kubeflow
```

This produces the result shown in Example 4-10.

Example 4-10. Argo execution log

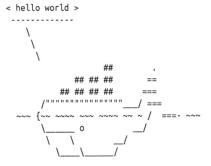

```
< hello world >
 -------------
    \
     \
      \
                    ##        .
              ## ## ##       ==
              ## ## ## ##    ===
          /"""""""""""""""""___/ ===
     ~~~ {~~ ~~~~ ~~~ ~~~~ ~~ ~ /  ===- ~~~
          _____ o          __/
           \    \        __/
            _____/
```

You can also delete a specific workflow; see Example 4-11.

Example 4-11. Deleting Argo execution

```
$ argo delete hello-world-wsxbr -n kubeflow
```

Alternatively, you can get pipeline execution information using the Argo UI, as seen in Figure 4-5.

Figure 4-5. Argo UI for pipeline execution

Installing Argo UI

By default, Kubeflow does not provide access to the Argo UI. To enable access, you have to do the following:

- Make sure that your Argo UI deployment corresponds to the UI provided in code in this book's GitHub repo (*https://oreil.ly/Kubeflow_for_ML_ch04_install*).

- Create a virtual service by applying the YAML provided in code in this book's GitHub repo (*https://oreil.ly/Kubeflow_for_ML_ch04_vsyaml*).

- Point your browser to *<cluster main url>/argo*.

You can also look at the details of the flow execution graph by clicking a specific workflow, as seen in Figure 4-6.

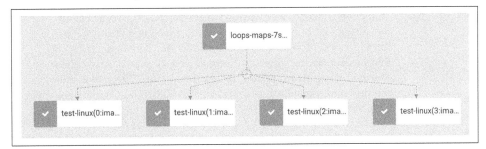

Figure 4-6. Argo UI execution graph

For any Kubeflow pipeline you run, you can also view that pipeline in the Argo CLI/UI. Note that because ML pipelines are using the Argo CRD, you can also see the result of the pipeline execution in the Argo UI (as in Figure 4-7).

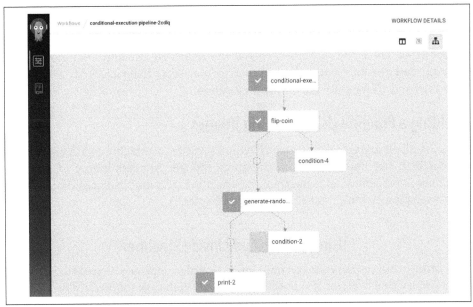

Figure 4-7. Viewing Kubeflow pipelines in Argo UI

Currently, the Kubeflow community is actively looking at alterna-tive foundational technologies for running Kubeflow pipelines, one of which is Tekton (*https://tekton.dev*). The paper by A. Singh et al., "Kubeflow Pipelines with Tekton" (*https://oreil.ly/rrg-V*), gives "ini-tial design, specifications, and code for enabling Kubeflow Pipe-lines to run on top of Tekton." The basic idea here is to create an intermediate format that can be produced by pipelines and then executed using Argo, Tekton, or other runtimes. The initial code for this implementation is found in this Kubeflow GitHub repo (*https://oreil.ly/nes4r*).

What Kubeflow Pipelines Adds to Argo Workflow

Argo underlies the workflow execution; however, using it directly requires you to do awkward things. First, you must define your workflow in YAML, which can be diffi-cult. Second, you must containerize your code, which can be tedious. The main advantage of KF Pipelines is that you can use Python APIs for defining/creating pipe-lines, which automates the generation of much of the YAML boilerplate for workflow definitions and is extremely friendly for data scientists/Python developers. Kubeflow Pipelines also has hooks that add building blocks for machine learning-specific components. These APIs not only generate the YAML but can also simplify container creation and resource usage. In addition to the APIs, Kubeflow adds a recurring scheduler and UI for configuration and execution.

Building a Pipeline Using Existing Images

Building pipeline stages directly from Python provides a straightforward entry point. It does limit our implementation to Python, though. Another feature of Kubeflow Pipelines is the ability to orchestrate the execution of a multilanguage implementa-tion leveraging prebuilt Docker images (see Chapter 9).

Using Custom Code Inside Pipelines

In order to use custom code and tools inside Kubeflow Pipelines, it needs to be pack-aged into a container: see this Kubeflow documentation page (*https://oreil.ly/tTZBD*). Once the container is uploaded to an accessible repository, it can be included in the pipeline. Pipelines allow the user to configure some of the container execution through environment variables and pass data between pipeline components. Environ-ment variables can be set using Kubernetes Python library (*https://oreil.ly/WdJNl*). Include the Kubernetes library and then implement the code:

```
from kubernetes import client as k8s_client

data = dsl.ContainerOp(
    name='updatedata',
    image='lightbend/recommender-data-update-publisher:0.2') \
    .add_env_variable(k8s_client.V1EnvVar(name='MINIO_KEY', value='minio')) ❶
```

❶ Here we set the environment variable MINIO_KEY to the value of minio.

The way you can pass parameters between steps (containers), depends on the Argo runtime that you are using. For example, in the case of the docker runtime, you can pass parameters by value. Those parameters are exposed by the image. If you are using the k8api runtime, then the only way to pass parameters is through the file.

In addition to our previous imports, we also want to import the Kubernetes client, which allows us to use Kubernetes functions directly from Python code (see Example 4-12).

Example 4-12. Exporting Kubernetes client

```
from kubernetes import client as k8s_client
```

Again, we create a client and experiment to run our pipeline. As mentioned earlier, experiments group the runs of pipelines. You can only create a given experiment once, so Example 4-13 shows how to either create a new experiment or use an existing one.

Example 4-13. Obtaining pipeline experiment

```
client = kfp.Client()
exp = client.get_experiment(experiment_name ='mdupdate')
```

Now we create our pipeline (Example 4-14). The images used need to be accessible, and we're specifying the full names, so they resolve. Since these containers are pre-built, we need to configure them for our pipeline.

The pre-built containers we are using have their storage configured by the MINIO_* environment variables. So we configure them to use our local MinIO install by calling add_env_variable.

In addition to the automatic dependencies created when passing parameters between stages, you can also specify that a stage requires a previous stage with after. This is most useful when there is an external side effect, like updating a database.

Example 4-14. Example recommender pipeline

```
@dsl.pipeline(
  name='Recommender model update',
  description='Demonstrate usage of pipelines for multi-step model update'
)
def recommender_pipeline():
    # Load new data
  data = dsl.ContainerOp(
      name='updatedata',
      image='lightbend/recommender-data-update-publisher:0.2') \
    .add_env_variable(k8s_client.V1EnvVar(name='MINIO_URL',
        value='http://minio-service.kubeflow.svc.cluster.local:9000')) \
    .add_env_variable(k8s_client.V1EnvVar(name='MINIO_KEY', value='minio')) \
    .add_env_variable(k8s_client.V1EnvVar(name='MINIO_SECRET', value='minio123'))
    # Train the model
  train = dsl.ContainerOp(
      name='trainmodel',
      image='lightbend/ml-tf-recommender:0.2') \
    .add_env_variable(k8s_client.V1EnvVar(name='MINIO_URL',
          value='minio-service.kubeflow.svc.cluster.local:9000')) \
    .add_env_variable(k8s_client.V1EnvVar(name='MINIO_KEY', value='minio')) \
    .add_env_variable(k8s_client.V1EnvVar(name='MINIO_SECRET', value='minio123'))
  train.after(data)
    # Publish new model
  publish = dsl.ContainerOp(
      name='publishmodel',
      image='lightbend/recommender-model-publisher:0.2') \
    .add_env_variable(k8s_client.V1EnvVar(name='MINIO_URL',
          value='http://minio-service.kubeflow.svc.cluster.local:9000')) \
    .add_env_variable(k8s_client.V1EnvVar(name='MINIO_KEY', value='minio')) \
    .add_env_variable(k8s_client.V1EnvVar(name='MINIO_SECRET', value='minio123')) \
    .add_env_variable(k8s_client.V1EnvVar(name='KAFKA_BROKERS',
          value='cloudflow-kafka-brokers.cloudflow.svc.cluster.local:9092')) \
    .add_env_variable(k8s_client.V1EnvVar(name='DEFAULT_RECOMMENDER_URL',
          value='http://recommendermodelserver.kubeflow.svc.cluster.local:8501')) \
    .add_env_variable(k8s_client.V1EnvVar(name='ALTERNATIVE_RECOMMENDER_URL',
          value='http://recommendermodelserver1.kubeflow.svc.cluster.local:8501'))
  publish.after(train)
```

Since the pipeline definition is just code, you can make it more compact by using a loop to set the MinIO parameters instead of doing it on each stage.

As before, we need to compile the pipeline, either explicitly with `compiler.Com piler().compile` or implicitly with `create_run_from_pipeline_func`. Now go ahead and run the pipeline (as in Figure 4-8).

Figure 4-8. Execution of recommender pipelines example

Kubeflow Pipeline Components

In addition to container operations which we've just discussed, Kubeflow Pipelines also exposes additional operations with components. Components expose different Kubernetes resources or external operations (like `dataproc`). Kubeflow components allow developers to package machine learning tools while abstracting away the specifics on the containers or CRDs used.

We have used Kubeflow's building blocks fairly directly, and we have used the `func_to_container` component.[6] Some components, like `func_to_container`, are available as Python code and can be imported like normal. Other components are specified using Kubeflow's `component.yaml` system and need to be loaded. In our opinion, the best way to work with Kubeflow components is to download a specific tag of the repo, allowing us to use `load_component_from_file`, as shown in Example 4-15.

Example 4-15. Pipeline release

```
wget https://github.com/kubeflow/pipelines/archive/0.2.5.tar.gz
tar -xvf 0.2.5.tar.gz
```

---

6 Many of the standard components are in this Kubeflow GitHub repo (*https://oreil.ly/0WX6k*).

There is a `load_component` function that takes a component's name and attempts to resolve it. We don't recommend using this function since it defaults to a search path that includes fetching, from Github, the master branch of the pipelines library, which is unstable.

We explore data preparation components in depth in the next chapter; however, let's quickly look at a file-fetching component as an example. In our recommender example earlier in the chapter, we used a special prebuilt container to fetch our data since it was not already in a persistent volume. Instead, we can use the Kubeflow GCS component `google-cloud/storage/download/` to download our data. Assuming you've downloaded the pipeline release as in Example 4-15, you can load the component with `load_component_from_file` as in Example 4-16.

Example 4-16. Load GCS download component

```
gcs_download_component = kfp.components.load_component_from_file(
    "pipelines-0.2.5/components/google-cloud/storage/download/component.yaml")
```

When a component is loaded, it returns a function that produces a pipeline stage when called. Most components take parameters to configure their behavior. You can get a list of the components' options by calling `help` on the loaded component, or looking at the *component.yaml*. The GCS download component requires us to configure what we are downloading with `gcs_path`, shown in Example 4-17.

Example 4-17. Loading pipeline storage component from relative path and web link

```
dl_op = gcs_download_component(
    gcs_path=
    "gs://ml-pipeline-playground/tensorflow-tfx-repo/tfx/components/testdata/external/csv"
) # Your path goes here
```

In Chapter 5, we explore more common Kubeflow pipeline components for data and feature preparation.

Advanced Topics in Pipelines

All of the examples that we have shown so far are purely sequential. There are also cases in which we need the ability to check conditions and change the behavior of the pipeline accordingly.

Conditional Execution of Pipeline Stages

Kubeflow Pipelines allows conditional executions via dsl.Condition. Let's look at a very simple example, where, depending on the value of a variable, different calculations are executed.

A simple notebook implementing this example follows. It starts with the imports necessary for this, in Example 4-18.

Example 4-18. Importing required components

```
import kfp
from kfp import dsl
from kfp.components import func_to_container_op, InputPath, OutputPath
```

Once the imports are in place, we can implement several simple functions, as shown in Example 4-19.

Example 4-19. Functions implementation

```
@func_to_container_op
def get_random_int_op(minimum: int, maximum: int) -> int:
    """Generate a random number between minimum and maximum (inclusive)."""
    import random
    result = random.randint(minimum, maximum)
    print(result)
    return result

@func_to_container_op
def process_small_op(data: int):
    """Process small numbers."""
    print("Processing small result", data)
    return

@func_to_container_op
def process_medium_op(data: int):
    """Process medium numbers."""
    print("Processing medium result", data)
    return

@func_to_container_op
def process_large_op(data: int):
    """Process large numbers."""
    print("Processing large result", data)
    return
```

We implement all of the functions directly using Python (as in the previous example). The first function generates an integer between 0 and 100, and the next three constitute a simple skeleton for the actual processing. The pipeline is implemented as in Example 4-20.

Example 4-20. Pipeline implementation

```
@dsl.pipeline(
    name='Conditional execution pipeline',
    description='Shows how to use dsl.Condition().'
)
def conditional_pipeline():
    number = get_random_int_op(0, 100).output ❶
    with dsl.Condition(number < 10): ❷
        process_small_op(number)
    with dsl.Condition(number > 10 and number < 50): ❷
        process_medium_op(number)
    with dsl.Condition(number > 50): ❷
        process_large_op(number)

kfp.Client().create_run_from_pipeline_func(conditional_pipeline, arguments={}) ❸
```

❶ Depending on the number we get here…

❷ We will continue on to one of these operations.

❸ Note here that we are specifying empty arguments—required parameter.

Finally, the execution graph, as shown in Figure 4-9.

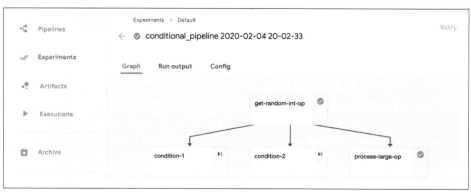

Figure 4-9. Execution of conditional pipelines example

From this graph, we can see that the pipeline really splits into three branches and process-large-op execution is selected in this run. To validate that this is correct, we look at the execution log, shown in Figure 4-10.

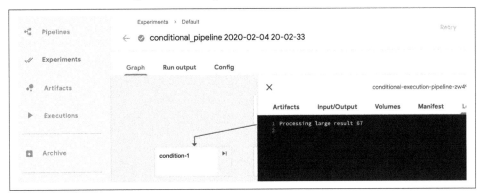

Figure 4-10. Viewing conditional pipeline log

Here we can see that the generated number is 67. This number is larger than 50, which means that the *process_large_op* branch should be executed.[7]

Running Pipelines on Schedule

We have run our pipeline manually. This is good for testing, but is often insufficient for production environments. Fortunately, you can run pipelines on a schedule, as described on thisKubeflow documentation page (*https://oreil.ly/8v3fb*). First, you need to upload a pipeline definition and specify a description. When this is done, you can create a periodic run by creating a run and selecting a run type of "Recurring," then following the instructions on the screen, as seen in Figure 4-11.

In this figure we are setting a pipeline to run every day.

 When creating a periodic run we are specifying how often to run a pipeline, not when to run it. In the current implementation, the time of execution is defined by when the run is created. Once it is created, it is executed immediately and then executed with the defined frequency. If, for example, a daily run is created at 10 am, it will be executed at 10 am daily.

Setting periodic execution of pipelines is an important functionality, allowing you to completely automate pipeline execution.

---

7 A slightly more complex example of conditional processing (with nested conditions) can be found in this GitHub site (*https://oreil.ly/WBwD1*).

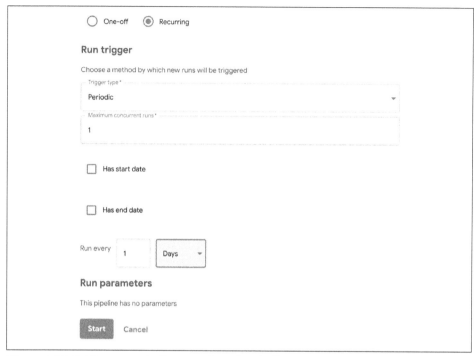

Figure 4-11. Setting up periodic execution of a pipeline

Conclusion

You should now have the basics of how to build, schedule, and run some simple pipelines. You also learned about the tools that pipelines use for when you need to debug. We showed how to integrate existing software into pipelines, how to implement conditional execution inside a pipeline, and how to run pipelines on a schedule.

In our next chapter, we look at how to use pipelines for data preparation with some examples.

# CHAPTER 5

Data and Feature Preparation

Machine learning algorithms are only as good as their training data. Getting good data for training involves data and feature preparation.

Data preparation is the process of sourcing the data and making sure it's valid. This is a multistep process[1] that can include data collection, augmentation, statistics calculation, schema validation, outlier pruning, and various validation techniques. Not having enough data can lead to overfitting, missing significant correlations, and more. Putting in the effort to collect more records and information about each sample during data preparation can considerably improve the model.[2]

Feature preparation (sometimes called *feature engineering*) refers to transforming the raw input data into features that the machine learning model can use.[3] Poor feature preparation can lead to losing out on important relations, such as a linear model with nonlinear terms not expanded, or a deep learning model with inconsistent image orientation.

Small changes in data and feature preparation can lead to significantly different model outputs. The iterative approach is the best for both feature and data preparation, revisiting them as your understanding of the problem and model changes.

---

1 See the TFX documentation (*https://www.tensorflow.org/tfx*) for a good summary if you are new to data preparation.

2 The positive impact of using more data in training is made clear in A. Halevy et al., "The Unreasonable Effectiveness of Data," IEEE Intelligent Systems 24, no. 2 (March/April 2009): 8-12, *https://oreil.ly/YI820*, and T. Schnoebelen, "More Data Beats Better Algorithms," Data Science Central, September 23, 2016, *https://oreil.ly/oLe1R*.

3 For the formal definition, see "Six Steps to Master Machine Learning with Data Preparation" (*https://oreil.ly/qyKTT*).

Kubeflow Pipelines makes it easier for us to iterate our data and feature preparation. We will explore how to use hyperparameter tuning to iterate in Chapter 10.

In this chapter, we will cover different approaches to data and feature preparation and demonstrate how to make them repeatable by using pipelines. We assume you are already familiar with local tools. As such, we'll start by covering how to structure our local code for pipelines, and then move on to more scalable distributed tools. Once we've explored the tools, we'll put them together in a pipeline, using the examples from "Introducing Our Case Studies" on page 10.

Deciding on the Correct Tooling

There are a wide variety of data and feature preparation tools.[4] We can categorize them into distributed and local. Local tools run on a single machine and offer a great amount of flexibility. Distributed tools run on many machines so they can handle larger and more complex tasks. With two very distinct paths of tooling, making the wrong decision here can require substantial changes in code later.

If the input data size is relatively small, a single machine offers you all of the tools you are used to. Larger data sizes tend to require distributed tools for the entire pipeline or just as a sampling stage. Even with smaller datasets, distributed systems, like Apache Spark, Dask, or TFX with Beam, can be faster but may require learning new tools.[5]

Using the same tool for all of the data and feature preparation activities is not necessary. Using multiple tools is especially common when working with different datasets where using the same tools would be inconvenient. Kubeflow Pipelines allows you to split the implementation into multiple steps and connect them (even if they use different languages) into a cohesive system.

Local Data and Feature Preparation

Working locally limits the scale of data but offers the most comprehensive range of tools. A common way to implement data and feature preparation is with Jupyter notebooks. In Chapter 4, we covered how to turn parts of the notebook into a pipeline, and here we'll look at how to structure our data and feature prep code to make this easy.

Using notebooks for data preparation can be a great way to start exploring the data. Notebooks can be especially useful at this stage since we often have the least amount

---

4 There are too many tools to cover here, but this blog post (*https://oreil.ly/Iv9xi*) includes many.

5 Datasets tend to grow over time rather than shrinking, so starting with distributed tooling can help you scale your work.

of understanding, and because using visualizations to understand our data can be quite beneficial.

Fetching the Data

For our mailing list example, we use data from public archives on the internet. Ideally, you want to connect to a database, stream, or other data repository. However, even in production, fetching web data can be necessary. First, we'll implement our data-fetching algorithm, which takes an Apache Software Foundation (ASF) project's email list location along with the year from which to fetch messages. Example 5-1 returns the path to the records it fetches so we can use that as the input to the next pipeline stage.

 The function downloads at *most* one year of data, and it sleeps between calls. This is to prevent overwhelming the ASF mail archive servers. The ASF is a charity; please be mindful of that when downloading data and do not abuse this service.

Example 5-1. Downloading the mailing list data

```
def download_data(year: int) -> str:

    # The imports are inline here so Kubeflow can serialize the function correctly.
    from datetime import datetime
    from lxml import etree
    from requests import get
    from time import sleep

    import json

    def scrapeMailArchives(mailingList: str, year: int, month: int):
        #Ugly xpath code goes here. See the example repo if you're curious.

    datesToScrape =  [(year, i) for i in range(1,2)]

    records = []
    for y,m in datesToScrape:
        print(m,"-",y)
        records += scrapeMailArchives("spark-dev", y, m)
    output_path = '/data_processing/data.json'
    with open(output_path, 'w') as f:
        json.dump(records, f)

    return output_path
```

This code downloads all of the mailing list data for a given year and saves it to a known path. In this example, a persistent volume needs to be mounted there to allow this data to move between stages, when we make our pipeline.

You may have a data dump as part of the machine learning pipeline, or a different system or team may provide one. For data on GCS or a PV, you can use the built-in components `google-cloud/storage/download` or `filesystem/get_subdirectory` to load the data instead of writing a custom function.

Data Cleaning: Filtering Out the Junk

Now that we've loaded our data, it's time to do some simple data cleaning. Local tools are more common, so we'll focus on them first. While data cleaning often depends on domain expertise, there are standard tools to assist with common tasks. A first step can be validating input records by checking the schema. That is to say, we check to see if the fields are present and are the right type.

To check the schema in the mailing list example, we ensure a sender, subject, and body all exist. To convert this into an independent component, we'll make our function take a parameter for the input path and return the file path to the cleaned records. The amount of code it takes to do this is relatively small, shown in Example 5-2.

Example 5-2. Data cleaning

```
def clean_data(input_path: str) -> str:
    import json
    import pandas as pd

    print("loading records...")
    with open(input_path, 'r') as f:
        records = json.load(f)
    print("records loaded")

    df = pd.DataFrame(records)
    # Drop records without a subject, body, or sender
    cleaned = df.dropna(subset=["subject", "body", "from"])

    output_path_hdf = '/data_processing/clean_data.hdf'
    cleaned.to_hdf(output_path_hdf, key="clean")

    return output_path_hdf
```

There are many other standard data quality techniques besides dropping missing fields. Two of the more popular ones are imputing missing data[6] and analyzing and removing outliers that may be the result of incorrect measurements. Regardless of which additional general techniques you decide to perform, you can simply add them to your data-cleaning function.

---

6 See this blog post (*https://oreil.ly/t5xal*) on some common techniques for imputing missing data.

Domain specific data cleaning tools can also be beneficial. In the mailing list example, one potential source of noise in our data could be spam messages. One way to solve this would be by using SpamAssassin. We can add this package to our container as shown in Example 5-3. Adding system software, not managed by pip, on top of the notebook images is a bit more complicated because of permissions. Most containers run as root, making it simple to install new system packages. However, because of Jupyter, the notebook containers run as a less privileged user. Installing new packages like this requires switching to the root user and back, which is not common in other Dockerfiles.

Example 5-3. Installing SpamAssassin

```
ARG base
FROM $base
# Run as root for updates
USER root
# Install SpamAssassin
RUN apt-get update && \
    apt-get install -yq spamassassin spamc && \
    apt-get clean && \
    rm -rf /var/lib/apt/lists/* && \
    rm -rf /var/cache/apt
# Switch back to the expected user
USER jovyan
```

After you created this Dockerfile, you'll want to build it and push the resulting image somewhere that the Kubeflow cluster can access, as in Example 2-8.

Pushing a new container is not enough to let Kubeflow know that we want to use it. When constructing a pipeline stage with `func_to_container_op`, you then need to specify the `base_image` parameter to the `func_to_container_op` function call. We'll show this when we bring the example together as a pipeline in Example 5-35.

Here we see the power of containers again. You can add the tools we need on top of the building blocks provided by Kubeflow rather than making everything from scratch.

Once the data is cleaned, it's time to make sure you have enough of it, or if not, explore augmenting your data.

Formatting the Data

The correct format depends on which tool you're using to do the feature preparation. If you're sticking with the same tool you used for data preparation, an output can be the same as input. Otherwise, you might find this a good place to change formats. For example, when using Spark for data prep and TensorFlow for training, we often implement conversion to TFRecords here.

Feature Preparation

How to do feature preparation depends on the problem. With the mailing list example, we can write all kinds of text-processing functions and combine them into features, as shown in Example 5-4.

Example 5-4. Writing and combining text-processing functions into features

```
df['domains'] = df['links'].apply(extract_domains)
df['isThreadStart'] = df['depth'] == '0'

# Arguably, you could split building the dataset away from the actual witchcraft.
from sklearn.feature_extraction.text import TfidfVectorizer

bodyV = TfidfVectorizer()
bodyFeatures = bodyV.fit_transform(df['body'])

domainV = TfidfVectorizer()

def makeDomainsAList(d):
    return ' '.join([a for a in d if not a is None])

domainFeatures = domainV.fit_transform(
    df['domains'].apply(makeDomainsAList))

from scipy.sparse import csr_matrix, hstack

data = hstack([
    csr_matrix(df[[
        'containsPythonStackTrace', 'containsJavaStackTrace',
        'containsExceptionInTaskBody', 'isThreadStart'
    ]].to_numpy()), bodyFeatures, domainFeatures
])
```

So far, the example code is structured to allow you to turn each function into a separate pipeline stage; however, other options exist. We'll examine how to use the entire notebook as a pipeline stage in "Putting It Together in a Pipeline" on page 88.

There are data preparation tools beyond notebooks and Python, of course. Notebooks are not always the best tool as they can have difficulty with version control. Python doesn't always have the libraries (or performance) you need. So we'll now look at how to use other available tools.

Custom Containers

Pipelines are not just limited to notebooks or even to specific languages.[7] Depending on the project, you may have a regular Python project, custom tooling, Python 2, or even FORTRAN code as an essential component.

For instance, in Chapter 9 we will use Scala to perform one step in our pipeline. Also, in "Using RStats" on page 190, we discuss how to get started with an RStats container.

Sometimes you won't be able to find a container that so closely matches your needs as we did here. In these cases, you can take a generic base image and build on top of it, which we look at more in Chapter 9.

Beyond the need for custom containers, another reason you might choose to move beyond notebooks is to explore distributed tools.

Distributed Tooling

Using a distributed platform makes it possible to work with large datasets (beyond a single machine memory) and can provide significantly better performance. Often the time when we need to start using distributed tooling is when our problem has outgrown our initial notebook solution.

The two main data-parallel distributed systems in Kubeflow are Apache Spark and Google's Dataflow (via Apache Beam). Apache Spark has a larger install base and variety of formats and libraries supported. Apache Beam supports TensorFlow Extended (TFX), an end-to-end ML tool, which integrates smoothly into TFServing for model inference. As it's the most tightly integrated, we'll start with exploring TFX on Apache Beam and then continue to the more standard Apache Spark.

TensorFlow Extended

The TensorFlow community has created an excellent set of integrated tools for everything from data validation to model serving. At present, TFX's data tools are all built on top of Apache Beam, which has the most support for distributed processing on Google Cloud. If you want to use Kubeflow's TFX components, you are limited to a single node; this may change in future versions.

---

7 Have some VB6 code you really need to run? Check out Chapter 9, on going beyond TensorFlow, and make a small sacrifice of wine.

Apache Beam's Python support outside of Google Cloud's Dataflow is not as mature. TFX is a Python tool, so scaling it depends on Apache Beam's Python support. You can scale the job by using the GCP only Dataflow component. As Apache Beam's support for Apache Flink and Spark improves, support may be added for scaling the TFX components in a portable manner.[8]

Kubeflow includes many of the TFX components in its pipeline system. TFX also has its own concept of pipelines. These are separate from Kubeflow pipelines, and in some cases TFX can be an alternative to Kubeflow. Here we will focus on the data and feature preparation components, since those are the simplest to be used with the rest of the Kubeflow ecosystem.

Keeping your data quality: TensorFlow data validation

It's crucial to make sure data quality doesn't decline over time. Data validation allows us to ensure that the schema and distribution of our data are only evolving in expected ways and catch data quality issues before they become production issues. TensorFlow Data Validation (TFDV) gives us the ability to validate our data.

To make the development process more straightforward, you should install TFX and TFDV locally. While the code can be evaluated inside of Kubeflow only, having the library locally will speed up your development work. Installing TFX and TFDV is a simple pip install, shown in Example 5-5.[9]

Example 5-5. Installing TFX and TFDV

```
pip3 install tfx tensorflow-data-validation
```

Now let's look at how to use TFX and TFDV in Kubeflow's pipelines. The first step is loading the relevant components that we want to use. As we discussed in the previous chapter, while Kubeflow does have a load_component function, it automatically resolves on master making it unsuitable for production use cases. So we'll use load_component_from_file along with a local copy of Kubeflow components from Example 4-15 to load our TFDV components. The basic components we need to load are: an example generator (think data loader), schema, statistics generators, and the validator itself. Loading the components is illustrated in Example 5-6.

---

8 There is a compatibility matrix available on this Apache page (*https://oreil.ly/bD1vf*), although currently Beam's Python support requires launching an additional Docker container, making support on Kubernetes more complicated.

9 While TFX automatically installs TFDV, if you have an old installation and you don't specify tensorflow-data-validation, you may get an error of Could not find a version that satisfies the requirement so we illustrate explicitly installing both here.

Example 5-6. Loading the components

```
tfx_csv_gen = kfp.components.load_component_from_file(
    "pipelines-0.2.5/components/tfx/ExampleGen/CsvExampleGen/component.yaml")
tfx_statistic_gen = kfp.components.load_component_from_file(
    "pipelines-0.2.5/components/tfx/StatisticsGen/component.yaml")
tfx_schema_gen = kfp.components.load_component_from_file(
    "pipelines-0.2.5/components/tfx/SchemaGen/component.yaml")
tfx_example_validator = kfp.components.load_component_from_file(
    "pipelines-0.2.5/components/tfx/ExampleValidator/component.yaml")
```

In addition to the components, we also need our data. The current TFX components pass data between pipeline stages using Kubeflow's file_output mechanism. This places the output into MinIO, automatically tracking the artifacts related to the pipeline. To use TFDV on the recommender example's input, we first download it using a standard container operation, as in Example 5-7.

Example 5-7. Download recommender data

```
fetch = kfp.dsl.ContainerOp(name='download',
                            image='busybox',
                            command=['sh', '-c'],
                            arguments=[
                                'sleep 1;'
                                'mkdir -p /tmp/data;'
                                'wget ' + data_url +
                                ' -O /tmp/data/results.csv'
                            ],
                            file_outputs={'downloaded': '/tmp/data'})
# This expects a directory of inputs not just a single file
```

 If we had the data on a persistent volume (say, data fetched in a previous stage), we could then use the filesystem/get_file component.

Once you have the data loaded, TFX has a set of tools called example generators that ingest data. These support a few different formats, including CSV and TFRecord. There are also example generators for other systems, including Google's BigQuery. There is not the same wide variety of formats supported by Spark or Pandas, so you may find a need to preprocess the records with another tool.[10] In our recommender example, we use the CSV component, as shown in Example 5-8.

---

10 While technically not a file format, since TFX can accept Pandas dataframes, a common pattern is to load with Pandas first.

Example 5-8. Using CSV component

```
records_example = tfx_csv_gen(input_base=fetch.output)
```

Now that we have a channel of examples, we can use this as one of the inputs for TFDV. The recommended approach for creating a schema is to use TFDV to infer the schema. To be able to infer the schema, TFDV first needs to compute some summary statistics of our data. Example 5-9 illustrates the pipeline stages for both of these steps.

Example 5-9. Creating the schema

```
stats = tfx_statistic_gen(input_data=records_example.output)
schema_op = tfx_schema_gen(stats.output)
```

If we infer the schema each time, we are unlikely to catch schema changes. Instead, you should save the schema and reuse it in future runs for validation. The pipeline's run web page has a link to the schema in MinIO, and you can either fetch it or copy it somewhere using another component or container operation.

Regardless of where you persist the schema, you should inspect it. To inspect the schema, you need to import the TFDV library, as shown in Example 5-10. Before you start using a schema to validate data, you should inspect the schema. To inspect the schema, download the schema locally (or onto your notebook) and use the dis play_schema function from TFDV, as shown in Example 5-11.

Example 5-10. Download the schema locally

```
import tensorflow_data_validation as tfdv
```

Example 5-11. Display the schema

```
schema = tfdv.load_schema_text("schema_info_2")
tfdv.display_schema(schema)
```

If needed, the schema_util.py script (downloadble from the TensorFlow GitHub repo (*https://oreil.ly/qjHeI*)) provides the tools to modify your schema (be it for evolution or incorrect inference).

Now that we know we're using the right schema, let's validate our data. The validate component takes in both the schema and the statistics we've generated, as shown in Example 5-12. You should replace the schema and statistics generation components with downloads of their outputs at production time.

Example 5-12. Validating the data

```
tfx_example_validator(stats=stats.outputs['output'],
                      schema=schema_op.outputs['output'])
```

 Check the size of the rejected records before pushing to production. You may find that the data format has changed, and you need to use the schema evolution guide and possibly update the rest of the pipeline.

TensorFlow Transform, with TensorFlow Extended on Beam

The TFX program for doing feature preparation is called TensorFlow Transform (TFT) and integrates into the TensorFlow and Kubeflow ecosystems. As with TFDV, Kubeflow's TensorFlow Transform component currently does not scale beyond single node processing. The best benefit of TFT is its integration into the TensorFlow Model Analysis tool, simplifying feature preparation during inference.

We need to specify what transformations we want TFT to apply. Our TFT program should be in a file separate from the pipeline definition, although it is possible to inline it as a string. To start with, we need some standard TFT imports, as shown in Example 5-13.

Example 5-13. TFT imports

```
import tensorflow as tf
import tensorflow_transform as tft
from tensorflow_transform.tf_metadata import schema_utils
```

Now that we've got the imports, it's time to create the entry point into our code for the component, shown in Example 5-14.

Example 5-14. Creating the entry point

```
def preprocessing_fn(inputs):
```

Inside this function is where we do our data transformations to produce our features. Not all features need to be transformed, which is why there is also a copy method to mirror the input to the output if you're only adding features. With our mailing list example, we can compute the vocabulary, as shown in Example 5-15.

Example 5-15. Compute the vocabulary

```
outputs = {}
# TFT business logic goes here
outputs["body_stuff"] = tft.compute_and_apply_vocabulary(inputs["body"],
                                                          top_k=1000)
return outputs
```

This function does not support arbitrary python code. All transformations must be expressed as TensorFlow or TensorFlow Transform operations. TensorFlow operations operate on one tensor at a time, but in data preparation we often want to compute something over all of our input data, and TensorFlow Transform's operations give us this ability. See the TFT Python docs (*https://oreil.ly/4j0mv*) or call `help(tft)` to see some starting operations.

Once you've written the desired transformations, it is time to add them to the pipeline. The simplest way to do this is with Kubeflow's `tfx/Transform` component. Loading the component is the same as the other TFX components, illustrated in Example 5-6. Using this component is unique in requiring the transformation code to be passed in as a file uploaded to either S3 or GCS. It also needs the data, and you can use the output from TFDV (if you used it) or load the examples as we did for TFDV. Using the TFT component is illustrated in Example 5-16.

Example 5-16. Using the TFT component

```
transformed_output = tfx_transform(
    input_data=records_example.output,
    schema=schema_op.outputs['output'],
    module_file=module_file)  # Path to your TFT code on GCS/S3
```

Now you have a machine learning pipeline that has feature preparation along with a critical artifact to transform requests at serving time. The close integration of TensorFlow Transform can make model serving much less complicated. TensorFlow Transform with Kubeflow components doesn't have the power for all projects, so we'll look at distributed feature preparation next.

Distributed Data Using Apache Spark

Apache Spark is an open source distributed data processing tool that can run on a variety of clusters. Kubeflow supports Apache Spark through a few different components so you can access cloud-specific features. Since you may not be familiar with Spark we'll briefly introduce Spark's Dataset/Dataframe APIs in the context of data and feature preparation. If you want to go beyond the basics, we recommend *Learning Spark*, *Spark: The Definitive Guide*, or *High Performance Spark* as resources to improve your Spark skills.

Here our code is structured to go in as a single stage for all of the feature and data preparation, since once you're at scale, writing and loading the data between steps is costly.

Spark in Jupyter

Spark is not preinstalled in the notebook images. You can use pip inside your notebook to install Spark, but this does not support complex environments. Instead, take the notebook container you're working with and add Spark with a new Dockerfile, as shown in Example 5-17.

Example 5-17. Adding Spark

```
# See https://www.kubeflow.org/docs/notebooks/custom-notebook/
ARG base
FROM $base
ARG sparkversion
ARG sparkrelease
ARG sparkserver https://www-us.apache.org/dist/spark
# We need to run as root for updates
USER root

# Set an environment variable for where we are going to put Spark
ENV SPARK_HOME /opt/spark

# Install Java because Spark needs it
RUN apt-get update && \
    apt-get install -yq openjdk-8-jre openjdk-8-jre-headless && \
    apt-get clean && \
    rm -rf /var/lib/apt/lists/*

# Install Spark
RUN set -ex && \
    rm /bin/sh && \
    ln -sv /bin/bash /bin/sh

RUN  echo "Setting up $sparkversion"
RUN  cd /tmp && \
    (wget ${sparkserver}/spark-${sparkversion}/${sparkrelease}.tgz) && \
    cd /opt && tar -xvf /tmp/${sparkrelease}.tgz && \
    rm /tmp/${sparkrelease}.tgz && mv ${sparkrelease} spark && \
    cd spark/python && pip install -e .
# Fix permissions
WORKDIR /opt/spark/work-dir
RUN chmod -R 777 /opt/spark/

# Switch the user back; using jovyan as a user is bad but the base image
# depends on it.
USER jovyan
# Install some common tools
pip install pandas numpy scipy pyarrow
```

The Spark workers don't have a way to connect to our notebook server so we can't send data and requests back and forth. To enable this, you can create a service using the name of the notebook to make it discoverable. The service definition exposes two ports, as shown in Example 5-18, for a user in the "programmerboo" namespace with a notebook named "spark-test-2." Once you've written the service definition, all that is needed is to run `kubectl apply -f my_spark_service.yaml`.

Example 5-18. Sample service definition

```
apiVersion: v1
kind: Service
metadata:
  name: spark-driver
  namespace: kubeflow-programmerboo
spec:
  selector:
    notebook-name: spark-test-2
  ports:
    - port: 39235
      targetPort: 39235
      name: spark-driver-port
    - port: 39236
      targetPort: 39236
      name: spark-block-port
```

When we make the SparkContext, we'll configure it to use this service as the hostname. Jupyter notebooks make important activities like testing and version management challenging. Notebooks are great for the exploration phase, but as you move on, you should consider using a Spark operator.

Spark operators in Kubeflow

Using Kubeflow's native Spark operator EMR, or Dataproc is best once you've moved beyond the experimental phase. The most portable operator is the native Spark operator, which does not depend on any specific cloud. To use any of the operators, you need to package the Spark program and store it on either a distributed filesystem (such as GCS, S3, and so on) or put it inside a container.

If you're working in Python or R, we recommend building a Spark container so you can install your dependencies. With Scala or Java code, this is less critical. If you put the application inside of a container, you can reference it with `local:///`. You can use the gcr.io/spark-operator/spark-py:v2.4.5 container as the base or build your own container—follow Spark on Kubernetes instructions, or see Chapter 9. Example 5-19 shows how to install any requirements and copy the application. If you decide to update the application, you can still use the container, just configure the main resource with a distributed filesystem.

We cover building custom containers additionally in Chapter 9.

Example 5-19. Installing requirements and copying the application

```
# Use the Spark operator image as base
FROM gcr.io/spark-operator/spark-py:v2.4.5
# Install Python requirements
COPY requirements.txt /
RUN pip3 install -r /requirements.txt
# Now you can reference local:///job/my_file.py
RUN mkdir -p /job
COPY *.py /job

ENTRYPOINT ["/opt/entrypoint.sh"]
```

Two cloud-specific options for running Spark are the Amazon EMR and Google Dataproc components in Kubeflow. However, they each take different parameters, meaning that you will need to translate your pipeline.

The EMR components allow you to set up clusters, submit jobs, and clean up the clusters. The two cluster task components are `aws/emr/create_cluster` for the start and `aws/emr/delete_cluster`. The component for running a PySpark job is `aws/emr/submit_pyspark_job`. If you are not reusing an external cluster, it's important to trigger the delete component regardless whether the submit_pyspark_job component succeeds.

While they have different parameters, the workflow for Dataproc clusters mirrors that of EMR. The components are similarly named, with `gcp/dataproc/create_clus ter/` and `gcp/dataproc/delete_cluster/` for the life cycle and `gcp/dataproc/ submit_pyspark_job/` for running our job.

Unlike the EMR and Dataproc components, the Spark operator does not have a component. For Kubernetes operators without components, you can use the dsl.ResourceOp to call them. Example 5-20 illustrates using the ResourceOp to launch a Spark job.

Example 5-20. Using the ResourceOp to launch a Spark job

```
resource = {
    "apiVersion": "sparkoperator.k8s.io/v1beta2",
    "kind": "SparkApplication",
    "metadata": {
        "name": "boop",
        "namespace": "kubeflow"
    },
    "spec": {
        "type": "Python",
        "mode": "cluster",
        "image": "gcr.io/boos-demo-projects-are-rad/kf-steps/kubeflow/myspark",
        "imagePullPolicy": "Always",
        # See the Dockerfile OR use GCS/S3/...
        "mainApplicationFile": "local:///job/job.py",
        "sparkVersion": "2.4.5",
        "restartPolicy": {
```

```
            "type": "Never"
        },
        "driver": {
            "cores": 1,
            "coreLimit": "1200m",
            "memory": "512m",
            "labels": {
                "version": "2.4.5",
            },
            # also try spark-operatoroperator-sa
            "serviceAccount": "spark-operatoroperator-sa",
        },
        "executor": {
            "cores": 1,
            "instances": 2,
            "memory": "512m"
        },
        "labels": {
            "version": "2.4.5"
        },
    }
}
```

```
@dsl.pipeline(name="local Pipeline", description="No need to ask why.")
def local_pipeline():

    rop = dsl.ResourceOp(
        name="boop",
        k8s_resource=resource,
        action="create",
        success_condition="status.applicationState.state == COMPLETED")
```

 Kubeflow doesn't apply any validation to ResourceOp requests. For example, in Spark, the job name must be able to be used as the start of a valid DNS name, and while in container ops container names are rewritten, ResourceOps just directly passes through requests.

Spark Basics

Apache Spark has APIs available in Python, R, Scala, and Java, with some third-party support for other languages. We'll use the Python interface, as it is popular in the machine learning community. The first thing needed in any Spark program is a Spark session or context (as in Example 5-21).

Example 5-21. Launching your Spark session

```
from pyspark.sql import SparkSession
from pyspark.sql.functions import col, to_date
from pyspark.sql.types import *
session = SparkSession.builder.getOrCreate()
```

This example was so simple because it reads its configuration from the environment it is called in. This works with the Spark operator, which does much of the setup for us. When working in a notebook, though, we need to provide some extra information so the executors can connect back to the notebook. Once you've set up the service so the notebook and the driver can communicate, as described in Example 5-18, you would then configure your Spark session to tell the executors to use this service, as shown in Example 5-22.

Example 5-22. Configuring your Spark session

```
.config("spark.driver.bindAddress",
        "0.0.0.0").config("spark.kubernetes.namespace",
                          "kubeflow-programmerboo").
config("spark.master", "k8s://https://kubernetes.default").config(
    "spark.driver.host",
    "spark-driver.kubeflow-programmerboo.svc.cluster.local").config(
        "spark.kubernetes.executor.annotation.sidecar.istio.io/inject",
        "false").config("spark.driver.port",
                        "39235").config("spark.blockManager.port", "39236")
```

Also, we need the versions of Python to match, since a version mismatch may cause serialization and function errors. To do this we add `os.environ["PYSPARK_PYTHON"]` = "python3.6" to our notebook and install Python 3.6 in Spark's worker container, as in Example 5-23.

Example 5-23. Installing Python 3.6 in Spark's worker container

```
ARG base
FROM $base

USER root

# Install libraries we need to build Python 3.6
RUN apt-get update && \
    DEBIAN_FRONTEND=noninteractive apt-get install -y -q \
    make build-essential libssl-dev zlib1g-dev libbz2-dev \
    libreadline-dev libsqlite3-dev wget curl llvm libncurses5-dev \
    libncursesw5-dev xz-utils tk-dev libffi-dev liblzma-dev && \
    rm -rf /var/cache/apt

# Install Python 3.6 to match the notebook
RUN cd /tmp && \
    wget https://www.python.org/ftp/python/3.6.10/Python-3.6.10.tgz && \
    tar -xvf Python-3.6.10.tgz && \
    cd Python-3.6.10 && \
    ./configure && \
    make -j 8 && \
    make altinstall

RUN python3.6 -m pip install pandas pyarrow==0.11.0 spacy
# We depend on Spark being on the PYTHONPATH so no pip install
USER 185
```

Using MinIO, Kubeflow's built-in S3-like service, requires some additional configuration. Example 5-24 illustrates how to configure Spark to use MinIO in Kubeflow.

Example 5-24. Configuring Spark to use MinIO

```
.config("spark.hadoop.fs.s3a.endpoint",
        "minio-service.kubeflow.svc.cluster.local:9000").config(
            "fs.s3a.connection.ssl.enabled",
                "false").config("fs.s3a.path.style.access", "true")
# You can also add an account using the minio command as described in
# Chapter 1.
.config("spark.hadoop.fs.s3a.access.key",
        "minio").config("spark.hadoop.fs.s3a.secret.key", "minio123")
```

 MinIO only works out of the box with Spark 3 or higher.

Now that we've got Spark up and running, it's time to look at the basic tasks you will want to do for data preparation and cleaning in Spark.

Reading the input data

Spark supports a wide variety of data sources, including (but not limited to): Parquet, JSON, JDBC, ORC, JSON, Hive, CSV, ElasticSearch, MongoDB, Neo4j, Cassandra, Snowflake, Redis, Riak Time Series, etc.[11] Loading data is very straightforward, and often all that is needed is specifying the format. For instance, in our mailing list example, reading the Parquet-formatted output of our data preparation stage is done as in Example 5-25.

Example 5-25. Reading our data's Parquet-formatted output

```
initial_posts = session.read.format("parquet").load(fs_prefix +
                                        "/initial_posts")
ids_in_reply = session.read.format("parquet").load(fs_prefix + "/ids_in_reply")
```

If this had instead been formatted as JSON, we would only have to change "parquet" to "JSON."[12]

---

11 There is no definitive list, although many vendors list their formats on this Spark page (*https://spark-packages.org*).

12 Of course, since most formats have slight variations, they have configuration options if the defaults don't work.

> ## Fetching Input Data
>
> We can also speed up our data fetching by using a block of our Python code to fetch our data in parallel. If we look back at the mailing list example, we could download each year on a different computer. Or if we wanted to look at multiple projects, we could also fetch by project. We can do this by using `parallelize`, which gives us a distributed list, and `flatMap`, which runs a Python function on the different executors. For example, `sc.parallelize([1, 2, 3]).map(fetchRecord)` effectively runs the `fetchRecords` function in parallel 3 times with the inputs 1, 2, and 3, respectively, and concatenates the results.

Validating the schema

We often believe we know the fields and types of our data. Spark can quickly discover the schema when our data is in a self-describing format like Parquet. In other formats, like JSON, the schema isn't known until Spark reads the records. Regardless of the data format, it is good practice to specify the schema and ensure the data matches it, as shown in Example 5-26. Errors during data load are easier to debug than errors during model deployment.

Example 5-26. Specifying the schema

```
ids_schema = StructType([
    StructField("In-Reply-To", StringType(), nullable=True),
    StructField("message-id", StringType(), nullable=True)
])
ids_in_reply = session.read.format("parquet").schema(ids_schema).load(
    fs_prefix + "/ids_in_reply")
```

You can configure Spark to handle corrupted and nonconforming records by dropping them, keeping them, or stopping the process (i.e., failing the job). The default is permissive, which keeps the invalid records while setting the fields to null, allowing us to handle schema mismatch with the same techniques for missing fields.

Handling missing fields

In many situations, some of our data is missing. You can choose to drop records with missing fields, fall back to secondary fields, impute averages, or leave as is. Spark's built-in tools for these tasks are inside `DataFrameNaFunctions`. The correct solution depends on both your data and the algorithm you end up using. The most common is to drop records and make sure that we have not filtered out too many records, illustrated using the mailing list data in Example 5-27.

Example 5-27. Dropping records

```
initial_posts_count = initial_posts.count()
initial_posts_cleaned = initial_posts.na.drop(how='any',
                                              subset=['body', 'from'])
initial_posts_cleaned_count = initial_posts_cleaned.count()
```

Filtering out bad data

Detecting incorrect data can be challenging. However, without performing at least some data cleaning, the model may train on noise. Often, determining bad data depends on the practitioner's domain knowledge of the problem.

A common technique supported in Spark is outlier removal. However, naively applying this can remove valid records. Using your domain experience, you can write a custom validation function and remove any records that do not match it using Spark's `filter` function, as illustrated with our mailing list example in Example 5-28.

Example 5-28. Filtering out bad data

```
def is_ok(post):
    # Your special business logic goes here
    return True


spark_mailing_list_data_cleaned = spark_mailing_list_data_with_date.filter(
    is_ok)
```

Using Spark SQL

If you're a pro at SQL and less so with Scala or Python, you can also directly write SQL queries. After you've loaded data, you can give the data names with register-TempTable and then use the SQL function on the Spark session (see Example 5-29).

Example 5-29. Using Spark SQL

```
ids_in_reply.registerTempTable("cheese")
no_text = session.sql("select * from cheese where body = '' AND subject = ''")
```

Saving the output

Once you have the data ready, it's time to save the output. If you're going to use Apache Spark to do feature preparation, you can skip this step for now.

If you want to go back to single-machine tools, it's often simplest to save to a persistent volume. To do this, bring the data back to the main program by calling `toPandas()`, as shown in Example 5-30. Now you can save the data in whatever format the next tool expects.

Example 5-30. Saving to a persistent volume

```
initial_posts.toPandas()
```

If the data is large, or you otherwise want to use an object store, Spark can write to many different formats (just as it can load from many different formats). The correct format depends on the tool you intend to use for feature preparation. Writing to Parquet is shown in Example 5-31.

Example 5-31. Writing to Parquet

```
initial_posts.write.format("parquet").mode('overwrite').save(fs_prefix +
                                                    "/initial_posts")
ids_in_reply.write.format("parquet").mode('overwrite').save(fs_prefix +
                                                    "/ids_in_reply")
```

Now you've seen a variety of different tools you can use to source and clean the data. We've looked at the flexibility of local tools, the scalability of distributed tools, and the integration from TensorFlow Extended. With the data in shape, let's now make sure the right features are available and get them in a usable format for the machine learning model.

Distributed Feature Preparation Using Apache Spark

Apache Spark has a large number of built-in feature preparation tools, in `pyspark.ml.feature`, that you can use to generate features. You can use Spark in the same way as you did during data preparation. You may find using Spark's own ML pipeline an easy way to put together multiple feature preparation stages.

For the Spark mailing list example, we have textual input data. To allow us to train a variety of models, converting this into word vectors is our preferred form of feature prep. Doing so involves first tokenizing the data with Spark's Tokenizer. Once we have the tokens, we can train a Word2Vec model and produce our word vectors. Example 5-32 illustrates how to prepare features for the mailing list example using Spark.

Example 5-32. Preparing features for the mailing list

```
tokenizer = Tokenizer(inputCol="body", outputCol="body_tokens")
body_hashing = HashingTF(inputCol="body_tokens",
                        outputCol="raw_body_features",
                        numFeatures=10000)
body_idf = IDF(inputCol="raw_body_features", outputCol="body_features")
body_word2Vec = Word2Vec(vectorSize=5,
                        minCount=0,
                        numPartitions=10,
                        inputCol="body_tokens",
                        outputCol="body_vecs")
```

```
assembler = VectorAssembler(inputCols=[
    "body_features", "body_vecs", "contains_python_stack_trace",
    "contains_java_stack_trace", "contains_exception_in_task"
],
                        outputCol="features")
```

With this final distributed feature preparation example, you're ready to scale up to handle larger data sizes if they ever come your way. If you're working with smaller data, you've seen how you can use the same simple techniques of containerization to continue to work with your favorite tools. Either way, you're almost ready for the next stage in the machine learning pipeline.

Putting It Together in a Pipeline

We have shown how to solve individual problems in data and feature preparation, but now we need to bring it all together. In our local example, we wrote our functions with the types and returned parameters to make it easy to put into a pipeline. Since we return the path of where our output is in each stage, we can use the function outputs to create the dependency graph for us. Putting these functions together into a pipeline is illustrated in Example 5-33.

Example 5-33. Putting the functions together

```
@kfp.dsl.pipeline(name='Simple1', description='Simple1')
def my_pipeline_mini(year: int):
    dvop = dsl.VolumeOp(name="create_pvc",
                        resource_name="my-pvc-2",
                        size="5Gi",
                        modes=dsl.VOLUME_MODE_RWO)
    tldvop = dsl.VolumeOp(name="create_pvc",
                        resource_name="tld-volume-2",
                        size="100Mi",
                        modes=dsl.VOLUME_MODE_RWO)
    download_data_op = kfp.components.func_to_container_op(
        download_data, packages_to_install=['lxml', 'requests'])
    download_tld_info_op = kfp.components.func_to_container_op(
        download_tld_data,
        packages_to_install=['requests', 'pandas>=0.24', 'tables'])
    clean_data_op = kfp.components.func_to_container_op(
        clean_data, packages_to_install=['pandas>=0.24', 'tables'])

    step1 = download_data_op(year).add_pvolumes(
        {"/data_processing": dvop.volume})
    step2 = clean_data_op(input_path=step1.output).add_pvolumes(
        {"/data_processing": dvop.volume})
    step3 = download_tld_info_op().add_pvolumes({"/tld_info": tldvop.volume})


kfp.compiler.Compiler().compile(my_pipeline_mini, 'local-data-prep-2.zip')
```

You can see that the feature preparation step here follows the same general pattern of all of the local components. However, the libraries that we need for our feature preparation are a bit different, so we've changed the `packages_to_install` value to install Scikit-learn, as shown in Example 5-34.

Example 5-34. Installing Scikit-learn

```
prepare_features_op = kfp.components.func_to_container_op(
    prepare_features,
    packages_to_install=['pandas>=0.24', 'tables', 'scikit-learn'])
```

 When you start exploring a new dataset, you may find it easier to use a notebook as usual, without the pipeline components. When possible following the same general structure you would with pipelines will make it easier to productionize your exploratory work.

These steps don't specify the container to use. For the container with SpamAssassin you've just built, you write it as in Example 5-35.

Example 5-35. Specifying a container

```
clean_data_op = kfp.components.func_to_container_op(
    clean_data,
    base_image="{0}/kubeflow/spammassisan".format(container_registry),
    packages_to_install=['pandas>=0.24', 'tables'])
```

Sometimes the cost of writing our data out in between stages is too expensive. In our recommender example, unlike in the mailing list example, we've chosen to put data and feature prep together into a single pipeline stage. In our distributed mailing list example, we build one single Spark job as well. In these cases, our entire work so far is just one stage. Using a single stage allows us to avoid having to write the file out in between, but can complicate debugging.

Using an Entire Notebook as a Data Preparation Pipeline Stage

If you don't want to turn the individual parts of the data preparation notebook into a pipeline, you can use the entire notebook as one stage. You can use the same containers used by JupyterHub to run the notebook programmatically.

To do this, you'll need to make a new `Dockerfile`, specify that it is based on top of another container using `FROM`, and then add a `COPY` directive to package the notebook inside the new container. Since the census data example has a preexisting notebook, that's the approach we've taken in Example 5-36.

Example 5-36. Using an entire notebook as data preparation

```
FROM gcr.io/kubeflow-images-public/tensorflow-1.6.0-notebook-cpu

COPY ./ /workdir /
```

If you require additional Python dependencies, you can use the RUN directive to install them. Putting the dependencies in the container can help speed up the pipeline, especially for complicated packages. For our mailing list example, the Dockerfile would look like Example 5-37.

Example 5-37. Using RUN to add Python dependencies to the container

```
RUN pip3 install --upgrade lxml pandas
```

We can use this container like any other in the pipeline with dsl.ContainerOp, as we did with the recommender example in Chapter 4. Now you have two ways to use notebooks in Kubeflow, and we'll cover options beyond notebooks next.

> Does the notebook need GPU resources? When specifying the dsl.ContainerOp, add a call to set_gpu_limit and specify either nvidia or amd depending on the desired GPU type.

Conclusion

Now you have your data ready to train a model. We've seen how there is no one-size-fits-all approach to feature and data preparation; our different examples needed different tooling. We've also seen how the methods can require changing within the same problem, like when we expanded the scope of the mailing list example to include more data. The amount and quality of the features, and the data to produce them, are critical to the success of the machine learning projects. You can test this by running the examples with smaller data sizes and comparing the models.

It's also important to remember that data and feature preparation is not a one-and-done activity, and you may want to revisit this step as you develop this model. You may find that there is a feature you wish you had, or that a feature you thought would perform well isn't suggesting data quality issues. In the coming chapters, as we train our models and serve them, feel free to revisit the data and feature preparation.

# CHAPTER 6

Artifact and Metadata Store

Machine learning typically involves dealing with a large amount of raw and intermediate (transformed) data where the ultimate goal is creating and deploying the model. In order to understand our model it is necessary to be able to explore datasets used for its creation and transformations (data lineage). The collection of these datasets and the transformation applied to them is called the *metadata of our model*.[1]

Model metadata is critical for *reproducibility* in machine learning;[2] reproducibility is critical for reliable production deployments. Capturing the metadata allows us to understand variations when rerunning jobs or experiments. Understanding variations is necessary to iteratively develop and improve our models. It also provides a solid foundation for model comparisons. As Pete Warden defined it in this post (*https://oreil.ly/dQZjL*):

> To reproduce results, code, training data, and the overall platform need to be recorded accurately.

The same information is also required for other common ML operations—model comparison, reproducible model creation, etc.

There are many different options for tracking the metadata of models. Kubeflow has a built-in tool for this called Kubeflow ML Metadata (*https://oreil.ly/0rVN1*).[3] The goal of this tool is to help Kubeflow users understand and manage their ML workflows by tracking and managing the metadata that the workflows produce. Another tool for

---

1 For a good background on metadata for machine learning, and an overview of what to capture refer to this blog post (*https://oreil.ly/3zA6K*) written by Luigi Patruno.

2 For more on this topic, see this blog post (*https://oreil.ly/H1B81*) by Jennifer Villa and Yoav Zimmerman.

3 Note that Kubeflow ML Metadata is different from ML Metadata (*https://oreil.ly/ALXsm*), which is part of TFX (*https://oreil.ly/vHYGz*).

tracking metadata that we can integrate into our Kubeflow pipelines is MLflow Tracking. It provides API and UI for logging parameters, code versions, metrics, and output files when running your machine learning code and for later visualizing the results.

In this chapter we will discuss the capabilities of Kubeflow's ML Metadata project and show how it can be used. We will also consider some shortcomings of this implementation and explore usage of additional third-party software: MLflow (*https://mlflow.org*).[4]

Kubeflow ML Metadata

Kubeflow ML Metadata (*https://oreil.ly/7WOp1*) is a library for recording and retrieving metadata associated with model creation. In the current implementation, Kubeflow Metadata provides only Python APIs. To use other languages, you need to implement the language-specific Python plug-in to be able to use the library. To understand how it works, we will start with a simple artificial example showing the basic capabilities of Kubeflow Metadata using a very simple notebook (based on this demo (*https://oreil.ly/Sm3ML*)).[5]

Implementation of Kubeflow Metadata starts with required imports, as shown in Example 6-1.

Example 6-1. Required imports

```
from kfmd import metadata
import pandas
from datetime import datetime
```

In Kubeflow Metadata, all the information is organized in terms of a workspace, run, and execution. You need to define a workspace so Kubeflow can track and organize the records. The code in Example 6-2 shows how this can be done.

Example 6-2. Define a workspace

```
ws1 = metadata.Workspace(
    # Connect to metadata-service in namespace kubeflow.
    backend_url_prefix="metadata-service.kubeflow.svc.cluster.local:8080",
    name="ws1",
    description="a workspace for testing",
    labels={"n1": "v1"})
```

---

4 MLflow was initially developed by Databricks and currently is part of the Linux Foundation (*https://oreil.ly/Fscza*).

5 The complete code for this notebook is located in this book's GitHub repo (*https://oreil.ly/Kubeflow_for_ML_ch06*).

```
r = metadata.Run(
    workspace=ws1,
    name="run-" + datetime.utcnow().isoformat("T") ,
    description="a run in ws_1",
)
exec = metadata.Execution(
    name = "execution" + datetime.utcnow().isoformat("T") ,
    workspace=ws1,
    run=r,
    description="execution example",
)
```

Workspace, run, and execution can be defined multiple times in the same or different applications. If they do not exist, they will be created; if they already exist, they will be used.

Kubeflow does not automatically track the datasets used by the application. They have to be explicitly registered in code. Following a classic MNIST example data sets registration in Metadata should be implemented as shown in Example 6-3.

Example 6-3. Metadata example

```
data_set = exec.log_input(
        metadata.DataSet(
            description="an example data",
            name="mytable-dump",
            owner="owner@my-company.org",
            uri="file://path/to/dataset",
            version="v1.0.0",
            query="SELECT * FROM mytable"))
```

In addition to data, Kubeflow Metadata allows you to store information about your model and its metrics. The code implementing it is presented in Example 6-4.

Example 6-4. Another metadata example

```
model = exec.log_output(
    metadata.Model(
            name="MNIST",
            description="model to recognize handwritten digits",
            owner="someone@kubeflow.org",
            uri="gcs://my-bucket/mnist",
            model_type="neural network",
            training_framework={
                "name": "tensorflow",
                "version": "v1.0"
            },
            hyperparameters={
                "learning_rate": 0.5,
                "layers": [10, 3, 1],
                "early_stop": True
```

```
        },
        version="v0.0.1",
        labels={"mylabel": "l1"}))
metrics = exec.log_output(
    metadata.Metrics(
        name="MNIST-evaluation",
        description="validating the MNIST model to recognize handwritten digits",
        owner="someone@kubeflow.org",
        uri="gcs://my-bucket/mnist-eval.csv",
        data_set_id=data_set.id,
        model_id=model.id,
        metrics_type=metadata.Metrics.VALIDATION,
        values={"accuracy": 0.95},
        labels={"mylabel": "l1"}))
```

These code snippets will implement all of the main steps for storing model creation metadata:

1. Define workspace, run, and execution.

2. Store information about data assets used for model creation.

3. Store information about the created model, including its version, type, training framework, and hyperparameters used for its creation.

4. Store information about model evaluation metrics.

In real-world implementations these snippets should be used in the actual code to capture metadata used for data preparation, machine learning, etc. See Chapter 7 for examples of where and how this information is captured.

Collecting metadata is useful only if there are ways to view it. Kubeflow Metadata provides two ways of viewing it—programmatically, and using Metadata UI.

Programmatic Query

The following functionality is available for programmatic query.

First, we list all the models in the workspace, as shown in Example 6-5.

Example 6-5. List all models

```
pandas.DataFrame.from_dict(ws1.list(metadata.Model.ARTIFACT_TYPE_NAME))
```

In our code we created only a single model, which is returned as a result of this query (see Table 6-1).

Table 6-1. List of models

id	workspace	run		create_time	description	model_type
0	2	ws1	run-2020-01-10T22:13:20.959882	2020-01-10T22:13:26.324443Z	model to recognize handwritten digits	neural network

name	owner	version	uri	training_framework
MNIST	someone@kubeflow.org	v0.0.1	gcs://my-bucket/mnist	{name: tensorflow, version: v1.0}

Next, we get basic lineage (see Example 6-6). In our case we created a single model, so the returned lineage will contain only the ID of this model.

Example 6-6. Basic lineage

```
print("model id is " + model.id) ❶
```

❶ Returns model id is 2.

Then we find the execution that produces this model. In our toy application we created a single execution. An ID of this execution is returned as a result of this query, as shown in Example 6-7.

Example 6-7. Find the execution

```
output_events = ws1.client.list_events2(model.id).events
execution_id = output_events[0].execution_id
print(execution_id) ❶
```

❶ Returns 1.

Finally, we find all events related to that execution, as illustrated in Example 6-8.

Example 6-8. Getting all related events

```
all_events = ws1.client.list_events(execution_id).events
assert len(all_events) == 3
print("\nAll events related to this model:")
pandas.DataFrame.from_dict([e.to_dict() for e in all_events])
```

In our case we used a single input that was used to create a model and metrics. So the result of this query looks as shown in Table 6-2.

Table 6-2. Query result as a table

	artifact_id	execution_id	path	type	milliseconds_since_epoch
0	1	1	None	INPUT	1578694406318
1	2	1	None	OUTPUT	1578694406338
2	3	1	None	OUTPUT	1578694406358

Kubeflow Metadata UI

In addition to providing APIs for writing code to analyze metadata, the Kubeflow Metadata tool provides a UI, which allows you to view metadata without writing code. Access to the Metadata UI is done through the main Kubeflow UI, as seen in Figure 6-1.

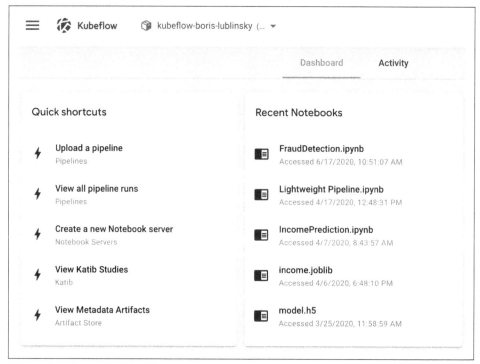

Figure 6-1. Accessing Metadata UI

Once you click the Artifact Store, you should see the list of available artifacts (logged metadata events), as in Figure 6-2.

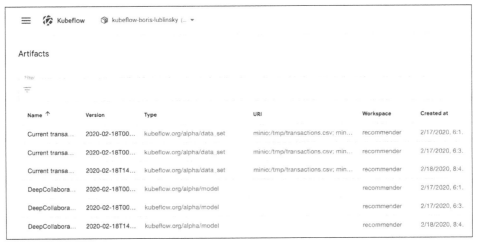

Figure 6-2. List of artifacts in the Artifact Store UI

From this view we can click the individual artifact and see its details, as shown in Figure 6-3.

Figure 6-3. Artifact view

Kubeflow Metadata provides some basic capabilities for storing and viewing of machine learning metadata; however, its capabilities are extremely limited, especially in terms of viewing and manipulating stored metadata. A more powerful implementation of machine learning metadata management is done by MLflow. Though MLflow isn't part of Kubeflow distribution, it's very easy to deploy it alongside Kubeflow and use it from Kubeflow-based applications, as described in the next section.

Using MLflow's Metadata Tools with Kubeflow

MLflow is an open source platform for managing the end-to-end machine learning life cycle. It includes three primary functions:

MLflow Tracking (https://oreil.ly/appTI)
> Tracking experiments to record and compare parameters and results

MLflow Projects (https://oreil.ly/YmBmS)
> Packaging ML code in a reusable, reproducible form in order to share with other data scientists or transfer to production

MLflow Models (https://oreil.ly/WN0nm)
> Managing and deploying models from a variety of ML libraries to a variety of model serving and inference platforms

For the purposes of our Kubeflow metadata discussion we will only discuss deployment and usage of MLflow tracking components—an API and UI for logging parameters, code versions, metrics, and output files when running your machine learning code and for visualizing the results. MLflow Tracking lets you log and query experiments using Python (*https://oreil.ly/BfpRU*), REST (*https://oreil.ly/pGC0j*), R (*https://oreil.ly/5xKAK*), and Java (*https://oreil.ly/AUUXL*) APIs, which significantly extends the reach of APIs, allowing you to store and access metadata from different ML components.

MLflow Tracking is organized around the concept of runs, which are executions of some piece of data science code. Each run records the following information:

Code version
> Git commit hash used for the run, if it was run from an MLflow Project

Start and end time
> Start and end time of the run

Source
> Name of the file to launch the run, or the project name and entry point for the run if run from an MLflow Project

Parameters
> Key-value input parameters of your choice. Both keys and values are strings.

Metrics
> Key-value metrics, where the value is numeric. Each metric can be updated throughout the course of the run (for example, to track how your model's loss function is converging), and MLflow records and lets you visualize the metric's full history.

Artifacts

Output files in any format. Here you can record images (such as PNG files), models (for example, a pickled Scikit-learn model), and data files (for example, a Parquet file) as artifacts.

Most of the MLflow examples (*https://oreil.ly/oik7f*) use local MLflow installations, which is not appropriate for our purposes. For our implementation we need a cluster-based installation, allowing us to write metadata from different Docker instances and view them centrally. Following the approach outlined in the project MLflow Tracking Server based on Docker and AWS S3 (*https://oreil.ly/5DdRC*), the overall architecture of such MLflow Tracking component deployment is presented in Figure 6-4.

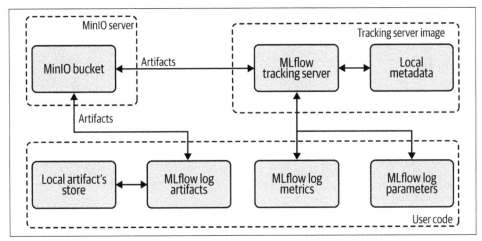

Figure 6-4. Overall architecture of MLflow components deployment

The main components of this architecture are:

- MinIO server, already part of the Kubeflow installation
- MLflow tracking server—the MLflow UI component—an additional component that needs to be added to Kubeflow installation to support MLflow usage
- User code such as notebook, Python, R, or Java application

Creating and Deploying an MLflow Tracking Server

MLflow Tracking Server allows you to record MLflow runs to local files, to a SQLAlchemy-compatible database, or remotely to a tracking server. In our implementation we are using a remote server.

An MLflow Tracking Server has two components for storage: a backend store and an artifact store. The backend store is where MLflow Tracking Server stores experiment and run metadata as well as parameters, metrics, and tags for runs. MLflow supports two types of backend stores: file store and database-backed store. For simplicity we will be using a file store. In our deployment, this file store is part of the Docker image, which means that this data is lost in the case of server restart. If you need longer-term storage, you can either use an external filesystem, like NFS server, or a database. The artifact store is a location suitable for large data (such as an S3 bucket or shared NFS filesystem) and is where clients log their artifact output (for example, models). To make our deployment cloud independent, we decided to use MinIO (part of Kubeflow) as an artifact store. Based on these decisions, a Docker file for building the MLflow Tracking Server looks like Example 6-9 (similar to the implementation in this GitHub repo (*https://oreil.ly/VOe9f*)).

Example 6-9. MLflow Tracking Server

```
FROM python:3.7

RUN pip3 install --upgrade pip && \
    pip3 install mlflow --upgrade && \
    pip3 install awscli --upgrade  && \
    pip3 install boto3 --upgrade

ENV PORT 5000
ENV AWS_BUCKET bucket
ENV AWS_ACCESS_KEY_ID aws_id
ENV AWS_SECRET_ACCESS_KEY aws_key
ENV FILE_DIR /tmp/mlflow

RUN mkdir -p /opt/mlflow
COPY run.sh /opt/mlflow
RUN chmod -R 777 /opt/mlflow/

ENTRYPOINT ["/opt/mlflow/run.sh"]
```

Here we first load MLflow code (using pip), set environment variables, and then copy and run the startup script. The start-up script used here looks like Example 6-10.[6]

Example 6-10. MLflow startup script

```
#!/bin/sh
mkdir -p $FILE_DIR

mlflow server \
    --backend-store-uri file://$FILE_DIR \
    --default-artifact-root s3://$AWS_BUCKET/mlflow/artifacts \
    --host 0.0.0.0 \
    --port $PORT
```

---

6 This is a simplified implementation. For complete implementation, see this book's GitHub repo (*https://oreil.ly/Kubeflow_for_ML_ch06_MLflow*).

This script sets an environment and then verifies that all required environment variables are set. Once validation succeeds, an MLflow server is started. Once the Docker is created, the Helm command in Example 6-11 (the Helm chart is located on this book's GitHub repo (*https://oreil.ly/Kubeflow_for_ML_ch06_mlflowchart*)) can be used to install the server.

Example 6-11. Installing MLflow server with Helm

```
helm install <location of the Helm chart>
```

This Helm chart installs three main components implementing the MLflow Tracking Server:

Deployment (https://oreil.ly/GYQwv)
Deploying MLflow server itself (single replica). The important parameters here are the environment, including MinIO endpoint, credentials, and bucket used for artifact storage.

Service (https://oreil.ly/RZq4U)
Creating a Kubernetes service exposing MLflow deployment

Virtual service (https://oreil.ly/-myuN)
Exposing MLflow service to users through the Istio ingress gateway used by Kubeflow

Once the server is deployed, we can get access to the UI, but at this point it will say that there are no available experiments. Let's now look at how this server can be used to capture metadata.[7]

Logging Data on Runs

As an example of logging data, let's look at some simple code.[8] We will start by installing required packages, shown in Examples 6-11 and 6-12.

Example 6-12. Install required

```
!pip install pandas --upgrade --user
!pip install mlflow --upgrade --user ❶
!pip install joblib --upgrade --user
!pip install numpy --upgrade --user
!pip install scipy --upgrade --user
```

---

7 Here we are showing usage of Python APIs. For additional APIs (R, Java, REST) refer to the MLflow documentation (*https://oreil.ly/QaeM1*).

8 The code here is adapted from this article (*https://oreil.ly/nVB_s*) by Jean-Michel Daignan.

```
!pip install scikit-learn --upgrade --user
!pip install boto3 --upgrade --user ❶
```

❶ Here mlflow and boto3 are the packages required for metadata logging, while the rest are used for machine learning itself.

Once these packages are installed, we can define required imports, as shown in Example 6-13.

Example 6-13. Import required libraries

```
import time
import json
import os
from joblib import Parallel, delayed

import pandas as pd
import numpy as np
import scipy

from sklearn.model_selection import train_test_split, KFold
from sklearn.metrics import mean_squared_error, mean_absolute_error
from sklearn.metrics import r2_score, explained_variance_score
from sklearn.exceptions import ConvergenceWarning

import mlflow
import mlflow.sklearn
from mlflow.tracking import MlflowClient

from warnings import simplefilter
simplefilter(action='ignore', category = FutureWarning)
simplefilter(action='ignore', category = ConvergenceWarning)
```

Here again, os and the last three imports are required for MLflow logging, while the rest are used for machine learning. Now we need to define the environment variables (see Example 6-14) required for proper access to the MinIO server for storing artifacts.

Example 6-14. Set environment variables

```
os.environ['MLFLOW_S3_ENDPOINT_URL'] = \
    'http://minio-service.kubeflow.svc.cluster.local:9000'
os.environ['AWS_ACCESS_KEY_ID'] = 'minio'
os.environ['AWS_SECRET_ACCESS_KEY'] = 'minio123'
```

Note here that in addition to the tracking server itself, MLFLOW_S3_ENDPOINT_URL is defined not only in the tracking server definition, but also in the code that actually captures the metadata. This is because, as we mentioned previously, user code writes to the artifact store directly, bypassing the server.

Here we skip the majority of the code (the full code can be found on this book's Git-Hub repo (*https://oreil.ly/Kubeflow_for_ML_ch06_MLflow*)) and concentrate only on the parts related to the MLflow logging. The next step (see Example 6-15) is connecting to the tracking server and creating an experiment.

Example 6-15. Create experiment

```
remote_server_uri = "http://mlflowserver.kubeflow.svc.cluster.local:5000"
mlflow.set_tracking_uri(remote_server_uri)
experiment_name = "electricityconsumption-forecast"
mlflow.set_experiment(experiment_name)
```

Once connected to the server and creating (choosing) an experiment, we can start logging data. As an example, let's look at the code for storing KNN regressor (*https://oreil.ly/g5yH3*) information, in Example 6-16.

Example 6-16. Sample KNN model

```
def train_knnmodel(parameters, inputs, tags, log = False):
    with mlflow.start_run(nested = True):

.............................................. .
        # Build the model
        tic = time.time()
        model = KNeighborsRegressor(parameters["nbr_neighbors"],
                            weights = parameters["weight_method"])
        model.fit(array_inputs_train, array_output_train)
        duration_training = time.time() - tic

        # Make the prediction
        tic1 = time.time()
        prediction = model.predict(array_inputs_test)
        duration_prediction = time.time() - tic1

        # Evaluate the model prediction
        metrics = evaluation_model(array_output_test, prediction)

        # Log in mlflow (parameter)
        mlflow.log_params(parameters)

        # Log in mlflow (metrics)
        metrics["duration_training"] = duration_training
        metrics["duration_prediction"] = duration_prediction
        mlflow.log_metrics(metrics)

        # Log in mlflow (model)
        mlflow.sklearn.log_model(model, f"model")

        # Save model
        #mlflow.sklearn.save_model(model,
                        f"mlruns/1/{uri}/artifacts/model/sklearnmodel")

        # Tag the model
        mlflow.set_tags(tags)
```

In this code snippet, we can see how different kinds of data about model creation and prediction test statistics are logged. The information here is very similar to the information captured by Kubeflow Metadata and includes inputs, models, and metrics.

Finally, similar to Kubeflow Metadata, MLflow allows you to access this metadata programmatically. The main APIs provided by MLflow include what you see in Example 6-17.

Example 6-17. Getting the runs for a given experiment

```
df_runs = mlflow.search_runs(experiment_ids="0")  ❶
print("Number of runs done : ", len(df_runs))

df_runs.sort_values(["metrics.rmse"], ascending = True, inplace = True)  ❷
df_runs.head()
```

❶ Getting the the runs for a given experiment

❷ Sorting runs based on the specific parameters

MLflow will sort runs by root mean square error (rmse) and show the best ones.

For additional capabilities of the programmatic runs querying, consult the MLflow documentation (*https://oreil.ly/Jistd*).

With all the capabilities of running programmatic queries, the most powerful way to evaluate runs' metadata is through the MLflow UI, which we will cover next.

Using the MLflow UI

The Tracking UI in MLflow lets you visualize, search, and compare runs, as well as download run artifacts or metadata for analysis in other tools. Because MLflow is not part of Kubeflow, its access is not provided by Kubeflow UI. Based on the provided virtual service, the MLflow UI is available at *<Kubeflow Istio ingress gateway URL>/ mlflow*.

Figure 6-5 shows the results produced by the run described. It is possible to filter results using the search box. For example, if we want to see only results for the KNN model, then the search criteria `tags.model="knn"` can be used. You can also use more complex filters, such as `tags.model="knn"` and `metrics.duration_prediction < 0.002`, which will return results for the KNN model for which prediction duration is less than 0.002 sec.

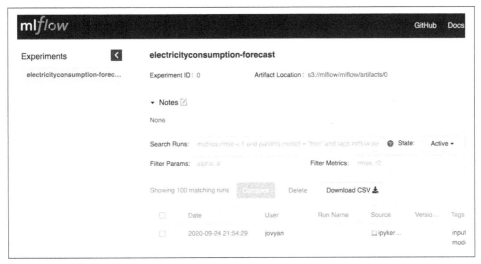

Figure 6-5. MLflow main page

By clicking the individual run we can see its details, as shown in Figure 6-6.

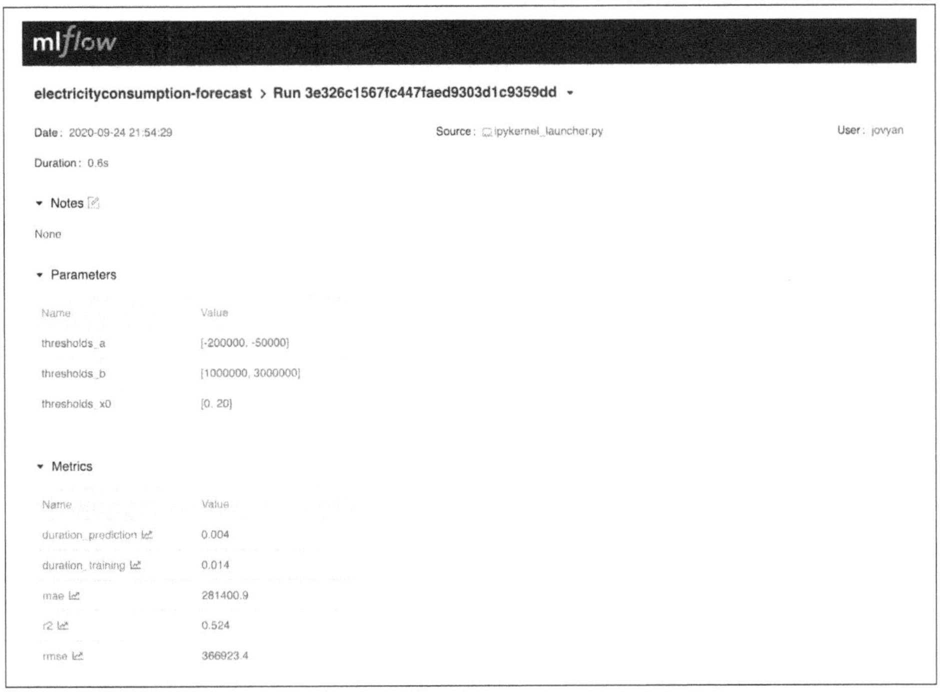

Figure 6-6. View of the individual run

Alternatively, we can compare several runs by picking them and clicking compare, as seen in Figure 6-7.

Figure 6-7. Run comparison view

We can also view metrics comparison for multiple runs, as in Figure 6-8.[9]

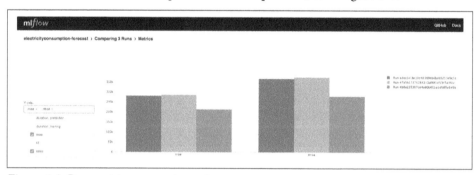

Figure 6-8. Run metrics comparison view

Conclusion

In this chapter we have shown how the Kubeflow Metadata component of the Kubeflow deployment supports storing and viewing ML metadata. We have also discussed shortcomings of this implementation, including its Python-only support and weak UI. Last, we covered how to supplement Kubeflow with components with similar functionality—MLflow and additional capabilities that can be achieved in this case.

In Chapter 7, we explore using Kubeflow with TensorFlow to train and serve models.

---

9 Also see the MLflow documentation (*https://oreil.ly/w9u7n*) for additional UI capabilities.

Training a Machine Learning Model

In Chapter 5, we learned how to prepare and clean up our data, which is the first step in the machine learning pipeline. Now let's take a deep dive into how to use our data to train a machine learning model.

Training is often considered the "bulk" of the work in machine learning. Our goal is to create a function (the "model") that can accurately predict results that it hasn't seen before. Intuitively, model training is very much like how humans learn a new skill— we observe, practice, correct our mistakes, and gradually improve. In machine learning, we start with an initial model that might not be very good at its job. We then put the model through a series of training steps, where training data is fed to the model. At each training step, we compare the prediction results produced by our model with the true results, and see how well our model performed. We then tinker with the parameters to this model (for example, by changing how much weight is given to each feature) to attempt to improve the model's accuracy. A good model is one that makes accurate predictions without overfitting to a specific set of inputs.

In this chapter, we are going to learn how to train machine learning models using two different libraries—TensorFlow and Scikit-learn. TensorFlow has native, first-class support in Kubeflow, while Scikit-learn does not. But as we will see in this chapter, both libraries can be easily integrated with Kubeflow. We'll demonstrate how you can experiment with models in Kubeflow's notebooks, and how you can deploy these models to production environments.

Building a Recommender with TensorFlow

Let us first take a look at TensorFlow—an open source framework for machine learning developed by Google. It is currently one of the most popular libraries for machine learning–powered applications, in particular for implementing deep learning. TensorFlow has great support for computational tasks on a variety of hardware, including CPUs, GPUs, and TPUs. We chose TensorFlow for this tutorial because its high-level APIs are user-friendly and abstract away many of the gory details.

What Is Deep Learning?

In recent years, *deep learning*—a category of algorithms that leverage artificial neural networks to progressively extract higher-level features from input data—has become increasingly popular. Deep learning has the ability to leverage hidden layers in the neural network to learn highly abstract models of the input.

Deep learning algorithms can be found in many everyday applications, like image recognition and natural language processing. The multiple hidden layers of neural networks allow these algorithms to discover increasingly abstract details from data. For example, while the initial layer in an image classification neural network might discover only object edges, the deeper layer may learn more complex features and classify the objects in the images.

Let's get acquainted with TensorFlow with a simple tutorial. In Chapter 1 we introduced our case studies, one of which is a product recommendation system for customers. In this chapter, we will be implementing this system with TensorFlow. Specifically, we will do two things:

1. Use TensorFlow to train a model for product recommendation.
2. Use Kubeflow to wrap the training code and deploy it to a production cluster.

TensorFlow's high-level Keras API makes it relatively easy to implement our model. In fact, the bulk of the model can be implemented with less than 50 lines of Python code.

 Keras is the high-level TensorFlow API for deep learning models. It has a user-friendly interface and high extensibility. As an added bonus, Keras has many common neural network implementations straight out of the box, so you can get a model up and running right away.

Let's begin by selecting a model for our recommender. We begin with a simple assumption—that if two people (Alice and Bob) have similar opinions on a set of products, then they are also more likely to think similarly about other products. In other words, Alice is more likely to have the same preferences as Bob than would a randomly chosen third person. Thus, we can build a recommendation model using just the users' purchase history. This is the idea of collaborative filtering—we collect preferential information from many users (hence "collaborative") and use this data to make selective predictions (hence "filtering").

To build this recommender model, we will need a few things:

Users' purchasing history
> We will use the example input data from this GitHub repo (*https://oreil.ly/F-8rS*).

Data storage
> To make sure that our model works across different platforms, we'll use MinIO as the storage system.

Training model
> The implementation that we are using is based on a Keras model on GitHub (*https://oreil.ly/hTGQf*).

We will first experiment with this model using Kubeflow's notebook servers, and then deploy the training job to our cluster using Kubeflow's TFJob APIs.

Getting Started

Let's get started by downloading the prerequisites. You can download the notebook from this book's GitHub repo (*https://oreil.ly/Kubeflow_for_ML_ch07*). To run the notebook, you will need a running Kubeflow cluster that includes a MinIO service. Review "Support Components" on page 33 to configure MinIO. Make sure that MinIO Client ("mc") is also installed.

We also need to prepare the data to facilitate training: you can download the user purchase history data from this GitHub site (*https://oreil.ly/BK6XS*). Then you can use MinIO Client to create the storage objects, as shown in Example 7-1.

Example 7-1. Setting up prerequisites

```
# Port-forward the MinIO service to http://localhost:9000
kubectl port-forward -n kubeflow svc/minio-service 9000:9000 &

# Configure MinIO host
mc config host add minio http://localhost:9000 minio minio123

# Create storage bucket
mc mb minio/data
```

```
# Copy storage objects
mc cp go/src/github.com/medium/items-recommender/data/recommend_1.csv \\
        minio/data/recommender/users.csv
mc cp go/src/github.com/medium/items-recommender/data/trx_data.csv \\
        minio/data/recommender/transactions.csv
```

Starting a New Notebook Session

Now let's start by creating a new notebook. You can do this by navigating to the "Notebook Servers" panel in your Kubeflow dashboard, then clicking "New Server" and following the instructions. For this example, we use the `tensorFlow-1.15.2-notebook-cpu:1.0` image.[1]

When the notebook server starts up, click the "Upload" button in the top right corner and upload the `Recommender_Kubeflow.ipynb` file. Click the file to start a new session.

The first few sections of the code involve importing libraries and reading the training data from MinIO. Then we normalize the input data so that we are ready to start training. This process is called feature preparation, which we discussed in Chapter 5. In this chapter we'll focus on the model training part of the exercise.

TensorFlow Training

Now that our notebook is set up and the data is prepared, we can create a TensorFlow session, as shown in Example 7-2.[2]

Example 7-2. Creating a TensorFlow session

```
# Create TF session and set it in Keras
sess = tf.Session()
K.set_session(sess)
K.set_learning_phase(1)
```

For the model class, we use the code in Example 7-3 for collaborative filtering.

---

1 Currently Kubeflow provides CPU and GPU images with TensorFlow 1.15.2 and 2.1.0, or you can use a custom image.

2 The examples in this chapter use TensorFlow 1.15.2. Examples with TensorFlow 2.1.0 can be found on this Kubeflow GitHub site (*https://oreil.ly/I71lt*).

Example 7-3. DeepCollaborativeFiltering learning

```python
class DeepCollaborativeFiltering(Model):
    def __init__(self, n_customers, n_products, n_factors, p_dropout = 0.2):
        x1 = Input(shape = (1,), name="user")

        P = Embedding(n_customers, n_factors, input_length = 1)(x1)
        P = Reshape((n_factors,))(P)

        x2 = Input(shape = (1,), name="product")

        Q = Embedding(n_products, n_factors, input_length = 1)(x2)
        Q = Reshape((n_factors,))(Q)

        x = concatenate([P, Q], axis=1)
        x = Dropout(p_dropout)(x)

        x = Dense(n_factors)(x)
        x = Activation('relu')(x)
        x = Dropout(p_dropout)(x)

        output = Dense(1)(x)

        super(DeepCollaborativeFiltering, self).__init__([x1, x2], output)

    def rate(self, customer_idxs, product_idxs):
        if (type(customer_idxs) == int and type(product_idxs) == int):
            return self.predict([np.array(customer_idxs).reshape((1,)),\
                    np.array(product_idxs).reshape((1,))])

        if (type(customer_idxs) == str and type(product_idxs) == str):
            return self.predict( \
                    [np.array(customerMapping[customer_idxs]).reshape((1,)),\
                    np.array(productMapping[product_idxs]).reshape((1,))])

        return self.predict([
            np.array([customerMapping[customer_idx] \
                    for customer_idx in customer_idxs]),
                np.array([productMapping[product_idx] \
                    for product_idx in product_idxs])
        ])
```

This is the basis of our model class. It includes a constructor with some code to instantiate the collaborative filtering model using Keras APIs, and a "rate" function that we can use to make a prediction using our model—namely, what rating a customer would give to a particular product.

We can create an instance of the model, as in Example 7-4.

Example 7-4. Model creation

```python
model = DeepCollaborativeFiltering(n_customers, n_products, n_factors)
model.summary()
```

Now we are ready to start training our model. We can do this by setting a few hyper-parameters, as shown in Example 7-5.

Example 7-5. Setting Training configuration

```
bs = 64
val_per = 0.25
epochs = 3
```

These are hyperparameters that control the training process. They are typically set before training begins, unlike model parameters, which are learned from the training process. Setting the right values for hyperparameters can significantly impact the effectiveness of your model. For now, let's just set some default values for them. In Chapter 10 we'll look at how to use Kubeflow to tune hyperparameters.

We are now ready to run the training code. See Example 7-6.

Example 7-6. Fitting model

```
model.compile(optimizer = 'adam', loss = mean_squared_logarithmic_error)
model.fit(x = [customer_idxs, product_idxs], y = ratings,
        batch_size = bs, epochs = epochs, validation_split = val_per)
print('Done training!')
```

Once the training is complete, you should see results like in Example 7-7.

Example 7-7. Model training results

```
Train on 100188 samples, validate on 33397 samples
Epoch 1/3
100188/100188 [==============================]
- 21s 212us/step - loss: 0.0105 - val_loss: 0.0186
Epoch 2/3
100188/100188 [==============================]
- 20s 203us/step - loss: 0.0092 - val_loss: 0.0188
Epoch 3/3
100188/100188 [==============================]
- 21s 212us/step - loss: 0.0078 - val_loss: 0.0192
Done training!
```

Congratulations: you've successfully trained a TensorFlow model in a Jupyter note-book. But we're not quite done yet—to make use of our model later, we should first export it. You can do this by setting up the export destination using MinIO Client, as shown in Example 7-8.

Example 7-8. Setting export destination

```
directorystream = minioClient.get_object('data', 'recommender/directory.txt')
directory = ""
for d in directorystream.stream(32*1024):
    directory += d.decode('utf-8')
arg_version = "1"
export_path = 's3://models/' + directory + '/' + arg_version + '/'
print ('Exporting trained model to', export_path)
```

Once you have set up your export destination, you can then export the model, as in Example 7-9.

Example 7-9. Exporting the model

```
# Inputs/outputs
tensor_info_users = tf.saved_model.utils.build_tensor_info(model.input[0])
tensor_info_products = tf.saved_model.utils.build_tensor_info(model.input[1])
tensor_info_pred = tf.saved_model.utils.build_tensor_info(model.output)

print ("tensor_info_users", tensor_info_users.name)
print ("tensor_info_products", tensor_info_products.name)
print ("tensor_info_pred", tensor_info_pred.name)

# Signature
prediction_signature = (tf.saved_model.signature_def_utils.build_signature_def(
        inputs={"users": tensor_info_users, "products": tensor_info_products},
        outputs={"predictions": tensor_info_pred},
        method_name=tf.saved_model.signature_constants.PREDICT_METHOD_NAME))
# Export
legacy_init_op = tf.group(tf.tables_initializer(), name='legacy_init_op')
builder = tf.saved_model.builder.SavedModelBuilder(export_path)
builder.add_meta_graph_and_variables(
      sess, [tf.saved_model.tag_constants.SERVING],
      signature_def_map={
        tf.saved_model.signature_constants.DEFAULT_SERVING_SIGNATURE_DEF_KEY:
          prediction_signature,
      },
      legacy_init_op=legacy_init_op)
builder.save()
```

Now we're ready to use this model to serve predictions, as we'll learn in Chapter 8. But before that, let's look at how to deploy this training job using Kubeflow.

Deploying a TensorFlow Training Job

So far we have done some TensorFlow training using Jupyter notebooks, which is a great way to prototype and experiment. But soon we may discover that our prototype is insufficient—perhaps we need to refine the model using more data, or perhaps we need to train the model using specialized hardware. Sometimes we may even need to continuously run the training job because our model is constantly evolving. Perhaps most importantly, our model has to be deployable to production, where it can serve actual customer requests.

In order to handle these requirements, our training code must be easily packageable and deployable to various different environments. One of the ways to achieve this is to use TFJob—a Kubernetes custom resource (implemented using Kubernetes operator `tf-operator`) that you can use to run TensorFlow training jobs on Kubernetes.

Why Should You Use TFJobs?

There are many challenges to deploying our training code to a production environment. To name a few:

- What kind of infrastructure do we have to work with? Are we running in the cloud or on-premises?

- Who has access to the training job and its data? Can we share a training job with our teammates?

- How do we scale up the training job? How do we clean up the resources when we are done?

- What do we do with the model after we've trained it? How do we export the model so we can make use of it?

Typically, these problems require the user to implement a large amount of "glue code" to work with the underlying infrastructure. Such code is likely to differ greatly depending on the environment and the technical constraints, which means that developing this technical stack could be much more time-consuming than the model itself.

These are the problems that Kubeflow aims to solve. Since Kubeflow's architecture is entirely based on Kubernetes, all of Kubernetes' scalable and portable features are available to Kubeflow. Applications in Kubernetes are developed as "cloud native" microservices. In the case of machine learning training, if you want to scale up a training job, simply increase the number of desired replicas and the underlying system will take care of that for you. The same Kubeflow job that runs on Amazon Cloud can easily be exported to a different cluster running Google Cloud or even to on-premises.

Kubeflow makes it easy to configure TensorFlow jobs on a Kubernetes cluster by orchestrating them as custom resources. Custom resources are extensions to the core Kubernetes API that store collections of API objects. By using custom resources, developers only need to provide a "desired state" of their applications, and the underlying controllers will take care of the rest.

We'll start by deploying our recommender as a single-container TFJob. Since we already have a Python notebook, exporting it as a Python file is fairly simple—just select "File," then "Download as" and select "Python." This should save your notebook as a ready-to-execute Python file.

The next step is to package the training code in a container. This can be done with the Dockerfile, as seen in Example 7-10.

Example 7-10. TFJob Dockerfile

```
FROM  tensorflow/tensorflow:1.15.2-py3
RUN pip3 install --upgrade pip
RUN pip3 install pandas --upgrade
RUN pip3 install keras --upgrade
RUN pip3 install minio --upgrade
RUN mkdir -p /opt/kubeflow
COPY Recommender_Kubeflow.py /opt/kubeflow/
ENTRYPOINT ["python3", "/opt/kubeflow/Recommender_Kubeflow.py"]
```

Next, we need to build this container along with its required libraries, and push the container image to a repository:

```
docker build -t kubeflow/recommenderjob:1.0 .
docker push kubeflow/recommenderjob:1.0
```

Once that's done, we are ready to create the specification for a TFJob, as in Example 7-11.

Example 7-11. Single-container TFJob example

```
apiVersion: "kubeflow.org/v1"   ❶
kind: "TFJob"                    ❷
metadata:
  name: "recommenderjob"        ❸
spec:
  tfReplicaSpecs:               ❹
    Worker:
      replicas: 1
    restartPolicy: Never
    template:
      spec:
        containers:
        - name: tensorflow image: kubeflow/recommenderjob:1.0
```

❶ The `apiVersion` field specifies which version of the TFJob custom resource you are using. The corresponding version (in this case v1) needs to be installed in your Kubeflow cluster.

❷ The `kind` field identifies the type of the custom resource—in this case a TFJob.

❸ The `metadata` field is common to all Kubernetes objects and is used to uniquely identify the object in the cluster—you can add fields like name, namespace, and labels here.

❹ The most important part of the schema is `tfReplicaSpecs`. This is the actual description of your TensorFlow training cluster and its desired state. For this example, we just have a single worker replica. In the following section, we'll examine this field further.

There are a few other optional configurations for your TFJob, including:

`activeDeadlineSeconds`
How long to keep this job active before the system can terminate it. If this is set, the system will kill the job after the deadline expires.

`backoffLimit`
How many times to keep retrying this job before marking it as failed. For example, setting this to 3 means that if a job fails 3 times, the system will stop retrying.

`cleanPodPolicy`
Configures whether or not to clean up the Kubernetes pods after the job completes. Setting this policy can be useful to keep pods for debugging purposes. This can be set to All (all pods are cleaned up), Running (only running pods are cleaned up), or None (no pods are cleaned up).

Now deploy the TFJob to your cluster, as in Example 7-12.

Example 7-12. Deploying TFJob

```
kubectl apply -f recommenderjob.yaml
```

You can monitor the status of the TFJob with the command in Example 7-13.

Example 7-13. Viewing the state of TFJob

```
kubectl describe tfjob recommenderjob
```

This should display something like Example 7-14.

Example 7-14. TF Recommender job description

```
Status:
  Completion Time:  2019-05-18T00:58:27Z
  Conditions:
    Last Transition Time:  2019-05-18T02:34:24Z
    Last Update Time:      2019-05-18T02:34:24Z
    Message:               TFJob recommenderjob is created.
    Reason:                TFJobCreated
    Status:                True
    Type:                  Created
    Last Transition Time:  2019-05-18T02:38:28Z
    Last Update Time:      2019-05-18T02:38:28Z
    Message:               TFJob recommenderjob is running.
    Reason:                TFJobRunning
    Status:                False
    Type:                  Running
    Last Transition Time:  2019-05-18T02:38:29Z
    Last Update Time:      2019-05-18T02:38:29Z
    Message:               TFJob recommenderjob successfully completed.
    Reason:                TFJobSucceeded
    Status:                True
    Type:                  Succeeded
  Replica Statuses:
    Worker:
      Succeeded:  1
```

Note that the status field contains a list of job conditions, which represent when the job transitioned into each state. This is useful for debugging—if the job failed, the reason for the job's failure would appear here.

So far we have trained a fairly simple and straightforward model with a modest number of training samples. In real life, learning more complex models may require significantly more training samples or model parameters. Such models can be too large and computationally complex to be handled by one machine. This is where distributed training comes in.

Distributed Training

By now we've deployed a single-worker TensorFlow job with Kubeflow. It is called "single-worker" because everything from hosting the data to executing the actual training steps is done on a single machine. However, as models become more complex, a single machine is often insufficient—we may need to distribute the model or the training samples over several networked machines. TensorFlow supports a distributed training mode, in which training is performed in parallel over several worker nodes.

Distributed training typically comes in two flavors: data parallelism and model parallelism. In data parallelism, the training data is partitioned into chunks, and the same training code runs on each chunk. At the end of each training step, each worker communicates its updates to all other nodes. Model parallelism is the opposite—the same training data is used in all workers, but the model itself is partitioned. At the end of each step, each worker is responsible for synchronizing the shared parts of the model.

Distribution Strategies in TensorFlow

TensorFlow supports a number of different strategies for distributed training. These include:

Mirrored strategy
> This is a synchronous strategy, which means the training steps and gradients are synced across replicas. Copies of all variables in the model are replicated on each device across all workers.

TPU strategy
> Similar to mirrored strategy, but allows you to train on Google's TPUs.

Multiworker mirrored strategy
> Also similar to mirrored strategy, but uses CollectiveOps multiworker all-reduce to keep variables in sync.

Central storage strategy
> Instead of replicating variables across all workers, this strategy stores variables on a central CPU while replicating computational work across workers.

Parameter server strategy
> Nodes are classified as either workers or parameter servers. Each model parameter is stored on one parameter server, while computational work is replicated among workers.

The TFJob interface supports multiworker distributed training. Conceptually, a TFJob is a logical grouping of all resources related to a training job, including *pods* and *services*. In Kubeflow, each replicated worker or parameter server is scheduled on its own single-container pod. In order for the replicas to synchronize with each other, each replica needs to expose itself through an endpoint, which is a Kubernetes internal service. Grouping these resources logically under a parent resource (which is the TFJob) allows these resources to be co-scheduled and garbage collected together.

In this section we'll deploy a simple MNIST example with distributed training. The TensorFlow training code is provided for you at this GitHub repo (*https://oreil.ly/ySztV*).

Let's take a look at the YAML file for the distributed TensorFlow job in Example 7-15.

Example 7-15. Distributed TFJob example

```yaml
apiVersion: "kubeflow.org/v1"
kind: "TFJob"
metadata:
  name: "mnist"
  namespace: kubeflow
spec:
  cleanPodPolicy: None
  tfReplicaSpecs:
    Worker:
      replicas: 2
      restartPolicy: Never
      template:
        spec:
          containers:
            - name: tensorflow
              image: gcr.io/kubeflow-ci/tf-mnist-with-summaries:1.0
              command:
                - "python"
                - "/var/tf_mnist/mnist_with_summaries.py"
                - "--log_dir=/train/logs"
                - "--learning_rate=0.01"
                - "--batch_size=150"
              volumeMounts:
                - mountPath: "/train"
                  name: "training"
          volumes:
            - name: "training"
              persistentVolumeClaim:
                claimName: "tfevent-volume"
```

Note that the `tfReplicaSpecs` field now contains a few different replica types. In a typical TensorFlow training cluster, there are a few possible possibilities:

Chief
    Responsible for orchestrating computational tasks, emitting events, and check-pointing the model

Parameter servers
    Provide a distributed data store for the model parameters

Worker
    This is where the computations and training actually happen. When a chief node is not explicitly defined (as in the preceding example), one of the workers acts as the chief node.

Evaluator
    The evaluators can be used to compute evaluation metrics as the model is trained.

Note also that a replica spec contains a number of properties that describe its desired state:

replicas
> How many replicas should be spawned for this replica type

template
> A PodTemplateSpec that describes the pod to create for each replica

restartPolicy
> Determines whether pods will be restarted when they exit. The allowed values are as follows:

> Always
>> Means the pod will always be restarted. This policy is good for parameter servers since they never exit and should always be restarted in the event of failure.

> OnFailure
>> Means the pod will be restarted if the pod exits due to failure. A nonzero exit code indicates a failure. An exit code of 0 indicates success and the pod will not be restarted. This policy is good for the chief and workers.

> ExitCode
>> Means the restart behavior is dependent on the exit code of the TensorFlow container as follows:
>>
>> - 0 indicates the process completed successfully and will not be restarted.
>> - 1–127 indicates a permanent error and that the container will not be restarted.
>> - 128–255 indicates a retryable error and the container will be restarted. This policy is good for the chief and workers.

Never
> This means pods that terminate will never be restarted. This policy should rarely be used, because Kubernetes will terminate pods for any number of reasons (e.g., node becomes unhealthy) and this will prevent the job from recovering.

Once you have the TFJob spec written, deploy it to your Kubeflow cluster:

```
kubectl apply -f dist-mnist.yaml
```

Monitoring the job status is similar to a single-container job:

```
kubectl describe tfjob mnist
```

This should output something like Example 7-16.

Example 7-16. TFJob execution result

```
Status:
  Completion Time:  2019-05-12T00:58:27Z
  Conditions:
    Last Transition Time:  2019-05-12T00:57:31Z
    Last Update Time:      2019-05-12T00:57:31Z
    Message:               TFJob dist-mnist-example is created.
    Reason:                TFJobCreated
    Status:                True
    Type:                  Created
    Last Transition Time:  2019-05-12T00:58:21Z
    Last Update Time:      2019-05-12T00:58:21Z
    Message:               TFJob dist-mnist-example is running.
    Reason:                TFJobRunning
    Status:                False
    Type:                  Running
    Last Transition Time:  2019-05-12T00:58:27Z
    Last Update Time:      2019-05-12T00:58:27Z
    Message:               TFJob dist-mnist-example successfully completed.
    Reason:                TFJobSucceeded
    Status:                True
    Type:                  Succeeded
  Replica Statuses:
    Worker:
      Succeeded:  2
```

Notice that the `Replica Statuses` field shows a breakdown of status by each replica type. The TFJob is successfully completed when all of its workers complete. If any worker has failed, then the TFJob's status would be failed as well.

Using GPUs

GPUs are processors that are composed of many smaller and specialized cores. Originally designed to render graphics, GPUs are increasingly used for massively parallel computational tasks, such as machine learning. Unlike CPUs, GPUs are ideal for distributing large workloads over its many cores and executing them concurrently.

To use GPUs for training, your Kubeflow cluster needs to be preconfigured to enable GPUs. Refer to your cloud provider's documentation on enabling GPU usage. After enabling GPUs on the cluster, you can enable GPUs on the specific replica type in the training spec by modifying the command-line arguments, as in Example 7-17.

Example 7-17. TFJob with GPU example

```
Worker:
  replicas: 4
  restartPolicy: Never
  template:
    spec:
      containers:
        - name: tensorflow
          image: kubeflow/tf-dist-mnist-test:1.0
```

```
    args:
  - python
  - /var/tf_dist_mnist/dist_mnist.py
  - --num_gpus=1
```

Using Other Frameworks for Distributed Training

Kubeflow is designed to be a multiframework machine learning platform. That means the schema for distributed training can easily be extended to other frameworks. As of the time of this writing, there are a number of operators written to provide first-class support for other frameworks, including PyTorch and Caffe2.

Example 7-18 shows what a PyTorch training job spec looks like.

Example 7-18. Pytorch Distributed Training Example

```
apiVersion: "kubeflow.org/v1"
kind: "PyTorchJob"
metadata:
  name: "pytorch-dist"
spec:
  pytorchReplicaSpecs:
    Master:
      replicas: 1
      restartPolicy: OnFailure
      template:
        spec:
          containers:
            - name: pytorch
              image: gcr.io/kubeflow-ci/pytorch-dist-sendrecv-test:1.0
    Worker:
      replicas: 3
      restartPolicy: OnFailure
      template:
        spec:
          containers:
            - name: pytorch
              image: gcr.io/kubeflow-ci/pytorch-dist-sendrecv-test:1.0
```

As you can see, the format is very similar to that of TFJobs. The only difference is in the replica types.

Training a Model Using Scikit-Learn

Thus far we have seen how to use the built-in operators in Kubeflow to train machine learning models. However, there are many frameworks and libraries for which there are no Kubeflow operators. In these cases you can still use your favorite frameworks in Jupyter notebooks[3] or in custom Docker images.

---

3 The languages currently supported by Jupyter notebooks include Python, R, Julia, and Scala.

Scikit-learn is an open source Python library for machine learning built on top of NumPy for high-performance linear algebra and array operations. The project started as scikits.learn, a Google Summer of Code project by David Cournapeau. Its name stems from the notion that it is a "SciKit" (SciPy Toolkit), a separately developed and distributed third-party extension to SciPy. Scikit-learn is one of the most popular machine learning libraries on GitHub, and one of the best-maintained. Training models with Scikit-learn is supported in Kubeflow as generic Python code, with no specific operators for distributed training.

The library supports state-of-the-art algorithms such as KNN, XGBoost, Random Forest, and SVM. Scikit-learn is widely used in Kaggle competitions and by prominent tech companies. Scikit-learn helps in preprocessing, dimensionality reduction (parameter selection), classification, regression, clustering, and model selection.

In this section, we will explore how to train models in Kubeflow by using Scikit-learn on the 1994 US Census dataset (*https://oreil.ly/9nQrt*). This example is based on this implementation (*https://oreil.ly/9hnha*) of Anchor explanations for income prediction, and leverages an extract from the 1994 census dataset. The dataset includes several categorical variables and continuous features, including age, education, marital status, occupation, salary, relationship, race, sex, native country, and capital gains and losses. We will use a Random Forest algorithm—an ensemble learning method for classification, regression, and other tasks that operates by constructing a multitude of decision trees at training time and outputting the class that is the mode of the classes (classification) or mean prediction (regression) of the individual trees.

You can download the notebook from this book's GitHub repo (*https://oreil.ly/Kube flow_for_ML_ch07_notebook*).

Starting a New Notebook Session

Let's start by creating a new notebook. Similar to TensorFlow training, you can do this by navigating to the "Notebook Servers" panel in your Kubeflow dashboard, then clicking "New Server" and following the instructions. For this example, we can use the tensorFlow-1.15.2-notebook-cpu:1.0 image.

When working in Kubeflow, an easy way to take advantage of GPU resources to accelerate your Scikit model is to switch to GPU type.

When the notebook server starts up, click the "Upload" button in the top right corner and upload the *IncomePrediction.ipynb* file. Click the file to start a new session.

Data Preparation

The first few sections of the notebook involve importing libraries and reading the data. Then we proceed to feature preparation.[4] For feature transformation we are using Scikit-learn pipelines. The pipeline makes it easier to feed the model with consistent data.

For our Random Forest training, we need to define ordinal (standardize data) and categorical (one-hot encoding) features, as in Example 7-19.

Example 7-19. Feature preparation

```
ordinal_features = [x for x in range(len(feature_names))
                if x not in list(category_map.keys())]
ordinal_transformer = Pipeline(steps=[
    ('imputer',  SimpleImputer(strategy='median')),
    ('scaler', StandardScaler())])

categorical_features = list(category_map.keys())
categorical_transformer = Pipeline(steps=[('imputer',
    SimpleImputer(strategy='median')),
    ('onehot', OneHotEncoder(handle_unknown='ignore'))])
```

 Many real-world datasets contain missing values, which are encoded by data-specific placeholders, such as blanks and NaNs. Such datasets are typically incompatible with Scikit-learn estimators, which assume that all values are numerical. There are multiple strategies to deal with such missing data. One basic strategy would be to discard entire rows and/or columns containing missing values, which comes at the price of losing data. A better strategy is to impute the missing values—to infer them from the known part of the data. Simple imputer is a Scikit-learn class that allows you to handle the missing data in the predictive model dataset by replacing the NaN values with specified predefined values.

Once features are defined, we can use a column transformer to combine them, as shown in Example 7-20.

Example 7-20. Combining columns using column transformer

```
preprocessor = ColumnTransformer(transformers=[
    ('num', ordinal_transformer, ordinal_features),
    ('cat', categorical_transformer, categorical_features)])
preprocessor.fit(X_train)
```

---

4 See Chapter 5 for an in-depth discussion of feature preparation.

Scikit-learn one-hot encoding is used to encode categorical features as a one-hot numeric array. The encoder transforms an array of integers or strings, replacing the values by categorical (discrete) features. The features are encoded using a one-hot (aka, one-of-K or dummy) encoding scheme. This creates a binary column for each category and returns a sparse matrix or dense array (depending on the sparse parameter).

The transformer itself looks like Example 7-21.

Example 7-21. Data transformer

```
ColumnTransformer(n_jobs=None, remainder='drop', sparse_threshold=0.3,
  transformer_weights=None,
  transformers=[('num',
    Pipeline(memory=None,
      steps=[
        ('imputer', SimpleImputer(add_indicator=False,
          copy=True,
          fill_value=None,
          missing_values=nan,
          strategy='median',
          verbose=0)),
        ('scaler', StandardScaler(copy=True,
          with_mean=True,
          with_std=True))],
        verbose=False),
      [0, 8, 9, 10]),
    ('cat',
    Pipeline(memory=None,
      steps=[('imputer', SimpleImputer(add_indicator=False,
        copy=True,
        fill_value=None,
        missing_values=nan,
        strategy='median',
        verbose=0)),
      ('onehot', OneHotEncoder(categories='auto',
        drop=None,
        dtype=<class 'numpy.float64'>,
        handle_unknown='ignore',
        sparse=True))],
      verbose=False),
    [1, 2, 3, 4, 5, 6, 7, 11])],
  verbose=False)
```

As a result of this transformation, we have our data in the form of features ready for training.

Scikit-Learn Training

Once we have our features prepared we can proceed with the training. Here we will use `RandomForestClassifier`, provided by the Scikit-learn library, as shown in Example 7-22.

Example 7-22. Using RandomForestClassifier

```
np.random.seed(0)
clf = RandomForestClassifier(n_estimators=50)
clf.fit(preprocessor.transform(X_train), Y_train)
```

 The set and specific features of machine learning algorithm(s) is one of the main drivers behind picking a specific framework for machine learning implementation. Even the same algorithm implementation in different frameworks provides slightly different features that might (or might not) be important for your specific dataset.

Once prediction is done, we can evaluate training results, as shown in Example 7-23.

Example 7-23. Evaluating training results

```
predict_fn = lambda x: clf.predict(preprocessor.transform(x))
print('Train accuracy: ', accuracy_score(Y_train, predict_fn(X_train)))
print('Test accuracy: ', accuracy_score(Y_test, predict_fn(X_test)))
```

Which returns the results in Example 7-24.

Example 7-24. Training results

```
Train accuracy:  0.9655333333333334
Test accuracy:  0.855859375
```

At this point the model is created and can be directly used by exporting it (see the next section). One of the most important attributes of a model is its explainability. Although model explainability is mostly used in model serving, it is also important for model creation, for two main reasons:

- If explainability is important for model serving during model creation, we often need to validate that the model that was created is explainable.
- Many of the model explanation methods require additional calculations during model creation.

Based on this, we will show how to implement model explainability[5] during model creation.

Explaining the Model

For model explanation, we are using anchors, which are part of Seldon's Alibi project (*https://oreil.ly/VSGxe*).

The algorithm provides model-agnostic (black box) and human-interpretable explanations suitable for classification models applied to images, text, and tabular data. The continuous features are discretized into quantiles (e.g., deciles), so they become more interpretable. The features in a candidate anchor are kept constant (same category or bin for discretized features) while we sample the other features from a training set, as in Example 7-25.

Example 7-25. Defining the tabular anchor

```
explainer = AnchorTabular(
    predict_fn, feature_names, categorical_names=category_map, seed=1)
explainer.fit(X_train, disc_perc=[25, 50, 75])
```

This creates the tabular anchor (Example 7-26).

Example 7-26. Tabular anchor

```
AnchorTabular(meta={
    'name': 'AnchorTabular',
    'type': ['blackbox'],
    'explanations': ['local'],
    'params': {'seed': 1, 'disc_perc': [25, 50, 75]}
})
```

Now we can get an anchor for the prediction of the first observation in the test set. An *anchor* is a sufficient condition—that is, when the anchor holds, the prediction should be the same as the prediction for this instance in Example 7-27.

Example 7-27. Prediction calculation

```
idx = 0
class_names = adult.target_names
print('Prediction: ', class_names[explainer.predictor( \
            X_test[idx].reshape(1, -1))[0]])
```

---

5 Refer to this blog post by Rui Aguiar (*https://oreil.ly/juWml*) for more information on model explainability.

Which returns a prediction calculation result as shown in Example 7-28.

Example 7-28. Prediction calculation result

```
Prediction:  <=50K
```

We set the precision threshold to 0.95. This means that predictions on observations where the anchor holds will be the same as the prediction on the explained instance at least 95% of the time. Now we can get an explanation (Example 7-29) for this prediction.

Example 7-29. Model explanation

```
explanation = explainer.explain(X_test[idx], threshold=0.95)
print('Anchor: %s' % (' AND '.join(explanation.anchor)))
print('Precision: %.2f' % explanation.precision)
print('Coverage: %.2f' % explanation.coverage)
```

Which returns a model explanation result as shown in Example 7-30.

Example 7-30. Model explanation result

```
Anchor: Marital Status = Separated AND Sex = Female
Precision: 0.95
Coverage: 0.18
```

This tells us that the main factors for decision are marital status (Separated) and sex (Female). Anchors might not be found for all points. Let's try getting an anchor for a different observation in the test set—one for which the prediction is >50K, shown in Example 7-31.

Example 7-31. Model explanation

```
idx = 6
class_names = adult.target_names
print('Prediction: ', class_names[explainer.predictor( \
                 X_test[idx].reshape(1, -1))[0]])

explanation = explainer.explain(X_test[idx], threshold=0.95)
print('Anchor: %s' % (' AND '.join(explanation.anchor)))
print('Precision: %.2f' % explanation.precision)
print('Coverage: %.2f' % explanation.coverage)
```

Which returns a model explanation result as shown in Example 7-32.

Example 7-32. Model explanation result

```
Prediction:  >50K
Could not find a result satisfying the 0.95 precision constraint.
Now returning the best non-eligible result.
Anchor: Capital Loss > 0.00 AND Relationship = Husband AND
    Marital Status = Married AND Age > 37.00 AND
    Race = White AND Country = United-States AND Sex = Male
Precision: 0.71
Coverage: 0.05
```

Due to the imbalanced dataset (roughly 25:75 high:low earner proportion), during the sampling stage feature ranges corresponding to low earners will be oversampled. As a result, the anchor in this case is not found. This is a feature because it can point out an imbalanced dataset, but it can also be fixed by producing balanced datasets to enable anchors to be found for either class.

Exporting Model

In order to use the created model for serving, we need to export the model. This is done using Scikit-learn functionality, as in Example 7-33.

Example 7-33. Exporting model

```
dump(clf, '/tmp/job/income.joblib')
```

This exports a model in Scikit-learn format, that can be used by, for example, Scikit-learn server for inference.

Integration into Pipelines

Regardless of which Python-based machine learning library you want to use, if Kubeflow doesn't have an operator for it, you can simply write your code as normal and then containerize it. To take the notebook we built in this chapter and use it as a pipeline stage, see "Using an Entire Notebook as a Data Preparation Pipeline Stage" on page 89. Here we can use `file_output` to upload the resulting model to our artifact tracking system, but you can also use the persistent volume mechanism.

Conclusion

In this chapter, we have taken a look at how to train machine learning models in Kubeflow using two very different frameworks: TensorFlow and Scikit-learn.

We learned how to build a collaborative filtering recommendation system using TensorFlow. We used Kubeflow to create a notebook session, where we've prototyped a TensorFlow model with Keras APIs, and then used the TFJob APIs to deploy our training job to a Kubernetes cluster. Finally, we've looked at how to use TFJob for distributed training.

We also learned how to train a generic Python model using Scikit-learn, a framework that is not natively supported by Kubeflow. Chapter 9 looks at how to integrate non-supported non-Python machine learning systems, which is a bit more complicated. While Kubeflow's first-party training operators can simplify your work, it's important to remember you aren't limited by this.

In Chapter 8 we will look at how to serve the model that we've trained in this chapter.

Model Inference

 We would like to acknowledge Clive Cox and Alejandro Saucedo from Seldon (*https://www.seldon.io*) for their great contributions to this chapter.

Most of the attention paid to machine learning has been devoted to algorithm development. However, models are not created for the sake of their creation, they are created to be put into production. Usually when people talk about taking a model "to production," they mean performing inference. As introduced in Chapter 1 and illustrated in Figure 1-1, a complete inference solution seeks to provide serving, monitoring, and updating functionality.

Model serving
    Puts a trained model behind a service that can handle prediction requests

Model monitoring
    Monitors the model server for any irregularities in performance—as well as the underlying model's accuracy

Model updating
    Fully manages the versioning of your models and simplifies the promotion and rollback between versions

This chapter will explore each of these core components and define expectations for their functionality. Given concrete expectations, we will establish a list of requirements that your ideal inference solution will satisfy. Lastly, we will discuss Kubeflow-supported inference offerings and how you can use them to satisfy your inference requirements.

Model Serving

The first step of model inference is model serving, which is hosting your model behind a service that you can interface with. Two fundamental approaches to model serving are *embedded*, where the models are deployed directly into the application, and *model serving as a service* (MaaS), where a separate service dedicated to model serving can be used from any application in the enterprise. Table 8-1 provides a comparison of these approaches.

Table 8-1. Comparing embedded with MaaS

Serving types	Advantages	Disadvantages
Embedded	• Delivers maximum performance • Features the simplest infrastructure • No need to plan for aberrant user behavior	• Model has to be deployed in every application using it • Application updates are required when the model type changes • All deployment strategies, for example blue-green, must be explicitly implemented
MaaS	• Simplifies integration with other technologies and organizational processes • Reuses model deployment across multiple stream-processing applications • Allows model serving on lower-power devices (e.g., phones) incapable of running complex models • Enables mini-batching for requests from multiple clients • Makes it easier to provide built-in capabilities, including model updates, explainability, drift detection, etc. • Enables advanced model deployment strategies like ensembles and multi-armed bandit, which require decoupling from application • Allows for separate scaling between application and model server, or running them on different devices like CPU and GPU	• Additional network hops decrease performance • Tight temporal coupling to the model server can impact overall service-level agreement

Kubeflow only supports a MaaS approach. As a result, we will not be discussing model embedding in this book.[1]

There are two main approaches for implementing MaaS: *model as code*, and *model as data*. Model as code uses model code directly in a service's implementation. Model as data uses a generic implementation that is driven by a model in an intermediate model format like PMML (*https://oreil.ly/ljhYw*), PFA (*https://oreil.ly/SsM9C*), ONNX

---

[1] If you are interested in learning more about model embedding, we suggest reading *Serving Machine Learning Models* by Boris Lublinsky (O'Reilly).

(*https://onnx.ai*), or TensorFlow's native format (*https://oreil.ly/KtkQS*). Both approaches are used in different model server implementations in Kubeflow. When determining which implementation to use, we recommended using model as data, as it allows for the exchange of models between serving instances to be standardized, thus providing portability across systems and the enablement of generic model serving solutions.

Most common serving implementations, like TFServing, ONNX Runtime, Triton, and TorchServe, use a model-as-data approach and leverage an intermediate model format. Some of these implementations support only one framework, while others support multiple. Unfortunately, each of these solutions uses different model formats and exposes unique proprietary serving APIs. None of these interfaces meet everyone's needs. The complexity and divergence of these API interfaces result in a differing UX and an inability to share features effectively. Furthermore, there is increased friction in swapping between model frameworks, as the interfaces behind these implementations are different.

There are a few strong industry players attempting to unify the open source community of model servers and decrease the friction between toggling model frameworks. Seldon is pioneering graph inferencing with Seldon Core; Bloomberg and IBM are investigating serverless model serving using solutions like Knative; and Google is further hardening its serving implementation for TensorFlow models.

In "Model Inference in Kubeflow" on page 137, we will discuss the serving solutions that Kubeflow offers and the work that has been done to unify these solutions into a single interface.

Model Serving Requirements

Model serving requires you to understand and manage the developmental operations (DevOps) and handle the analysis, experimentation, and governance of your models. This scope is wide, complicated, and universal among data scientists. We will now start scoping out the expectations you might want from a serving solution.

First, you want framework flexibility. Solutions like Kubeflow allow for your training to be implementation-agnostic (i.e., TensorFlow versus PyTorch). If you write an image classification inference service, it should not matter if the underlying model was trained using PyTorch, Scikit-learn, or TensorFlow—the service interface should be shared so that the user's API remains consistent.

Second, you want the ability to leverage hardware optimizers that match the needs of the algorithm. Sometimes fully fitted and tuned neural nets are quite deep, which means that even in the evaluation phase, you would benefit from hardware optimizers like GPUs or TPUs to infer the models.

Third, your model server should seamlessly interact with other components in an inference graph. An inference graph could comprise feature transformers, predictors, explainers, and drift detectors—all of which we will cover later.

Fourth, you should also have options to scale your serving instance, both explicitly and using autoscalers, regardless of the underlying hardware—i.e., cost per inference, latency. This is particularly important and difficult because GPU autoscaling relies on a combination of factors including: GPU/CPU utilization metrics, duty cycles, and more, and knowing which metric to use for autoscaling is not obvious. Also, the scaling of each of the components in your inference graph should be done separately due to differing algorithmic needs.

Fifth, you want a serving instance that exposes representational state transfer (REST) requests or general-purpose remote procedure calls (gRPC). If you have streaming inputs, you may want to support a streaming interface like Kafka.

Model Monitoring

Once you have a model served, you must monitor the model server in production. When we are talking about monitoring of the model server, we are talking not only about model serving insights but also about general monitoring used for any Kubernetes-based applications, including memory, CPU, networking, etc. We will explore model monitoring and model insight in more detail in "Monitoring Your Models" on page 151.

Model Accuracy, Drift, and Explainability

In generating model serving insights, the most common ML attributes to monitor are model accuracy, model drift, and explainability. *Model accuracy* refers to the validation accuracy of your training data. But as live data distributions begin to deviate from those of the original training data, this tends to result in *model drift*. In other words, model drift occurs when the feature distribution of the data sent to the model begins to significantly differ from the data used to train the model, causing the model to perform suboptimally. ML insight systems implement effective techniques for analyzing and detecting changes—*concept drift*—that might happen to your input data, and the detection of these drifts is critical for models running in production systems.

Another form of model insight that is increasingly gaining attention today is *model explainability*, or the ability to explain why a certain result was produced. More precisely, it answers:

- What features in the data did the model think are most important?

- For any single prediction from a model, how did each feature in the data affect that particular prediction?

- What interactions between features have the greatest effects on a model's predictions?

Beyond model insight, application monitoring traditionally relates to network observability, or telemetry, the enablement of log aggregation, and service-mesh-related metrics collection. These tools are useful in capturing data from a live serving instance. This infrastructure exposes enough queryable information for troubleshooting and alerting, should things go awry regarding reachability, utilization, or latency.

Model Monitoring Requirements

Monitoring model accuracy and model drift is hard. Luckily, this is a very active research space with a variety of open source solutions.[2] Your inference solution should enable you to plug in solutions that provide your desired functionality out of the box. Now, we will see what you may wish to have from your model monitoring component.

First, you want your inference service to provide ML insight out of the box and run in a microservice-based architecture in order to simplify the experimentation of drift detection and model explanation solutions.

Second, you want to enable the monitoring, logging, and tracing of your service. It should also support solutions like Prometheus, Kibana, and Zipkin, respectively, but then also be able to seamlessly support their alternatives.

Model Updating

If you wish to update your model and roll out a newer version or roll back to a previous version, you will want to deploy and run this updated version. However, the relationship between your current deployment and the new deployment can be defined in a variety of ways. When your inference system introduces multiple versions of your model serving instance, you can use either shadow or competing models:

---

2 Some references include: "Failing Loudly: An Empirical Study of Methods for Detecting Dataset Shift" (*https://oreil.ly/mJP-U*), "Detecting and Correcting for Label Shift with Black Box Predictors" (*https://oreil.ly/R5AuT*), "A Kernel Two-Sample Test" (*https://oreil.ly/P3ujL*), and "Monitoring and Explainability of Models in Production" (*https://oreil.ly/J0COf*).

Shadow models
> These are useful when considering the replacement of a model in production. You can deploy the new model alongside the current one and send the same production traffic to gather data on how the shadow model performs before promoting it.

Competing models
> These are a slightly more complex scenario, where you are trying multiple versions of a model in production to find out which one is better through tools like A/B testing.

Let's discuss the three main deployment strategies:

Blue-green deployments (https://oreil.ly/pXHA4)
> These reduce downtime and risk relating to version rollouts by having only one live environment, which serves all production traffic.

Canary deployments (https://oreil.ly/BOEQi)
> These enable rollout releases by allowing you to do percentage-based traffic between versions.

Pinned deployments
> These allow you to expose experimental traffic to a newer version, while keeping production traffic against the current version.

The added complexity of canary and pinned over blue-green comes from the infrastructure and routing rules required to ensure that traffic is being redirected to the right models. With this enablement, you can then gather data to make statistically significant decisions about when to start moving traffic. One statistical approach for traffic movement is A/B testing. Another popular approach for evaluating multiple competing models is multi-armed bandits (*https://oreil.ly/eDEsU*), which requires you to define a score or reward for each model and to promote models relative to their respective score.

Model Updating Requirements

Upgrading your model must be simple, so the deployment strategy that you use for upgrading should be easy to configure and simple to change (i.e., from pinned to canary). Your inference solution should also offer more-complex graph inferencing in its design. We will elaborate on what you need from your inference solution:

First, the toggle of deployment strategies—i.e., from pinned to canary—should be trivial. You can enable traffic-level routing in an abstracted way by abstracting the service plane, which will be defined in "Serverless and the Service Plane" on page 159.

Second, version changes should be tested and validated before promotion, and the corresponding upgrade should be logged.

Third, the underlying stack should enable you to configure the more complex deployment strategies common to graph inferencing literature.

Summary of Inference Requirements

With the requirements of model serving, monitoring, and updating all satisfied, you now have an inference solution that completes your model development life cycle (MDLC) story. This enables you to bring a model all the way from lab to production, and even handle the updating of this model should you want to tune or modify its construction. Now we will discuss the inference solutions that Kubeflow offers.

Some ML practitioners believe that continuous learning (CL) is fundamental in their production ML systems. CL is the ability of a model to learn continually from streaming data. In essence, the model will autonomously learn and adapt in production as new data comes in. Some even call this AutoML. With a complete MDLC solution that enables pipelines and canary deployments, you can design such a system using the tools available in Kubeflow.

Model Inference in Kubeflow

Model serving, monitoring, and updating within inference can be quite tricky because you need a solution that manages all of these expectations in a way that provides abstraction for first-time users and customizability for power users.

Kubeflow provides many options (*https://oreil.ly/GXjL4*) for model inference solutions. In this section, we will describe some of them, including TensorFlow Serving, Seldon Core, and KFServing. Table 8-2 presents a quick comparison of these solutions.

Table 8-2. Comparing different model inference approaches

Solution	Approach
TensorFlow Serving	• Single model type (TensorFlow) support • Some support for monitoring metrics (Prometheus) • With version 2.3, support for canarying via model version labels • Simplest infrastructure dependencies
Seldon Core	• Optimized Docker containers for popular libraries like TensorFlow, H2O, XGBoost, MXNet, etc. • Language wrappers that convert a Python file or a Java JAR into a fully fledged microservice • Support for inference pipelines that can consist of models, transformers, combiners and routers • Support for monitoring metrics and auditable request logs • Support for advanced deployment techniques—canary, blue-green, etc. • Support for advanced ML insights: explainers, outlier detectors, and adversarial attack detectors • More complex infrastructure dependencies
KFServing	• Adding serverless (Knative) and a standardized inference experience to Seldon Core, while providing extensibility for other model servers • Most complex infrastructure dependencies

TensorFlow Serving

One of the most popular serving implementations is TensorFlow Serving (*https://oreil.ly/AV0jU*) (TFServing), a model-serving implementation based on the TensorFlow export format (*https://oreil.ly/WOV9j*). TFServing implements a flexible, high-performance serving system for ML models, designed for production environments. The TFServing architecture is shown in Figure 8-1.

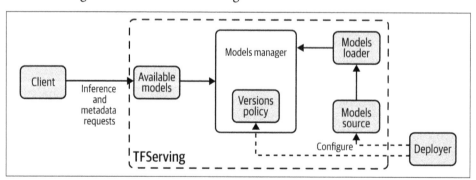

Figure 8-1. TFServing architecture

TFServing uses exported TensorFlow models as inputs and supports running predictions on them using HTTP or gRPC. TFServing can be configured (*https://oreil.ly/O8oE-*) to use either:

- A single (latest) version of the model
- Multiple, specific versions of the model

TensorFlow can be used both locally[3] and in Kubernetes.[4] A typical TFServing implementation within Kubeflow includes the following components:

- A Kubernetes deployment running the required amount of replicas
- A Kubernetes service providing access to the deployment
- An Istio virtual service that exposes the service through the Istio ingress gateway
- An Istio `DestinationRule` that defines policies for traffic routed to the service (These rules can specify configurations for load balancing, connection pool size, and outlier detection settings so that you can detect and evict unhealthy hosts from the load balancing pool.)

We will walk through an example of how these components are implemented (*https:// oreil.ly/copcG*) by extending our recommender example. To simplify your initial inference service, your example TFServing instance will be scoped to a deployment and a service that enables HTTP access. The Helm chart for this example can be found in the GitHub repo for this book (*https://oreil.ly/Kube flow_for_ML_ch08_Helm*).

The chart defines a Kubernetes deployment and service. The deployment uses the "standard" TFServing Docker image and, in its configuration spec, points to a serialized model at an S3 source location. This S3 bucket is managed by a local MinIO instance. The service exposes this deployment inside the Kubernetes cluster.

The chart can be deployed using the following command (assuming you are running Helm 3):

```
helm install <chart_location>
```

Now that you have the chart deployed, you need a way to interface with your inference solution. One method is to port forward (*https://oreil.ly/jWjfV*) your service, so that the traffic can be redirected to your localhost for testing. You can port-forward your service with Example 8-1.

Example 8-1. Port-forwarding TFServing services

```
kubectl port-forward service/recommendermodelserver 8501:8501
```

---

3 Refer to the TensorFlow documentation (*https://oreil.ly/NnBSc*) for details on using TFServing locally.

4 Refer to the TensorFlow documentation (*https://oreil.ly/Ac_Pr*) for details on using TFServing on Kubernetes.

The resulting traffic will be rerouted to `localhost:8051`.

You are now ready to interact with your TFServing inference solution. To start, you should validate the deployment by requesting model deployment information from your service:

```
curl http://localhost:8501/v1/models/recommender/versions/1
```

The expected output is shown in Example 8-2.

Example 8-2. TFServing Recommender model version status

```
{
 "model_version_status": [
  {
   "version": "1",
   "state": "AVAILABLE",
   "status": {
    "error_code": "OK",
    "error_message": ""
   }
  }
 ]
}
```

You can also get the model's metadata, including its signature definition, by issuing the following curl command:

```
curl http://localhost:8501/v1/models/recommender/versions/1/metadata
```

Now that your model is available and has the correct signature definition, you can predict against the service with the command seen in Example 8-3.

Example 8-3. Sending a request to your TFServing Recommender service

```
curl -X POST http://localhost:8501/v1/models/recommender/versions/1:predict\
-d '{"signature_name":"serving_default","inputs":\
{"products": [[1],[2]],"users" : [[25], [3]]}}'
```

The result from executing Example 8-3 is shown in Example 8-4.

Example 8-4. Output from your TFServing Recommender service

```
{
    "outputs": {
        "model-version": [
            "1"
        ],
        "recommendations": [
            [
                0.140973762
            ],
            [
```

```
                    0.0441606939
                ]
            ]
        }
    }
}
```

Your TensorFlow model is now behind a live inference solution. TFServing makes it easy to deploy new TensorFlow algorithms and experiments, while keeping the same server architecture and APIs. But the journey does not end there. For one, these deployment instructions create a service but do not enable access from outside of the cluster.[5] But we will now take a further look into all the capabilities of this particular solution against your inference requirements.

Review

If you are looking to deploy your TensorFlow model with the lowest infrastructure requirement, TFServing is your solution. However, this has limitations when you consider your inference requirements.

Model serving

Because TFServing only has production-level support for TensorFlow, it does not have the desired flexibility you would expect from a framework-agnostic inference service. It does, however, support REST, gRPC, GPU acceleration, mini-batching, and "lite" versions for serving on edge devices. Regardless of the underlying hardware, this support does not extend to streaming inputs or to built-in auto scaling.[6] Furthermore, the ability to extend the inference graph—beyond a Fairness Indicator—to include more advanced ML insights isn't supported in a first-class way. Despite providing basic serving and model analysis features for TensorFlow models, this inference solution does not satisfy your more advanced serving requirements.

Model monitoring

TFServing supports traditional monitoring via its integration (*https://oreil.ly/WigdN*) with Prometheus. This exposes both system information—such as CPU, memory, and networking—and TFServing-specific metrics; unfortunately, there is very little documentation (see the best source, on the TensorFlow site (*https://oreil.ly/czq_V*)). Also, there is no first-class integration with data visualization tools like Kibana or distributed tracing libraries like Jaeger. As such, TFServing does not provide the managed network observability capabilities you desire.

---

5 If you are using Istio as a service mesh, follow these instructions (*https://oreil.ly/Dg6Vp*) to add a virtual service (*https://oreil.ly/mu28a*).

6 You can, of course, scale it manually by changing the amount of deployed instances.

When it comes to advanced model serving insights, including model drift and explainability, some of them are available in TensorFlow 2.0 (*https://oreil.ly/_yunS*). Furthermore, the vendor lock-in to a proprietary serving solution complicates the plugability of model insight components. Since the deployment strategy of TFServing uses Kubeflow's infrastructure stack, it leverages a microservice approach. This allows TFServing deployments to be easily coupled with auxiliary ML components.

Model updating

TFServing is quite advanced in that it enables canary, pinned, and even rollback deployment strategies.[7] However, the strategies are limited to the manual labeling of existing model versions and do not include support for the introduction of in-flight model versions. So version promotion does not have a safe-rollout guarantee. Lastly, the strategies are embedded in the server and aren't extensible for other deployment strategies that might exist outside of TFServing.

Summary

TFServing provides extremely performant and sophisticated out-of-the-box integration for TensorFlow models, but it falls short on enabling more advanced features like framework extensibility, advanced telemetry, and plugable deployment strategies. Seeing these requirements unsatisfied, we will now look at how Seldon Core attempts to fill these gaps.

Seldon Core

Instead of just serving up single models behind an endpoint, Seldon Core enables data scientists to compose complex runtime inference graphs—by converting their machine learning code or artifacts into microservices. An inference graph, as visualized in Figure 8-2, can be composed of:

Models
Runtime inference executable for one or more ML models

Routers
Route requests to subgraphs, i.e., enabling A/B tests or multi-armed bandits

Combiners
Combine the responses from subgraphs, i.e., model ensemble

Transformers
Transform requests or responses, i.e., transform feature requests

---

7 See TFServing's deployment strategy configuration (*https://oreil.ly/ezM2g*) for more information.

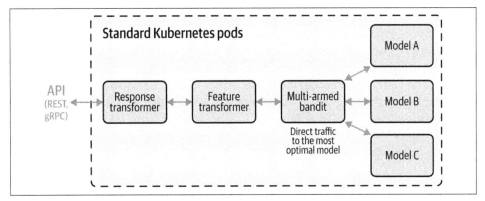

Figure 8-2. Seldon inference graph example

To understand how Seldon achieves this, we will explore its core components and feature set:

Prepackaged model servers
Optimized Docker containers for popular libraries such as TensorFlow, XGBoost, H2O, etc., which can load and serve model artifacts/binaries

Language wrappers
Tools to enable more custom machine learning models to be wrapped using a set of CLIs, which allow data scientists to convert a Python file or a Java JAR into a fully fledged microservice

Standardized API
Out-of-the-box APIs that can be REST or gRPC

Out of the box observability
Monitoring metrics and auditable request logs

Advanced machine learning insights
Complex ML concepts such as explainers, outlier detectors, and adversarial attack detectors abstracted into infrastructural components that can be extended when desired

Using all of these components, we walk through how to design an inference graph using Seldon.

Designing a Seldon Inference Graph

First, you will need to decide what components you want your inference graph to consist of. Will it be just a model server, or will you add a set of transformers, explainers, or outlier detectors to the model server? Luckily, it's really easy to add or remove components as you see fit, so we will start with just a simple model server.

Second, you need to containerize your processing steps. You can build each step of your inference graph with *model as data* or *model as code*. For model as data, you could use a prepackaged model server to load your model artifacts/binaries and avoid building a Docker container every time your model changes. For model as code, you would build your own prepackaged model server based on a custom implementation. Your implementation is enabled via a language wrapper that would containerize your code by exposing a high-level interface to your model's logic. This can be used for more complex cases, even use cases that may require custom OS-specific, or even external-system dependencies.

Next, you need to test your implementation. You can run your implementation locally, leveraging Seldon tools to verify that it works correctly. Local development is enabled by the underlying portability of Kubernetes and by Seldon's compatibility with Kubeflow's infrastructure stack.

Then, you can enable Seldon Core extensions. Some extensions include: Jaeger tracing integration, ELK request logging integration, Seldon Core analytics integration, or Istio/Ambassador ingress integration, to name a few.[8]

After enabling extensions, you can promote your local graph deployment to be hosted against a live Kubernetes cluster.

Lastly, you can hook up your inference graph into a continuous integration/continuous delivery (CI/CD) pipeline. Seldon components allow you to integrate seamlessly into CI/CD workflows, which enables you to use your preferred CI tool to connect your model sources into Seldon Core.

Now that you have scoped out a rather robust inference graph, we will walk through some examples after getting set up with Seldon on your Kubeflow cluster.

Setting up Seldon Core

Seldon Core 1.0 comes prepackaged with Kubeflow, so it should already be available to you. The Seldon Core installation will create a Kubernetes operator which will watch for SeldonDeployment resources that describe your inference graph. However, you can install a custom version of Seldon Core, as per the installation instructions, with Example 8-5.

---

8 Refer to the Seldon documentation for integration with Prometheus (*https://oreil.ly/_8xgR*), ELK (*https:// oreil.ly/DV5_b*), and Jaeger (*https://oreil.ly/7CIeM*).

Example 8-5. Helm install for a custom Seldon Core version

```
helm install seldon-core-operator \
    --repo https://storage.googleapis.com/seldon-charts  \
    --namespace default \
    --set istio.gateway=istio-system/seldon-gateway \
    --set istio.enabled=true
```

You must ensure that the namespace where your models will be served has an Istio gateway and an InferenceServing namespace label. An example label application would be:

```
kubectl label namespace kubeflow serving.kubeflow.org/inferenceservice=enabled
```

An example Istio gateway is shown in Example 8-6.

Example 8-6. Seldon Core Istio Gateway

```
kind: Gateway
metadata:
  name: seldon-gateway
  namespace: istio-system
spec:
  selector:
    istio: ingressgateway
  servers:
  - hosts:
    - '*'
    port:
      name: http
      number: 80
      protocol: HTTP
```

You should save Example 8-6 to a file and apply it using `kubectl`.

Packaging your model

As mentioned before, to run a model with Seldon Core you can either package it using a prepackaged model server[9] or a language wrapper.[10]

Creating a SeldonDeployment

After packaging your model you need to define an inference graph that connects a set of model components into a single inference system. Each of the model components can be one of the two options outlined in "Packaging your model" on page 145.

---

9 Currently supported prepackaged servers include MLflow server, SKLearn server, TensorFlow serving, and XGBoost server.

10 Currently supported is a language server for Python. Incubating are Java, R, NodeJS, and Go.

Some example graphs are shown in Figure 8-3.

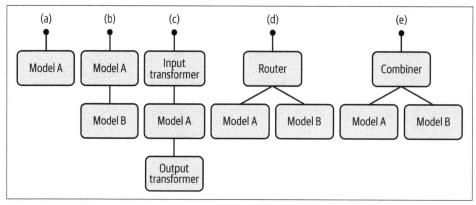

Figure 8-3. Seldon graph examples

The following list expands on the example inference graphs (a) to (e), as shown in Figure 8-3:

- (a) A single model
- (b) Two models in sequence. The output of the first will be fed into the input of the second.
- (c) A model with input and output transformers: the input transformer will be called, then the model and the response will be transformed by the output transformer
- (d) A router that will choose whether to send to model A or B
- (e) A combiner that takes the response from model A and B and combines into a single response[11]

In addition, SeldonDeployment can specify methods for each component. When your SeldonDeployment is deployed, Seldon Core adds a service orchestrator to manage the request and response flow through your graph.

An example SeldonDeployment, for inference graph (a) in Figure 8-3, appears in Example 8-7 as an example of what a prepackaged model server looks like.

---

11 Because Seldon implements the computational structure as a tree, the combiner executes in reverse order to combine output from all children.

Example 8-7. Simple Seldon Core prepackaged model server

```
apiVersion: machinelearning.seldon.io/v1
kind: SeldonDeployment
metadata:
 name: seldon-model
spec:
 name: test-deployment
 predictors:
 - componentSpecs:
   graph:
     name: classifier
     type: SKLEARN_SERVER
     modelUri: gs://seldon-models/sklearn/income/model
     children: []
   name: example
   replicas: 1
```

In the example you see that the SeldonDeployment has a list of `predictors`, each of which describes an inference graph. Each predictor has some core fields:

componentSpecs
    A list of Kubernetes PodSpecs, each of which will be used for a Kubernetes deployment.

graph
    A representation of the inference graph containing the name of each component, its type, and the protocol it respects. The name must match one container name from the componentSpecs section, unless it is a prepackaged model server (see subsequent examples).

Name
    The name of the predictor.

Replicas
    The number of replicas to create for each deployment in the predictor.

Type
    The detail on whether it is a prepackaged model server or a custom language wrapper model.

modelUri
    A URL where the model binary or weight are stored, which would be relevant for the respective prepackaged model server.

Another example for SeldonDeployment for (a) is shown in Example 8-8, using in this instance a custom language wrapper model.

Example 8-8. Simple Seldon Core custom language wrapper

```
apiVersion: machinelearning.seldon.io/v1
kind: SeldonDeployment
metadata:
 name: seldon-model
spec:
 name: test-deployment
 predictors:
 - componentSpecs:
   - spec:
       containers:
       - image: seldonio/mock_classifier_rest:1.3
         name: classifier
     graph:
       children: []
       endpoint:
         type: REST
       name: classifier
       type: MODEL
     name: example
     replicas: 1
```

In this example you have a small set of new sections:

Containers
> This is your Kubernetes container definition, where you are able to provide overrides to the details of your container, together with your Docker image and tag.

Endpoint
> In this case you can specify if the endpoint of your model will be REST or gRPC.

The definition of your inference graph is now complete. We will now discuss how to test your components individually or in unison on the cluster.

Testing Your Model

In order to test your components, you must interface with each using some request input. You can send requests directly using `curl`, `grpcurl`, or a similar utility, as well as by using the Python `SeldonClient` SDK.

There are several options for testing your model before deploying it.

Running your model directly with the Python client
> This allows for easy local testing outside of a cluster.

Running your model as a Docker container
> This can be used for all language wrappers—but not prepackaged inference servers—to test that your image has the required dependencies and behaves as you would expect.

Running your `SeldonDeployment` *in a Kubernetes dev client such as KIND (https:// oreil.ly/U-5XT)*

This can be used for any models and is a final test that your model will run as expected.

Python client for Python language wrapped models

You can define your Python model in a file called *MyModel.py*, as seen in Example 8-9.

Example 8-9. Seldon Core Python model class

```
class MyModel:
    def __init__(self):
      pass
    def predict(*args, **kwargs):
      return ["hello, "world"]
```

You are able to test your model by running the `microservice` CLI that is provided by the Python module (*https://oreil.ly/RH1Dg*). Once you install the Python `seldon-core` module you will be able to run the model with the following command:

```
> seldon-core-microservice MyModel REST --service-type MODEL
...
2020-03-23 16:59:17,366 - werkzeug:_log:122
- INFO: * Running on http://0.0.0.0:5000/
(Press CTRL+C to quit)
```

Now that your model microservice is running, you can send a request using curl, as seen in Example 8-10.

Example 8-10. Sending a request to your Seldon Core custom microservice

```
> curl -X POST \
>  -H 'Content-Type: application/json' \
>  -d '{"data": { "ndarray": [[1,2,3,4]]}}' \
>     http://localhost:5000/api/v1.0/predictions
{"data":{"names":[],"ndarray":["hello","world"]},"meta":{}}
```

You can see that the output of the model is returned through the API.[12]

---

12 You can also send requests using the Python client.

Local testing with Docker

If you are building language models with other wrappers, you can run the containers you build through your local Docker client. A good tool for building Docker containers from source code is S2I (*https://oreil.ly/Kgx_Q*). For this, you just have to run the Docker client with the command seen in Example 8-11.

Example 8-11. Exposing Seldon Core microservice in a local Docker client

```
docker run --rm --name mymodel -p 5000:5000 mymodel:0.1
```

This will run the model and export it on port 5000, so now you can send a request using curl, as seen in Example 8-12.

Example 8-12. Sending a request to your local Seldon Core microservice

```
> curl -X POST \
>   -H 'Content-Type: application/json' \
>   -d '{"data": { "ndarray": [[1,2,3,4]]}}' \
>       http://localhost:5000/api/v1.0/predictions

{"data":{"names":[],"ndarray":["hello","world"]},"meta":{}}
```

With this environment, you can rapidly prototype and effectively test, before serving your model in a live cluster.

Serving Requests

Seldon Core supports two ingress gateways, Istio and Ambassador. Because Kubeflow's installation uses Istio, we will focus on how Seldon Core works with the Istio Ingress Gateway. We will assume that the Istio gateway is at `<istioGateway>` and has a SeldonDeployment name `<deploymentName>` in namespace `<namespace>`. This means a REST endpoint will be exposed at:

```
http://<istioGateway>/seldon/<namespace>/<deploymentName>/api/v1.0/predictions.
```

A gRPC endpoint will be exposed at `<istioGateway>` and you should send header metadata in your request with:

- Key `seldon` and value `<deploymentName>`.
- Key `namespace` and value `<namespace>`.

The payload for these requests will be a SeldonMessage.[13]

---

13 A SeldonMessage can be defined as both an OpenAPI specification (*https://oreil.ly/lGoRK*) and a protobuffer definition (*https://oreil.ly/J-E70*).

A sample SeldonMessage, say for a simple `ndarray` representation, is shown in Example 8-13.

Example 8-13. SeldonMessage containing an ndarray

```
{
  "data": {
  "ndarray":[[1.0, 2.0, 5.0]]
  }
}
```

Payloads can also include simple tensors, TFTensors, as well as binary, string, or JSON data. An example request containing JSON data is shown in Example 8-14.

Example 8-14. SeldonMessage containing JSON data

```
{
  "jsonData": {
    "field1": "some text",
    "field2": 3
  }
}
```

Now that your inference graph is defined, tested, and running, you will want to get predictions back from it, and you also might want to monitor it in production to ensure it is running as expected.

Monitoring Your Models

In Seldon Core's design, deploying ML models is not treated differently from how one would deploy traditional applications. The same applies to monitoring and governance once the deployments are live. Traditional application monitoring metrics like request latency, load, and status code distribution are provided by exposing Prometheus metrics in Grafana.[14]

However, as data scientists we are mostly interested in how well the models are performing—the relationship between the live data coming in and the data the model was trained on and the reasons why specific predictions were made.

To address these concerns, Seldon Core provides the additional open source projects Alibi:Explain (*https://oreil.ly/tXxQr*) and Alibi:Detect (*https://oreil.ly/iowRX*), which focus specifically on advanced ML insights. These two projects implement the core algorithms for model explainability, outlier detection, data drift, and adversarial attack detection, respectively. We will now walk through examples of how Seldon

---

14 For more on how to enable this, see this Seldon documentation page (*https://oreil.ly/myFaS*).

Core enables model explainability and drift detection, via its integration of Alibi:Explain and Alibi:Detect.

Model explainability

Model explainability algorithms seek to answer the question: "Why did my model make this prediction on this instance?" The answer can come in many shapes, i.e., the most important features contributing to the model's prediction or the minimum change to features necessary to induce a different prediction.

Explainability algorithms are also distinguished by how much access to the underlying model they have. On one end of the spectrum there are "black box" algorithms that only have access to the model prediction endpoint and nothing else. In contrast, you have "white box" algorithms that have full access to the internal model architecture and allow for much greater insight (such as taking gradients). In the production scenario, however, the black-box case is much more prominent, so we will focus on that here.

Before discussing an example, we will describe the integration patterns that would arise from the use of black-box explanation algorithms. These algorithms typically work by generating a lot of similar-looking instances to the one being explained and then send both batch and sequential requests to the model to map out a picture of the model's decision-making process in the vicinity of the original instance. Thus, an explainer component will communicate with the underlying model, as the explanation is being computed. Figure 8-4 shows how this pattern is implemented. A model configured as a SeldonDeployment sits alongside an explainer component, which comes with its own endpoint. When the explainer endpoint is called internally the explainer communicates with the model to produce an explanation.

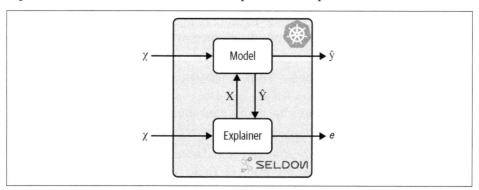

Figure 8-4. Seldon explainer component

In Figure 8-4, the explainer communicates directly with the production model. However, in a more realistic scenario, the underlying model would be a separate but identical deployment (i.e., in staging) to ensure that calls to the explainer don't degrade the performance of the production inference system.

To illustrate these techniques we will show a few examples.

Sentiment prediction model

Our first example is a sentiment prediction model that is trained on movie review data hosted by Cornell University (*https://oreil.ly/qOe2_*). You can launch this with an associated anchors explainer, using a SeldonDeployment like in Example 8-15.

Example 8-15. SeldonDeployment with Anchor Explainers

```
apiVersion: machinelearning.seldon.io/v1
kind: SeldonDeployment
metadata:
  name: movie
spec:
  name: movie
  annotations:
    seldon.io/rest-timeout: "10000"
  predictors:
  - graph:
      children: []
      implementation: SKLEARN_SERVER
      modelUri: gs://seldon-models/sklearn/moviesentiment
      name: classifier
    explainer:
      type: AnchorText
    name: default
    replicas: 1
```

Once deployed, this model can be queried via the Istio ingress as usual. You can then send the simple review `"This film has great actors"` to the model, as in Example 8-16.

Example 8-16. Sending a prediction request to your Seldon Core movie sentiment model

```
curl -d '{"data": {"ndarray":["This film has great actors"]}}' \
   -X POST http://<istio-ingress>/seldon/seldon/movie/api/v1.0/predictions \
   -H "Content-Type: application/json"
```

The response to the prediction request in Example 8-16 is seen in Example 8-17.

Example 8-17. Prediction response from your Seldon Core movie sentiment model

```
{
  "data": {
    "names": ["t:0","t:1"],
    "ndarray": [[0.21266916924914636,0.7873308307508536]]
  },
  "meta": {}
}
```

The model is a classifier and it is predicting with 78% accuracy that this is a positive review, which is correct. You can now try to explain the request, as seen in Example 8-18.

Example 8-18. Sending an explanation request to your Seldon Core movie sentiment model

```
curl -d '{"data": {"ndarray":["This movie has great actors"]}}' \
   -X POST http://<istio-ingress>/seldon/seldon/movie/explainer/api/v1.0/explain \
   -H "Content-Type: application/json"
```

The response to the explanation request in Example 8-18 is seen in Example 8-19 (curtailed without the examples section).

Example 8-19. Explanation response from your Seldon Core movie sentiment model

```
{
  "names": [
    "great"
  ],
  "precision": 1,
  "coverage": 0.5007,
  ...
  "instance": "This movie has great actors",
  "prediction": 1
  },
  "meta": {
    "name": "AnchorText"
  }
}
```

The key element in this example is that the explainer has identified the word *great* as being the reason the model predicted positive sentiment and suggests that this would occur 100% of the time for this model if a sentence contains the word *great* (reflected by the precision value).

US Census income predictor model example

Here is a second example, trained on the 1996 US Census data (*https://oreil.ly/kcmRm*), which predicts whether a person will have high or low income.[15] For this example, you also need to have an Alibi explainer sample the input dataset and identify categorical features to allow the explainer to give more intuitive results. The details for configuring an Alibi explainer can be found in the Alibi documentation (*https://oreil.ly/4i10y*) along with an in-depth review of the following data science example.

The SeldonDeployment resource is defined in Example 8-20.

Example 8-20. SeldonDeployment for income predictor

```
apiVersion: machinelearning.seldon.io/v1
kind: SeldonDeployment
metadata:
  name: income
spec:
  name: income
  annotations:
    seldon.io/rest-timeout: "100000"
  predictors:
  - graph:
      children: []
      implementation: SKLEARN_SERVER
      modelUri: gs://seldon-models/sklearn/income/model
      name: classifier
    explainer:
      type: AnchorTabular
      modelUri: gs://seldon-models/sklearn/income/explainer
    name: default
    replicas: 1
```

Once deployed, you can ask for a prediction with a curl request seen in Example 8-21.

Example 8-21. Sending a prediction request to your Seldon Core income predictor model

```
curl -d '{"data": {"ndarray":[[39, 7, 1, 1, 1, 1, 4, 1, 2174, 0, 40, 9]]}}' \
   -X POST http://<istio-ingress>/seldon/seldon/income/api/v1.0/predictions \
   -H "Content-Type: application/json"
```

The response to the prediction request in Example 8-21 is seen in Example 8-22.

---

15 See "Training a Model Using Scikit-Learn" on page 122 for more information on this model and how it is
   built.

Example 8-22. Prediction response from your Seldon Core income predictor model

```
{
    "data": {
      "names":["t:0","t:1"],
      "ndarray":[[1.0,0.0]]
    },
    "meta":{}
}
```

The model is predicting low income for this person. You can now get an explanation for this prediction with Example 8-23.

Example 8-23. Sending a explanation request to your Seldon Core income predictor model

```
curl -d '{"data": {"ndarray":[[39, 7, 1, 1, 1, 1, 4, 1, 2174, 0, 40, 9]]}}' \
    -X POST http://<istio-ingress>/seldon/seldon/income/explainer/api/v1.0/explain \
    -H "Content-Type: application/json"
```

The response to the explanation request in Example 8-23 is seen in Example 8-24, which we have shortened to not show all the examples returned.

Example 8-24. Explanation response from your Seldon Core income predictor model

```
{
  "names": [
    "Marital Status = Never-Married",
    "Occupation = Admin",
    "Relationship = Not-in-family"
  ],
  "precision": 0.9766081871345029,
  "coverage": 0.022,
  ...
}
```

The key takeaway is that this model will predict a low income classification 97% of the time if the input features are "Marital Status = Never-Married", "Occupation = Admin", and "Relationship = Not-in-family". So these are the key features from the input that influenced the model.

Outlier and drift detection

ML models traditionally do not extrapolate well outside of the training data distribution, and that impacts model drift. In order to trust and reliably act on model predictions, you must monitor the distribution of incoming requests via different types of detectors. Outlier detectors aim to flag individual instances that do not follow the original training distribution. An adversarial detector tries to spot and correct a carefully crafted attack with the intent to fool the model. Drift detectors check when the distribution of the incoming requests is diverging from a reference distribution, such as that of the training data.

If data drift occurs, the model performance can deteriorate, and it should be retrained. The ML model predictions on instances flagged by any of the detectors we've looked at should be verified before being used in real-life applications. Detectors typically return an outlier score at the instance or even the feature level. If the score is above a predefined threshold, the instance is flagged.

Outlier and drift detection are usually done asynchronously to the actual prediction request. In Seldon Core you can activate payload logging and send the requests to an external service that will do the outlier and drift detection outside the main request/response flow. An example architecture is shown in Figure 8-5, where Seldon Core's payload logger passes requests to components that process them asynchronously. The components that do the processing and alerting are managed via Knative Eventing, which is described in "Knative Eventing" on page 173. The use of Knative Eventing here is to provide late-binding event sources and event consumers, enabling asynchronous processing. The results can be passed on to alerting systems.

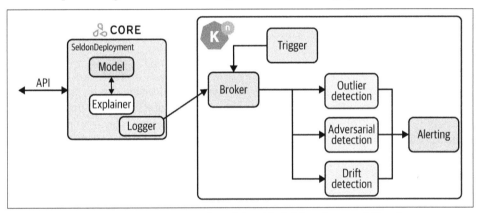

Figure 8-5. Data science monitoring of models with Seldon Core and Knative

Following are some examples that leverage outlier and drift detection using the architecture in Figure 8-5:

- An outlier detection example (*https://oreil.ly/p-Lfw*) for CIFAR10
- A drift detection example (*https://oreil.ly/z8jRG*) for CIFAR10

Review

Seldon Core is a solid choice as an inference solution when building an inference graph and hoping to simultaneously achieve model serving, monitoring, and updating guarantees. It sufficiently fills most of the gaps of TFServing while enabling data scientists to organically grow their inference graph as their use cases become more complex. It also allows many more features outside the scope of this overview, such as Canaries, Shadows, and powerful multistage inference pipelines.[16]

However, we will take a look at how it satisfies your inference requirements.

Model serving

Seldon Core clearly provides the functionality to extend an inference graph and support advanced ML insights in a first-class way. The architecture is also flexible enough to leverage other advanced ML insights outside of its managed offering. And Seldon Core is quite versatile, providing the expected serving flexibility because it is framework-agnostic. It provides support for both REST and gRPC, and GPU acceleration. It also can interface with streaming inputs using Knative Eventing. However, because the SeldonDeployment is running as a bare Kubernetes deployment, it does not provide GPU autoscaling, which we expect from hardware-agnostic autoscaling.

Model monitoring

Seldon Core seems to satisfy all of your model monitoring needs. Seldon Core's deployment strategy also uses Kubeflow's infrastructure stack, so it leverages a microservice approach. This is especially noticeable with Seldon Core's explainers and detectors being represented as separate microservices within a flexible inference graph. Seldon Core makes monitoring first-class by enabling monitoring, logging, and tracing with its support of Prometheus and Zipkin (*https://oreil.ly/stSIe*).

Model updating

Seldon Core is advanced in that it supports a variety of deployment strategies, including canary, pinned, and even multi-armed bandits. However, similar to TFServing, revision or version management isn't managed in a first-class way. This, again, means that version promotion does not have a safe-rollout guarantee. Lastly, as you can see by the options available for graph inferencing, in Figure 8-3, Seldon Core provides complete flexibility in growing your inference graph to support more complex deployment strategies.

---

16 See the Seldon Core documentation (*https://oreil.ly/4dPsn*) for further details.

Summary

Seldon Core works to fill in the gaps by providing extensibility and sophisticated out-of-the-box support for complex inference graphs and model insight. But it falls short with regards to the autoscaling of GPUs, its scale-to-zero capabilities, and revision management for safe model updating—features that are common to serverless applications. We will now explore how KFServing works to fill this gap by adding some recent Kubernetes additions, provided by Knative, to enable serverless workflows for TFServing, Seldon Core, and many more serving solutions.

KFServing

As seen with TFServing and Seldon Core, the production-grade serving of ML models is not a unique problem to any one research team or company. Unfortunately, this means that every in-house solution will use different model formats and expose unique proprietary serving APIs. Another problem facing both TFServing and Seldon Core is the lack of serverless primitives, like revision management and more sophisticated forms of autoscaling. These shortcomings are also found in most inference services. In order to unify the open source community of model servers, while filling the gaps that each model server had, Seldon, Google, Bloomberg, and IBM engaged with the open source community to collaboratively develop KFServing.

KFServing is a serverless inferencing solution that provides performant, high-abstraction interfaces for common ML frameworks like TensorFlow, XGBoost, Scikit-learn, PyTorch, and ONNX. By placing Knative on top of Kubeflow's cloud native stack, KFServing encapsulates the complexity of autoscaling, networking, health checking, and server configuration and brings cutting-edge serving features like GPU autoscaling, scale to zero, and canary rollouts to ML prediction services. This allows ML engineers to focus on critical data-science–related tooling like prediction services, transformers, explainability, and drift detectors.

Serverless and the Service Plane

KFServing's design primarily borrows from serverless web development. Serverless allows you to build and run applications and services without provisioning, scaling, or managing any servers. These server configurations are commonly referred to as the service plane, or control plane.

Naturally, serverless abstractions come with deployment simplicity and fluidity as there is limited infrastructure administration. However, serverless architecture depends heavily on event-based triggers for scaling its replicas, which we will talk about in "Escape hatches" on page 170. It allows you to focus solely on your application code.

One of the primary tenancies of KFServing is extending serverless application development to model serving. This is particularly advantageous for data scientists, as you want to only focus on the ML model that you are developing and the resulting input and output layers.

Data Plane

KFServing defines the *data plane*, which links all of the standard model serving components together and uses Knative to provide serverless abstractions for the service plane. A data plane is the protocol for how packets and requests are forwarded from one interface to another while also providing agency over service discovery, health checking, routing, load balancing, authentication/authorization, and KFServing's data plane architecture consists of a static graph of components—similar to Seldon Core's InferenceGraph—to coordinate requests for a single model. Advanced features like ensembling, A/B testing, and multi-armed bandits connect these services together, again taking inspiration from Seldon Core's deployment extensibility.

In order to understand the data plane's static graph, let's review some terminology used in Figure 8-6.

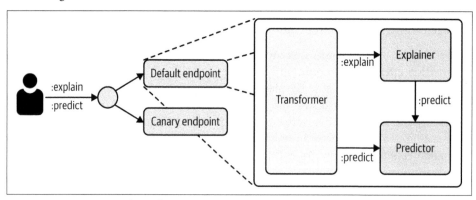

Figure 8-6. KFServing data plane

Endpoint
> KFServing instances are divided into two endpoints: *default* and *canary*. The endpoints allow users to safely make changes using the pinned and canary rollout strategies. Canarying is completely optional, enabling users to simply deploy with a blue-green deployment strategy against the default endpoint.

Component
> Each endpoint has multiple components: *predictor*, *explainer*, and *transformer*.

The only required component is the predictor, which is the core of the system. As KFServing evolves, it can seamlessly increase the number of supported components to enable use cases like Seldon Core's outlier detection. If you want, you can even introduce your own components and wire them together using the power of Knative's abstractions.

Predictor

The predictor is the workhorse of the KFServing instance. It is simply a model and a model server that is made available at a network endpoint.

Explainer

The explainer enables an optional alternative data plane that provides model explanations in addition to predictions. Users may define their own explanation container, which KFServing configures with relevant environment variables like a prediction endpoint. For common use cases, KFServing provides out-of-the-box explainers like Seldon Core's Alibi:Explain, which we learned about earlier.

Transformer

The transformer enables users to define a pre- and postprocessing step before the prediction and explanation workflows. Like the explainer, it is configured with relevant environment variables.

The last portion of the data plane is the prediction protocol[17] that KFServing uses. KFServing worked to define a set of HTTP/REST and gRPC APIs that must be implemented by compliant inference/prediction services. It is worth noting that KFServing standardized this prediction workflow, described in Table 8-3, across all model frameworks.

Table 8-3. KFServing V1 data plane

API	Verb	Path	Payload

Readiness	GET	/v1/models/
		<model_name>
			{
			  Response:{"name":<model_name>,"ready": true/false}
			}

Predict	POST	/v1/models/
		<model_name>:predict
			{
			  Request:{"instances": []},
			  Response:{"predictions": []}
			}

Explain	POST	/v1/models/
		<model_name>:explain
			{
			  Request:{"instances": []},
			  Response:{"predictions": [],"explanations": []}
			}

---

17 KFServing is continuously evolving, as is its protocol. You can preview the V2 protocol on this Kubeflow GitHub site (*https://oreil.ly/-duCU*). The second version of the data plane protocol addresses several issues found in the V1 data plane protocol, including performance and generality across a large number of model frameworks and servers.

Example Walkthrough

With the data plane defined, we will now walk through an example of how you can interface with a model served by KFServing.

Setting up KFServing

KFServing provides InferenceService, a serverless inference resource that describes your static graph, by providing a Kubernetes CRD for serving ML models on arbitrary frameworks. KFServing comes prepackaged with Kubeflow, so it should already be available. The KFServing installation[18] will create a Kubernetes operator in the kubeflow namespace, which will watch for InferenceService resources.

 Because Kubeflow's Kubernetes minimal requirement is 1.14, which does not support object selector, ENABLE_WEBHOOK_NAME SPACE_SELECTOR is enabled in the Kubeflow installation by default. If you are using Kubeflow's dashboard or profile controller to create user namespaces, labels are automatically added to enable KFServing to deploy models. If you are creating namespaces manually, you will need to run:

```
kubectl label namespace \
my-namespace serving.kubeflow.org/inferenceservice=enabled
```

to allow KFServing to deploy InferenceService in the namespace my-namespace, for example.

To check whether the KFServing controller is installed correctly, run the following command:

```
kubectl get pods -n kubeflow | grep kfserving
```

You can confirm that the controller is running by seeing a pod in the Running state. There is also a detailed troubleshooting guide you can follow on this Kubeflow GitHub site (*https://oreil.ly/YG_ut*).

Simplicity and extensibility

KFServing was fashioned to be simple for day-one users and customizable for seasoned data scientists. This is enabled via the interface that KFServing designed.

Now we will take a look at three examples of InferenceService.

Example 8-25 is for sklearn.

---

18 KFServing also supports standalone installation without Kubeflow. In fact, most production users of KFServing run it as a standalone installation.

Example 8-25. Simple sklearn KFServing InferenceService

```
apiVersion: "serving.kubeflow.org/v1alpha2"
kind: "InferenceService"
metadata:
  name: "sklearn-iris"
spec:
  default:
    predictor:
      sklearn:
        storageUri: "gs://kfserving-samples/models/sklearn/iris"
```

Example 8-26 is for `tensorflow`.

Example 8-26. Simple TensorFlow KFServing InferenceService

```
apiVersion: "serving.kubeflow.org/v1alpha2"
kind: "InferenceService"
metadata:
  name: "flowers-sample"
spec:
  default:
    predictor:
      tensorflow:
        storageUri: "gs://kfserving-samples/models/tensorflow/flowers"
```

Example 8-27 is for `pytorch`.

Example 8-27. Simple PyTorch KFServing InferenceService

```
apiVersion: "serving.kubeflow.org/v1alpha2"
kind: "InferenceService"
metadata:
  name: "pytorch-cifar10"
spec:
  default:
    predictor:
      pytorch:
        storageUri: "gs://kfserving-samples/models/pytorch/cifar10/"
        modelClassName: "Net"
```

Each of these will give you a serving instance—with an HTTP endpoint—that will serve a model using a requested framework server type. In each of these examples, a `storageUri` points to a serialized asset. The interface is mostly consistent across different models. The differences are in the framework specifications, i.e., `tensorflow` and `pytorch`. These framework specifications are common enough in that they share information like `storageUri` and Kubernetes resources requests, but they're also extensible in that they can enable framework-specific information like PyTorch's `ModelClassName`.

Clearly, this interface is simple enough to get started quite easily, but how extensible is it toward more complex deployment configurations and strategies? Example 8-28 exhibits some of the features that KFServing has to offer.

Example 8-28. Sophisticated Canary KFServing InferenceService

```
apiVersion: "serving.kubeflow.org/v1alpha2"
kind: "InferenceService"
metadata:
  name: "my-model"
spec:
  default:
    predictor:
      # 90% of traffic is sent to this model
      tensorflow:
        storageUri: "gs://kfserving-samples/models/tensorflow/flowers"
        serviceAccount: default
        minReplicas: 2
        maxReplicas: 10
        resources:
          requests:
            cpu: 1
            gpu: 1
            memory: 8Gi
  canaryTrafficPercent: 10
  canary:
    predictor:
      # 10% of traffic is sent to this model
      tensorflow:
        storageUri: "gs://kfserving-samples/models/tensorflow/flowers-2"
        serviceAccount: default
        minReplicas: 1
        maxReplicas: 5
        resources:
          requests:
            cpu: 1
            gpu: 1
            memory: 8Gi
```

The first extension is the ServiceAccount, which is used for authentication in the form of managed identities. If you wish to authenticate to S3 because your S3 should not be public, you need an identity attached to your InferenceService that validates you as a user. KFServing allows you to pass an identity mounted on the container and wires up the credentials through the ServiceAccount in a managed way. For example, say you are trying to access a model that may be stored on Minio. You would use your Minio identity information to create a secret beforehand, and then attach it to the service account. If you recall, we created a secret in MinIO in "MinIO" on page 34, so we just need to include KFServing-related annotations like in Example 8-29.

Example 8-29. KFServing-annotated MinIO secret

```
apiVersion: v1
data:
 awsAccessKeyID: xxxx
 awsSecretAccessKey: xxxxxxxxx
kind: Secret
metadata:
 annotations:
    serving.kubeflow.org/s3-endpoint: minio-service.kubeflow.svc.cluster.local:9000
    serving.kubeflow.org/s3-verifyssl: "0"
    serving.kubeflow.org/s3-usehttps: "0"
    serving.kubeflow.org/s3-region: us-east-1
 name: minioaccess
 namespace: my-namespace
```

And attach it to a service account like the one seen in Example 8-30.

Example 8-30. Service Account with attached MinIO secret

```
apiVersion: v1
kind: ServiceAccount
metadata:
  name: default
  namespace: my-namespace
secrets:
- name: default-token-rand6
- name: minioaccess
```

The second extension to notice is the min and max replicas. You would use these to control provisioning to allow you to meet demand, neither dropping requests nor overallocating.

The third extension is resource requests, which have preset defaults that you will almost always need to customize for your model. As you can see, this interface enables the use of hardware accelerators, like GPUs.

The last extension showcases the mechanism that KFServing uses to enable canary deployments. This deployment strategy assumes that you only want to focus on a two-way traffic split, as opposed to an *n*-way traffic split. In order to customize your deployment strategy, do the following:

- If you use just the default, like in your initial template, you get a standard blue-green deployment that comes with a Kubernetes deployment resource.
- If you include a canary, with canaryTrafficPercent == 0, you get a pinned deployment where you have an addressable default and canary endpoint. This is useful if you wish to send experimental traffic to your new endpoint, while keeping your production traffic pointed to your old endpoint.

- If you include canary, with `canaryTrafficPercent` > 0, you get a canary deployment that enables you to slowly increment traffic to your canary deployment, in a transparent way. In the previous example, you are experimenting with `flowers-2`, and as you slowly increment this `canaryTrafficPercentage` you can gain confidence that your new model will not break your current users.[19] Eventually, you would go to `100`, thereby flipping the canary and default, and you should then delete your old version.

Now that we understand some of the powerful abstractions that KFServing offers, let's use KFServing to host your product recommender example.

Recommender example

We will now put your product recommender example, from "Building a Recommender with TensorFlow" on page 108, behind an `InferenceService`.

 Because the `kubeflow` namespace is a system namespace, you are unable to create an `InferenceService` in the `kubeflow` namespace. As such, you must deploy your `InferenceService` in another namespace.

First, you'll define your `InferenceService` with the following 11 lines of YAML, as seen in Example 8-31.

Example 8-31. KFServing Recommender InferenceService

```
apiVersion: "serving.kubeflow.org/v1alpha2"
kind: "InferenceService"
metadata:
 name: "recommender"
 namespace: my-namespace
spec:
 default:
   predictor:
     tensorflow:
       serviceAccount: default
       storageUri: "s3://models/recommender"
```

---

19 You can still predict against a certain version by passing in a Host-Header in your request. For more information on rollouts, see this GitHub repo (*https://oreil.ly/ynNre*).

After running kubectl apply and waiting until your InferenceService is Ready, you should see:

```
$ kubectl get inferenceservices -n my-namespace
NAME        URL                                                          READY DEFAULT
recommender http://recommender.my-namespace.example.com/v1/models/recommender True  100
```

You can then curl your InferenceService as in Example 8-32.

Example 8-32. Sending a prediction request to your KFServing Recommender InferenceService

```
kubectl port-forward --namespace istio-system \
 $(kubectl get pod --namespace istio-system \
 --selector="app=istio-ingressgateway" \
 --output jsonpath='{.items[0].metadata.name}') \
 8080:80

curl -v -H "Host: recommender.my-namespace.example.com" \
http://localhost:8080/v1/models/recommender:predict -d \
'{"signature_name":"serving_default",
  "inputs": {"products": [[1],[2]],"users" : [[25], [3]]}}'
```

 If your curl returns a 404 Not Found error, this is a known Istio gateway issue that is present in Kubeflow 1.0.x. We recommend that you use Kubeflow 1.1 or above. A possible workaround is described in this GitHub issue (*https://oreil.ly/oyTi-*).

As an alternative to curl, you can also use the KFServing PythonSDK to send requests in Python.[20] In addition to an HTTP endpoint, this simple interface also provides all the serverless features that come with Kubeflow's stack and Knative, among them:

- Scale to zero
- GPU autoscaling
- Revision management (safe rollouts)
- Optimized containers
- Network policy and authentication
- Tracing
- Metrics

---

20 You can install the SDK by running pip install kfserving. You can get the KFServing SDK documentation on this GitHub site (*https://oreil.ly/Fl09j*) and examples on this GitHub site (*https://oreil.ly/g7nsa*) for creating, rolling out, promoting, and deleting an InferenceService.

As such, with only a few lines of YAML, KFServing provides production ML features, while also allowing data scientists to scale their deployments into the future. But how does KFServing enable these features in such an abstracted way?

We will now look at KFServing's underlying infrastructure stack and see how it promotes serverless, how its layers can be further customized, and what additional features exist.

Peeling Back the Underlying Infrastructure

By dissecting its infrastructure stack, you can see how KFServing enables serverless ML while also educating you on how to debug your inference solutions. KFServing is built in a cloud native way, as is Kubeflow. It benefits from the features of every layer below it. As seen in Figure 8-7, KFServing is built on the same stack as Kubeflow but is one of the few Kubeflow solutions that leverage Istio and Knative functionality quite heavily.

We will now walk through the role of each of these components, in greater detail than we did in previous chapters, to see what parts of these layers KFServing utilizes.

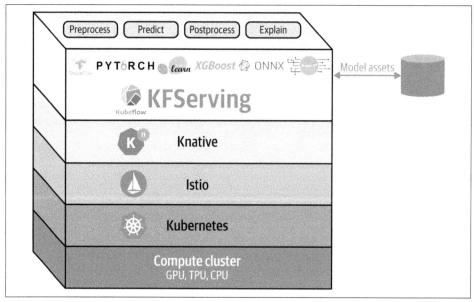

Figure 8-7. KFServing infrastructure stack

Going layer by layer

Hardware that runs your compute cluster is the base-building block for all the layers above. Your cluster could run a variety of hardware devices including CPUs, GPUs, or even TPUs. It is the responsibility of the layers above to simplify the toggling of hardware types and to abstract as much complexity as possible.

Kubernetes is the critical layer, right above the compute cluster, that manages, orchestrates, and deploys a variety of resources—successfully abstracting the underlying hardware. The main resources we will focus on are deployments, horizontal pod autoscalers (HPA), and ingresses. And since Kubernetes abstracts the underlying hardware, upon which deployments are run, this enables you to use hardware optimizers like GPUs within the upper levels of the stack.

Istio has been alluded to throughout this book, but we will talk about a few of its features that are particularly relevant to KFServing. Istio is an open source service mesh that layers transparently onto the Kubernetes cluster. It integrates into any logging platform, telemetry system, or policy system and promotes a uniform way to secure, connect, and monitor microservices. But what is a service mesh? Traditionally, each service instance is co-located with a sidecar network proxy. All network traffic (HTTP, REST, gRPC, etc.) from an individual service instance flows via its local sidecar proxy to the appropriate destination. Thus, the service instance is not aware of the network at large and only knows about its local proxy. In effect, the distributed system network has been abstracted away from the service programmer. Primarily, Istio expands upon Kubernetes resources, like ingresses, to provides service mesh fundamentals like:

- Authentication/Access control
- Ingress and egress policy management
- Distributed tracing
- Federation via multicluster ingress and routing
- Intelligent traffic management

These tools are all critical for production inference applications that require administration, security, and monitoring.

The last component of the KFServing infrastructure stack is Knative, which takes advantage of the abstractions that Istio provides. The KFServing project primarily borrows from Knative Serving and Eventing, the latter of which will be expanded on in "Knative Eventing" on page 173. As we described in "Knative" on page 38, Knative Serving builds on Kubernetes and Istio to support deploying and serving serverless applications. By building atop Kubernetes resources like deployments and HPAs, and Istio resources, like virtual services, Knative Serving provides:

- An abstracted service mesh
- CPU/GPU autoscaling (either queries per second (QPS) or metric-based)
- Revision management for safe rollouts and canary/pinned deployment strategies

These offerings are desirable for data scientists who want to limit their focus and energy to model development, and have scaling and versioning be handled for them in a managed way.

Escape hatches

KFServing's extensibility features escape hatches to the underlying layers of its stack. By building escape hatches into the `InferenceService` CRD, data scientists can further tune their production inference offering for security at the Istio level and their performance at the Knative level.

We will now walk through one example of how you can leverage these escape hatches, by tuning the autoscaling of your InferenceService.

To understand how to use this escape hatch, you need to understand how Knative enables autoscaling. There is a proxy in Knative Serving Pods called the queue proxy, which is responsible for enforcing request queue parameters (concurrency limits), and reporting concurrent client metrics to the autoscaler. The autoscaler, in turn, reacts to these metrics by bringing pods up and down. Every second, the queue proxy publishes the observed number of concurrent requests in that time period. KFServing by default sets the target concurrency (average number of in-flight requests per pod) to one. If we were to load the service with five concurrent requests, the autoscaler would try to scale up to five pods. You can customize the target concurrency by adding the example annotation `autoscaling.knative.dev/target`.

Let's look again at your InferenceService from Example 8-31.

```
apiVersion: "serving.kubeflow.org/v1alpha2"
kind: "InferenceService"
metadata:
 name: "recommender"
 namespace: my-namespace
spec:
 default:
   predictor:
     tensorflow:
       serviceAccount: default
       storageUri: "s3://models/recommender"
```

If you test this service by sending traffic in 30-second spurts while maintaining 5 in-flight requests, you will see that the autoscaler scales up your inference services to 5 pods.[21]

 There will be a cold-start time cost as a result of initially spawning pods and downloading the model, before being ready to serve. The cold start may take longer (to pull the serving image) if the image is not cached on the node that the pod is scheduled on.

By applying the annotation `autoscaling.knative.dev/target`, as seen in Example 8-33, the target concurrency will be set to five.

Example 8-33. Custom target concurrency via annotations in KFServing InferenceService

```
apiVersion: "serving.kubeflow.org/v1alpha2"
kind: "InferenceService"
metadata:
 name: "recommender"
 namespace: my-namespace
 annotations:
   autoscaling.knative.dev/target: "5"
spec:
 default:
   predictor:
     tensorflow:
       serviceAccount: default
       storageUri: "s3://models/recommender"
```

Which means, that if you load the service with five concurrent requests, you will see that you only need one pod for your inference service.

Debugging an InferenceService

With a fully abstracted interface, InferenceService enables many features while giving minimal exposure to the complexity under the hood. To properly debug your InferenceService, let's look at the request flow upon hitting your InferenceService.

The request flow when hitting your inference service, illustrated in Figure 8-8, is as follows:

---

21 You can further explore load testing on this Kubeflow GitHub site (*https://oreil.ly/zsTUE*). Two great load-testing frameworks are Hey (*https://oreil.ly/S0o6t*) and Vegeta (*https://oreil.ly/8hnd1*).

1. Traffic arrives through the Istio ingress gateway when traffic is external and through the Istio cluster local gateway when traffic is internal.

2. KFServing creates an Istio VirtualService to specify its top-level routing rules for all of its components. As such, traffic routes to that top-level VirtualService from the gateway.

3. Knative creates an Istio virtual service to configure the gateway to route the user traffic to the desired revision. Upon opening up the destination rules, you will see that the destination is a Kubernetes service for the latest ready Knative revision.

4. Once the revision pods are ready, the Kubernetes service will send the request to the queue-proxy.

   • If the queue proxy has more requests than it can handle, based on the concurrency of the KFServing container, then the autoscaler will create more pods to handle the additional requests.

5. Lastly, the queue proxy will send traffic to the KFServing controller.

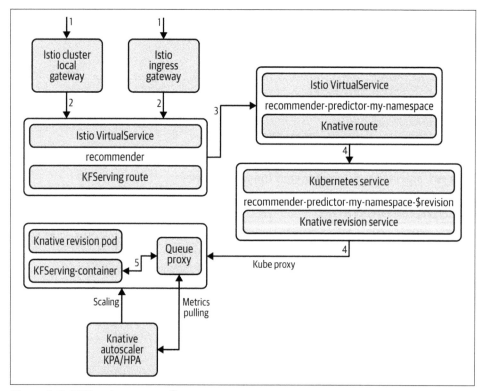

Figure 8-8. KFServing request flow

Where does this come in handy? Well, say you create your InferenceService but the Ready status is `false`:

```
kubectl get inferenceservice -n my-namespace recommender
NAME          URL   READY   DEFAULT TRAFFIC   CANARY TRAFFIC   AGE
recommender         False                                      3s
```

You can step through the resources that are created in the request flow and view each of their status objects to understand what the blocker is.[22]

Debugging performance

What if you deployed your InferenceService but its performance does not meet your expectations? KFServing provides various dashboards and tools to help investigate such issues. Using Knative, KFServing has many resources in its "debugging performance issues" guide (*https://oreil.ly/R5ASm*). You can also follow this Knative guide (*https://oreil.ly/MSiNX*) to access Prometheus and Grafana. Lastly, you can use request tracing, also known as distributed tracing, to see how much time is spent in each step of KFServing's request flow in Figure 8-8. You can use this Knative guide (*https://oreil.ly/STu7g*) to access request traces.

Knative Eventing

By bringing Knative into its stack, KFServing enabled serverless via Knative Serving and the use of event sources and event consumers via Knative Eventing.[23] We will take a look at how Knative Eventing works, and how you can extend your inference service with an event source.

Knative Eventing enforces a lambda-style architecture of event sources and event consumers with the following design principles:

- Knative Eventing services are loosely coupled.
- Event producers and event consumers are independent. Any producer or Source can generate events before there are active event consumers listening. Any event consumer can express interest in an event before there are producers that are creating those events.
- Other services can be connected to any Eventing system that:
  - Creates new applications without modifying the event producer or event-consumer.
  - Selects and targets specific subsets of events from their producers.

---

22 A detailed debugging guide can be found on this Kubeflow GitHub site (*https://oreil.ly/QWKsS*).

23 To learn more about Knative Eventing, see the documentation (*https://oreil.ly/LUmNH*).

Knative Eventing delivers events in two flavors: direct delivery from a source to a single service and fan-out delivery from a source to multiple endpoints using channels and subscriptions.

There are a variety of sources[24] that come out-of-the-box when installing Knative Eventing, one of which is KafkaSource.[25] If you look at Example 8-34, you will see how you would use KafkaSource to send events, received by Kafka, to your recommender example.

Example 8-34. KafkaSource that sends events to a KFServing Recommender InferenceService

```
apiVersion: sources.knative.dev/v1alpha1
kind: KafkaSource
metadata:
  name: kafka-source
spec:
  consumerGroup: knative-group
  # Broker URL. Replace this with the URLs for your Kafka cluster, which
  # is in the format of my-cluster-kafka-bootstrap.my-kafka-namespace:9092.
  bootstrapServers: my-cluster-kafka-bootstrap.my-kafka-namespace:9092.
  topics: recommender
  sink:
    ref:
      apiVersion: serving.kubeflow.org/v1alpha2
      kind: InferenceService
      name: recommender
```

As you can see by the simplicity of this specification, after setting up your Kafka resources, hooking Kafka into your InferenceService is as simple as 13 lines of YAML. You can find a more advanced end-to-end example with MinIO and Kafka on this Kubeflow GitHub site (*https://oreil.ly/_8oSZ*).

Additional features

KFServing contains a host of features that are continuously being improved. A comprehensive list of its capabilities can be found on this GitHub site (*https://oreil.ly/nJTCV*).

API documentation

For more on the APIs, consult the references for the KFServing Kubernetes APIs (*https://oreil.ly/iCBAD*) and the KFServing Python KFServing Python APIs (*https://oreil.ly/klfBR*).

---

24 Knative has a nonexhaustive list of event sources (*https://oreil.ly/uf1bA*).

25 To learn more about KafkaSource, see the documentation (*https://oreil.ly/nhKGY*).

Review

Building serverless on top of Seldon Core's graph inferencing, KFServing has produced a complete inference solution that sufficiently fills all the gaps of TFServing and Seldon Core. KFServing works to unify the entire community of model servers by running model servers as Knative components. With all of its functionality and promise, we will take a look at how KFServing manages to satisfy all your inference requirements.

Model serving

KFServing makes graph inference and advanced ML insights first-class while also defining a data plane that is extremely extensible for pluggable components. This flexibility allows data scientists to focus on ML insights without having to strain over how to include them in the graph.

KFServing is not only versatile in that it provides serving flexibility for a variety of frameworks, but it also standardizes the data plane across differing frameworks to reduce complexity in switching between model servers. It codifies the Kubernetes design pattern by moving common functionalities like request batching, logging, and pipelining into a sidecar. This, in turn, slims down the model server and creates a separation of concerns, as model services without these features can immediately benefit from deploying onto KFServing. It also provides support for REST, gRPC, and GPU acceleration and can interface with streaming inputs using Knative Eventing. And lastly, thanks to Knative Serving, KFServing provides GPU autoscaling, which you expect from hardware-agnostic autoscaling.

Model monitoring

By taking from Seldon Core and its infrastructure stack, KFServing meets all of your model monitoring needs. KFServing leverages the sophisticated model explainers and drift detectors of Seldon Core in a first-class way, while also paving a way for developers to define their own monitoring components in a highly flexible yet powerful data plane.

Furthermore, with all the networking capabilities enabled by having Istio and Knative in its infrastructure stack, KFServing provides extensible network monitoring and telemetry with support for Prometheus, Grafana, Kibana, Zipkin, and Jaeger, to name a few. These all satisfy your needs to monitor for Kubernetes metrics (memory/CPU container limits) and server metrics (queries per second and distributed tracing).

Model updating

KFServing's use of Knative was strategic in providing sophisticated model updating features. As such, KFServing satisfies all of your requirements regarding deployment strategies and version rollouts.

By leveraging Istio's virtual services and the simplicity of an abstracted CRD, KFServing makes the toggling of deployment strategies simple. It makes the flow from blue-green → pinned → canary as simple as changing a few lines of YAML. Furthermore, with the diverse and ever-expanding features of its underlying stack, KFServing is easily extensible to support more-complicated deployment strategies like multi-armed bandits.[26]

By using Knative Serving, KFServing adopts revision management that makes Kubernetes deployment immutable. This ensures safe rollout by health checking the new revisions pods before moving over the traffic. A revision enables:

- Automated and safe rollouts
- Bookkeeping for all revisions previously created
- Rollbacks to known, good configurations

This sufficiently satisfies your versioning requirements for models in development, in flight, and in production.

Summary

KFServing has developed a sophisticated inference solution that abstracts its complexity for day-one users while also enabling power users to take advantage of its diverse feature set. Building cloud native, KFServing seamlessly sits atop Kubeflow and finalizes the MDLC with its inference solution.

Conclusion

In this chapter we investigated various inference solutions that can be used within Kubeflow.

Based on what inference requirements you wish to prioritize and how deep you want your infrastructure stack to be, each of the solutions described has distinctive advantages. Having reviewed each of the offerings in detail, it might be worthwhile to reconsider Table 8-2 and see which inference solution is appropriate for your use case:

- TFServing provides extremely performant and sophisticated out-of-the-box integration for TensorFlow models.
- Seldon Core provides extensibility and sophisticated out-of-the-box support for complex inference graphs and model insight.

---

26 Check out examples of how ML Graph can be used to build complex graphs of ML components on this Seldon GitHub site (*https://oreil.ly/Ui-Xm*).

- KFServing provides a simpler opinionated deployment definition with serverless capabilities.

However, technology and development are shared between all these projects, and looking to the future, Seldon Core will even support the new KFServing data plane with the goal to provide easy interoperability and conversion. Other exciting features to expect from KFServing include multi-model serving, progressive rollouts, and more advanced graph inferencing techniques like pipelines and multi-armed bandit.

Now that you have completed the final step in your MDLC story, we will see how you can further customize Kubeflow to enable more advanced features in the next chapter.

# CHAPTER 9

Case Study Using Multiple Tools

In this chapter we're going to discuss what to do if you need to use "other" tools for your particular data science pipeline. Python has a plethora of tools for handling a wide array of data formats. RStats has a large repository of advanced math functions. Scala is the default language of big data processing engines such as Apache Spark and Apache Flink. Legacy programs that would be costly to reproduce exist in any number of languages.

A very important benefit of Kubeflow is that users no longer need to choose which language is best for their entire pipeline but can instead use the best language for each job (as long as the language and code are containerizable).

We will demonstrate these concepts through a comprehensive example denoising CT scans. Low-dose CT scans allow clinicians to use the scans as a diagnostic tool by delivering a fraction of the radiation dose—however, these scans often suffer from an increase in white noise. CT scans come in a format known as DICOM, and we'll use a container with a specialized library called `pydicom` to load and process the data into a `numpy` matrix.

Several methods for denoising CT scans exist; however, they often focus on the mathematical justification, not the implementation. We will present an open source method that uses a *singular value decomposition* (SVD) to break the image into components, the "least important" of which are often the noise. We use Apache Spark with the Apache Mahout library to do a singular value decomposition. Finally, we use Python again to denoise the CT scans and visualize the results.

The Denoising CT Scans Example

Computed tomography (CT) scans are used for a wide array of medical purposes. The scans work by taking X-rays from multiple angles and forming image "slices" that can then be stacked to create a 3D image of a person's insides. In the United States, health experts recommend a person receive no more than 100 milliSieverts (mSv) of radiation throughout their lives, which is equivalent to about 25 chest CT scans (at ~7 mSv each).

In the late twentieth and early twenty-first century, much research was done on what are known as "low-dose" CT scans. A low-dose chest CT scan only delivers 1 to 2 mSv of radiation, but at a cost of a much noisier image, which can be harder to read. These scans are popular tools for screening for lung cancer among habitual smokers.

The cost of this low-dose CT scan is that the resultant image is lower quality, or noisier. In the 2000s, much research was done on denoising these low-dose CT scans. Most of the papers present methods and results only (no code). Further, the FDA restricts what methods can be used for denoising CT scans, which has led to almost all solutions being proprietary and expensive. Denoising seeks to improve image quality by removing the white noise that is often present in these low-dose CT scans.

At the time of the writing of this book, the novel coronavirus more popularly known as COVID-19 has escalated into a global pandemic. It has been shown that chest CT scans are a more sensitive early-detection test than the reverse transcription polymerase chain reaction (RT-PCR) test, especially at early stages of infection.

As multiple repositories of CT scans are coming online and asking AI researchers to assist in fighting the pandemic, we have sought to add a method for denoising CT scans based entirely on off-the-shelf open source components. Namely we will use Python, Apache Spark, Apache Mahout (a Spark library specializing in distributed linear algebra), and Kubeflow.

We will not delve into the math of what we are doing here, but we strongly encourage you to consult this paper.[1]

In this example, we will instead focus on the "how" of doing this technique with Kubeflow, and encourage readers to add their own steps at the end of this pipeline, which can then be freely shared with other researchers.

---

[1] The full paper can be found here (*https://oreil.ly/OXrFs*).

Data Prep with Python

CT scan images are commonly stored in the DICOM format. In this format each "slice" of the image is stored in its own file, along with some metadata about the image, such as space between pixels, and space between slices. We want to read all of these files and create a 3D tensor of the pixel values. Then we want to "flatten" that tensor into a two-dimensional matrix, on which we can then perform a singular value decomposition.

There are several places where you can get DICOM file sets. For the paper, we retrieved some from *https://coronacases.org* (though downloading the DICOMs can be a bit tricky). Other places you can find DICOM files are CT scans from the Public Lung Image Database (*https://oreil.ly/fDXRn*), a CD you may have received from the doctor if you've ever had a CT scan, and other places online.[2] The important thing is, we need one directory of DICOM files that comprise a single CT scan. We will assume there exists *some* DICOM file set comprising a single CT scan in the directory /data/dicom.

Converting a DICOM image into a tensor is shockingly easy, if you have the right dependencies in place. We will use pydicom, which is a well-supported Python interface for working with DICOM images. Unfortunately, the pydicom Docker images do not include Grassroots DICOM (GDCM), which is required for converting the DICOM into a pixel array. Our solution to this problem was to use the pydicom Docker container as a base image, then build a compatible GDCM version. The resulting image we've named rawkintrevo/covid-prep-dicom. With pydicom and GDCM it's easy to convert DICOM images into tensors; we will use a Lightweight Python Function to do the rest (see Example 9-1).

Example 9-1. Lightweight Python function converts DICOMs to tensors

```
def dicom_to_matrix(input_dir: str, output_file: str) -> output_type:
    import pydicom ❶
    import numpy as np

    def dicom_to_tensor(path): ❷
        dicoms = [pydicom.dcmread(f"{path}/{f}") for f in listdir(path)]
        slices = [d for d in dicoms if hasattr(d, "SliceLocation")]
        slices = sorted(slices, key=lambda s: s.SliceLocation)

        img_shape = list(slices[0].pixel_array.shape)
        img_shape.append(len(slices))
        img3d = np.zeros(img_shape)

        for i, s in enumerate(slices):
```

---

2 The Radiological Society of North America (*https://oreil.ly/VI-V0*) hopes to publish a repository of COVID-19 CT scans soon.

```
        img2d = s.pixel_array
        img3d[:, :, i] = img2d

    return {"img3d": img3d, "img_shape": img_shape}

m = dicom_to_tensor(f"{input_dir}")
np.savetxt(output_file, m['img3d'].reshape((-1,m['img_shape'][2])), delimiter=",")  ❸
return None


dicom_to_matrix_op = comp.func_to_container_op(
        dicom_to_matrix,
        base_image='rawkintrevo/covid-prep-dicom:0.8.0.0')
```

❶ Our imports must occur within the function (not globally).

❷ This function reads the list of "slices," which themselves are 2D images, and stacks them into a 3D tensor.

❸ We use numpy to reshape the 3D tensor into a 2D matrix.

Next, let's consider denoising our CT scan using Apache Spark and Apache Mahout.

DS-SVD with Apache Spark

The mathematics behind distributed stochastic singular value decomposition (DS-SVD) are well beyond the scope of this book; however, we direct you to learn more in *Apache Mahout: Beyond MapReduce*, on the Apache Mahout website (*https://oreil.ly/ T3VUE*), or in the aforementioned paper.

We seek to decompose our CT scan into a set of features, and then drop the least important features, as these are probably noise. So let's jump into decomposing a CT scan with Apache Spark and Apache Mahout.

A significant feature of Apache Mahout is its "R-Like" domain-specific language, which makes math code written in Scala easy to read. In Example 9-2 we load our data into a Spark RDD, wrap that RDD in a Mahout distributed row matrix (DRM), and perform the DS-SVD on the matrix, which yields three matrices that we will then save.

Example 9-2. Decomposing a CT scan with Spark and Mahout

```
val pathToMatrix = "gs://covid-dicoms/s.csv"  ❶

val voxelRDD:DrmRdd[Int]  = sc.textFile(pathToMatrix)
  .map(s => dvec( s.split(",")
  .map(f => f.toDouble)))
  .zipWithIndex
  .map(o => (o._2.toInt, o._1))
```

```
val voxelDRM = drmWrap(voxelRDD) ❷

// k, p, q should all be cli parameters
// k is rank of the output, e.g., the number of eigenfaces we want out.
// p is oversampling parameter,
// and q is the number of additional power iterations
// Read https://mahout.apache.org/users/dim-reduction/ssvd.html
val k = args(0).toInt
val p = args(1).toInt
val q = args(2).toInt

val(drmU, drmV, s) = dssvd(voxelDRM.t, k, p, q) ❸

val V = drmV.checkpoint().rdd.saveAsTextFile("gs://covid-dicoms/drmV")
val U = drmU.t.checkpoint().rdd.saveAsTextFile("gs://covid-dicoms/drmU")

sc.parallelize(s.toArray,1).saveAsTextFile("gs://covid-dicoms/s") ❹
```

❶ Load the data.

❷ Wrap the RDD in a DRM.

❸ Perform the DS-SVD.

❹ Save the output.

And so in just a few lines of Scala we are able to execute an out-of-core singular value decomposition.

Visualization

There are lots of good libraries for visualization in R and Python, and we want to use one of these for visualizing our denoised DICOMs. We also want to save our final images to somewhere more persistent than a persistent volume container (PVC), so that we can come back later to view our images.

This phase of the pipeline will have three steps:

1. Download the DRMs that resulted from the DS-SVD.

2. Recombine the matrices into a DICOM, denoised by setting some of the diagonal values of the matrix *s* to zero.

3. Render a slice of the resulting DICOM visually.

> Visualization could be easily accomplished in R or Python. We will proceed in Python, but using the oro.dicom package in R. We have chosen Python because Google officially supports a Python API for interacting with Cloud Storage.

Downloading DRMs

Recall the DRM is really just a wrapper around an RDD. In the cloud storage bucket, it will be represented as a directory full of "parts" of the matrix. To download these files we use the helper function shown in Example 9-3.

Example 9-3. Helper function to download a directory from GCS

```
def download_folder(bucket_name = 'your-bucket-name',
                    bucket_dir = 'your-bucket-directory/',
                    dl_dir= "local-dir/"):
    storage_client = storage.Client()
    bucket = storage_client.get_bucket(bucket_name)
    blobs = bucket.list_blobs(prefix=bucket_dir)  # Get list of files
    for blob in blobs:
        filename = blob.name.replace('/', '_')
        blob.download_to_filename(dl_dir + filename)  # Download
```

At the time of writing, Mahout's integration with Python is sparse (there is no PySpark equivalent to this code).

Also, there are no helper functions for reading Mahout DRMs into Python NumPy arrays, so we must write another helper function to assist us with that (shown in Example 9-4).

Example 9-4. Helper function to read Mahout DRMs into NumPy matrices

```
def read_mahout_drm(path):
    data = {}
    counter = 0
    parts = [p for p in os.listdir(path) if "part"] ❶
    for p in parts:
        with open(f"{path}/{p}", 'r') as f:
            lines = f.read().split("\n")
            for l in lines[:-1]:
                counter +=1
                t = literal_eval(l)
                arr = np.array([t[1][i] for i in range(len(t[1].keys()))])
                data[t[0]] = arr
    print(f"read {counter} lines from {path}")
    return data
```

❶ Remember, most Mahout DRMs will be in "parts" of files, so we must iterate through the parts to reconstruct the matrix.

Recomposing the matrix into denoised images

In a singular value decomposition, the diagonal matrix of singular values are typically denoted with a sigma. In our code, however, we use the letter s. By convention, these values are typically ordered from most important to least important, and happily, this convention is followed in the Mahout implementation. To denoise the images, we

simply set the last few values of the diagonals to zero. The idea is that the least important basis vectors probably represent noise which we seek to get rid of (see
Example 9-5).

Example 9-5. A loop to write several images

```
percs = [0.001, 0.01, 0.05, 0.1, 0.3]

for p in range(len(percs)):
    perc = percs[p]
    diags = [diags_orig[i]
            if i < round(len(diags) - (len(diags) * perc))
            else 0
            for i in range(len(diags))] ❶
    recon = drmU_p5 @ np.diag(diags) @ drmV_p5.transpose() ❷
    composite_img = recon.transpose().reshape((512,512,301)) ❸
    a1 = plt.subplot(1,1,1)
    plt.imshow(composite_img[:, :, 150], cmap=plt.cm.bone) ❹
    plt.title(f"{perc*100}% denoised.  (k={len(diags)}, oversample=15, power_iters=2)")
    a1.set_aspect(1.0)
    plt.axis('off')
    fname = f"{100-(perc*100)}%-denoised-img.png"
    plt.savefig(f"/tmp/{fname}")
    upload_blob(bucket_name, f"/tmp/{fname}", f"/output/{fname}") ❺
```

❶ Set the last p% of the singular values to equal zero.

❷ @ is the "matrix multiplication" operator.

❸ We're presuming our original image was 512 x 512 x 301 slices, which may or
    may not be correct for your case.

❹ Take the 150th slice.

❺ We'll talk about this function in the next section.

Now in our bucket, we will have several images in the /output/ folder, named for
what percentage of denoising they have been through.

Our output was an image of one slice of the DICOM. Instead, we could have output
several full DICOM files (one for each level of denoising) that could then be viewed
in a DICOM viewer, though the full example is a bit involved and out of scope for this
text. We encourage you to read pydicom's documentation (*https://oreil.ly/_1-sT*) if you
are interested in this output.

The CT Scan Denoising Pipeline

To create our pipeline, we will first create a manifest for our Spark job, which will specify what image to use, what secrets to use to mount what buckets, and a wide array of other information. Then we will create a pipeline using our containers from earlier steps and the manifest we define, which will output a PNG of one slice of the DICOM image with varying levels of noise removed.

Spark operation manifest

Spark read/wrote the files from GCS because it has issues with ReadWriteOnce (RWO) PVCs. We'll need to download output from GCS, then upload.

The Apache Spark operator does not like to read from ReadWriteOnce PVCs. If your Kubernetes is using these operators, and you can't request ReadWriteMany (as, for example, is the case on GCP), then you will need to use some other storage for the original matrix which is to be decomposed.

Most of our containers to this point have used `ContainerOp`. As a Spark job may actually consist of several containers, we will use a more generic `ResourceOp`. Defining `ResourceOps` gives us much more power and control, but this comes at the cost of the pretty Python API. To define a `ResourceOp` we must define a manifest (see Example 9-6) and pass that to the `ResourceOp` creation (see the next section).

Example 9-6. Spark operation manifest

```
container_manifest = {
    "apiVersion": "sparkoperator.k8s.io/v1beta2",
    "kind": "SparkApplication",
    "metadata": {
        "name": "spark-app", ❶
        "namespace": "kubeflow"
    },
    "spec": {
        "type": "Scala",
        "mode": "cluster",
        "image": "docker.io/rawkintrevo/covid-basis-vectors:0.2.0",
        "imagePullPolicy": "Always",
        "hadoopConf": { ❷
            "fs.gs.project.id": "kubeflow-hacky-hacky",
            "fs.gs.system.bucket": "covid-dicoms",
            "fs.gs.impl" : "com.google.cloud.hadoop.fs.gcs.GoogleHadoopFileSystem",
            "google.cloud.auth.service.account.enable": "true",
            "google.cloud.auth.service.account.json.keyfile": "/mnt/secrets/user-gcp-sa.json",
        },
        "mainClass": "org.rawkintrevo.covid.App",
        "mainApplicationFile": "local:///covid-0.1-jar-with-dependencies.jar",
        # See the Dockerfile
        "arguments": ["245", "15", "1"],
        "sparkVersion": "2.4.5",
        "restartPolicy": {
```

```
            "type": "Never"
        },
        "driver": {
            "cores": 1,
            "secrets": [ ❷
                {"name": "user-gcp-sa",
                 "path": "/mnt/secrets",
                 "secretType": "GCPServiceAccount"
                }
            ],

            "coreLimit": "1200m",
            "memory": "512m",
            "labels": {
                "version": "2.4.5",
            },
            "serviceAccount": "spark-operatoroperator-sa", # also try spark-operatoroperator-sa
        },
        "executor": {
            "cores": 1,
            "secrets": [ ❷
                {"name": "user-gcp-sa",
                 "path": "/mnt/secrets",
                 "secretType": "GCPServiceAccount"
                }
            ],
            "instances": 4, ❸
            "memory": "4084m"
        },
        "labels": {
            "version": "2.4.5"
        },

    }
}
```

❶ Name of the app: you can check on progress in the console with `kubectl logs spark-app-driver`.

❷ Different cloud providers use slightly different configurations here.

❸ We're doing a decomposition on a very large matrix—you may want to give even more resources than this if you can spare them.

> Because we are accessing GCP, we need to base our image from `gcr.io/spark-operator/spark:v2.4.5-gcs-prometheus`, which has additional included JARs for accessing GCP (otherwise we would use `gcr.io/spark-operator/spark:v2.4.5`).

While this is tuned for GCP, with a very minimal change in configuration, specifically around the secrets, this could easily be ported to AWS or Azure.

If you are familiar with Kubernetes, you are probably used to seeing manifests represented as YAML files. Here we have created a manifest with a Python dictionary. Next we will use this dictionary in our pipeline definition to create a `ResourceOp`.

The pipeline

Finally, we have all of our necessary components. We will create a pipeline that strings them together into a repeatable operation for us.

To review, Example 9-7 does the following:

- Downloads CT scans from GCP to a local PVC.
- Converts the CT scans (DICOM files) into a matrix (*s.csv*).
- A Spark job does a distributed stochastic singular value decomposition and writes the output to GCP.
- The decomposed matrix is recomposed with some of the singular values set to zero—thus denoising the image.

Example 9-7. CT scan denoising pipeline

```
from kfp.gcp import use_gcp_secret
@kfp.dsl.pipeline(
    name="Covid DICOM Pipe v2",
    description="Visualize Denoised CT Scans"
)
def covid_dicom_pipeline():
    vop = kfp.dsl.VolumeOp(
        name="requisition-PVC",
        resource_name="datapvc",
        size="20Gi", #10 Gi blows up...
        modes=kfp.dsl.VOLUME_MODE_RWO
    )
    step1 = kfp.dsl.ContainerOp( ❶
        name="download-dicom",
        image="rawkintrevo/download-dicom:0.0.0.4",
        command=["/run.sh"],
        pvolumes={"/data": vop.volume}
    )
    step2 = kfp.dsl.ContainerOp( ❷
        name="convert-dicoms-to-vectors",
        image="rawkintrevo/covid-prep-dicom:0.9.5",
        arguments=[
            '--bucket_name', "covid-dicoms",
        ],
        command=["python", "/program.py"],
        pvolumes={"/mnt/data": step1.pvolume}
    ).apply(kfp.gcp.use_gcp_secret(secret_name='user-gcp-sa')) ❺
    rop = kfp.dsl.ResourceOp( ❸
        name="calculate-basis-vectors",
        k8s_resource=container_manifest,
```

```
        action="create",
        success_condition="status.applicationState.state == COMPLETED"
    ).after(step2)
    pyviz = kfp.dsl.ContainerOp( ❹
        name="visualize-slice-of-dicom",
        image="rawkintrevo/visualize-dicom-output:0.0.11",
        command=["python", "/program.py"],
        arguments=[
            '--bucket_name', "covid-dicoms",
        ],
    ).apply(kfp.gcp.use_gcp_secret(secret_name='user-gcp-sa')).after(rop)


kfp.compiler.Compiler().compile(covid_dicom_pipeline,"dicom-pipeline-2.zip")
client = kfp.Client()

my_experiment = client.create_experiment(name='my-experiments')
my_run = client.run_pipeline(my_experiment.id, 'my-run1', 'dicom-pipeline-2.zip')
```

❶ This container was not discussed, but it simply downloads images from a GCP bucket to our local PVC.

❷ Here we convert our DICOM into a matrix and upload it to a specified GCP bucket.

❸ This is the Spark job that calculates the singular value decomposition.

❹ This is where DICOM images are reconstructed.

❺ For GCP we use_gcp_secret, but similar functions exist for Azure and AWS.

For illustration, Figures 9-1 through 9-3 are slices of the DICOM image at various levels of denoising. As we are not radiology experts, we won't try to make any points about changes in quality or what is optimal, other than to point out that at 10% denoising we've probably gone too far, and at 30% we unquestionably have.

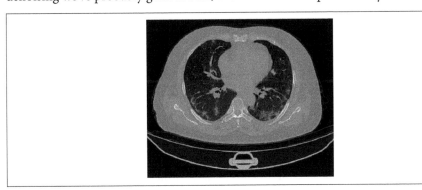

Figure 9-1. Original slice of DICOM

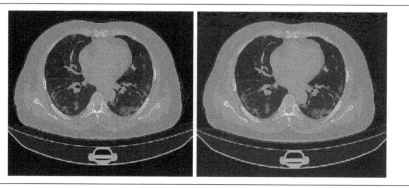

Figure 9-2. 1% denoised DICOM slice (left); 5% denoised DICOM slice (right)

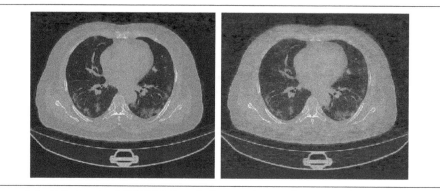

Figure 9-3. 10% denoised DICOM slice (left); .5% denoised DICOM slice (right)

Again we see that while this pipeline is now hardcoded for GCP, it can with only a few lines of updates be changed to work with AWS or Azure; specifically, how we mount secrets to the container. A significant advantage of this is that we are able to safely decouple passcodes from code.

Using RStats

Our examples have all been Python- or Scala-based, but remember—a container is just an OS that is going to run a program. As such, you can use any language that can exist in a container. To use an RStats script as a pipeline step:

1. Create a Docker container (probably from a preexisting images such as `r-base:latest`).

2. Create a program that takes command-line arguments.

3. Output the results to a mounted PVC or save to a cloud storage provider.

Sharing the Pipeline

A final important benefit of Kubeflow is the reproducibility of experiments. While often underscored in academia, reproducibiltiy is an important concept in business settings as well. By containerizing pipeline steps, we can remove hidden dependencies that allow a program to only run on one device—or, to put it another way, reproducibility prevents you from developing an algorithm that only runs on one person's machine.

The pipeline we present here should run on any Kubeflow deployment.[3] This also allows for rapid iteration. Any reader can use this pipeline as a basis and, for instance, could create a final step where some deep learning is performed on the denoised images and the original images to compare the effects of denoising.

Conclusion

We have now seen how to create very maintainable pipelines by leveraging containers that have most, if not all, of the required dependencies to make our program run. This not only removes the technical debt of having to maintain a system with all of these dependencies, but makes the program much more transferable, and our research much more easily transferable and reproducible.

There exists a large and exciting galaxy of Docker containers, and odds are you already have some steps Dockerized in preexisting containers. Being able to leverage these containers for Kubeflow Pipeline steps is certainly one of Kubeflow's biggest strengths.

---

3 With minor tuning for no GCE deployments.

# CHAPTER 10

Hyperparameter Tuning and Automated Machine Learning

In the previous chapters, we have seen how Kubeflow helps with the various phases of machine learning. But knowing what to do in each phase—whether it's feature preparation or training or deploying models—requires some amount of expert knowledge and experimentation. According to the "no free lunch" theorem (*https://oreil.ly/H_IHi*), no single model works best for every machine learning problem, therefore each model must be constructed carefully. It can be very time-consuming and expensive to fully build a highly performing model if each phase requires significant human input.

Naturally, one might wonder: is it possible to automate parts—or even the entirety—of the machine learning process? Can we reduce the amount of overhead for data scientists while still sustaining high model quality?

In machine learning, the umbrella term for solving these type of problems is *automated machine learning* (AutoML). It is a constantly evolving field of research, and has found its way to the industry with practical applications. AutoML seeks to simplify machine learning for experts and nonexperts alike by reducing the need for manual interaction in the more time-consuming and iterative phases of machine learning: feature engineering, model construction, and hyperparameter configuration.

In this chapter we will see how Kubeflow can be used to automate hyperparameter search and neural architecture search, two important subfields of AutoML.

AutoML: An Overview

AutoML refers to the various processes and tools that automate parts of the machine learning process. At a high level, AutoML refers to any algorithms and methodologies that seek to solve one or more of the following problems:

Data preprocessing
Machine learning requires data, and raw data can come from various sources and in different formats. To make raw data useful, human experts typically have to comb over the data, normalize values, remove erroneous or corrupted data, and ensure data consistency.

Feature engineering
Training models with too few input variables (or "features") can lead to inaccurate models. However, having too many features can also be problematic; the learning process would be slower and more resource-consuming, and overfitting problems can occur. Coming up with the right set of features can be the most time-consuming part of building a machine learning model. Automated feature engineering can speed up the process of feature extraction, selection, and transformation.

Model selection
Once you have all the training data, you need to pick the right training model for your dataset. The ideal model should be as simple as possible while still providing a good measure of prediction accuracy.

Hyperparameter tuning
Most learning models have a number of parameters that are external to the model, such as the learning rate, the batch size, and the number of layers in the neural network. We call these *hyperparameters* to distinguish them from model parameters that are adjusted by the learning process. Hyperparameter tuning is the process of automating the search process for these parameters in order to improve the accuracy of the model.

Neural architecture search
A related field to hyperparameter tuning is *neural architecture search* (NAS). Instead of choosing between a fixed range of values for each hyperparameter value, NAS seeks to take automation one step further and generates an entire neural network that outperforms handcrafted architectures. Common methodologies for NAS include reinforcement learning and evolutionary algorithms.

The focus of this chapter will be on the latter two problems—hyperparameter tuning and neural architecture search. As they are related, they can be solved using similar methodologies.

Hyperparameter Tuning with Kubeflow Katib

In Chapter 7, it was mentioned that we needed to set a few hyperparameters. In machine learning, hyperparameters refer to parameters that are set before the training process begins (as opposed to model parameters which are learned from the training process). Examples of hyperparameters include the learning rate, number of decision trees, number of layers in a neural network, etc.

The concept of hyperparameter optimization is very simple: select the set of hyperparameter values that lead to optimal model performance. A hyperparameter tuning framework is a tool that does exactly that. Typically, the user of such a tool would define a few things:

- The list of hyperparameters and their valid range of values (called the *search space*)
- The metrics used to measure model performance
- The methodology to use for the searching process

Kubeflow comes packaged with Katib (*https://oreil.ly/BW4TM*), a general framework for hyperparameter tuning. Among similar open source tools, Katib has a few distinguishing features:

It is Kubernetes native
This means that Katib experiments can be ported wherever Kubernetes runs.

It has multiframework support
Katib supports many popular learning frameworks, with first-class support for TensorFlow and PyTorch distributed training.

It is language-agnostic
Training code can be written in any language, as long as it is built as a Docker image.

 The name *katib* means "secretary" or "scribe" in Arabic, and is an homage to the Vizier framework that inspired its initial version ("vizier" being Arabic for a minister or high official).

In this chapter, we'll take a look at how Katib simplifies hyperparameter optimization.

Katib Concepts

Let's begin by defining a few terms that are central to the workflow of Katib (as illustrated in Figure 10-1):

Experiment

An experiment is an end-to-end process that takes a problem (e.g., tuning a training model for handwriting recognition), an objective metric (maximize the prediction accuracy), and a search space (range for hyperparameters), and produces a final set of optimal hyperparameter values.

Suggestion

A suggestion is one possible solution to the problem we are trying to solve. Since we are trying to find the combination of hyperparameter values that lead to optimal model performance, a suggestion would be one set of hyperparameter values from the specified search space.

Trial

A trial is one iteration of the experiment. Each trial takes a suggestion and executes a worker process (packaged through Docker) that produces evaluation metrics. Katib's controller then computes the next suggestion based on previous metrics and spawns new trials.

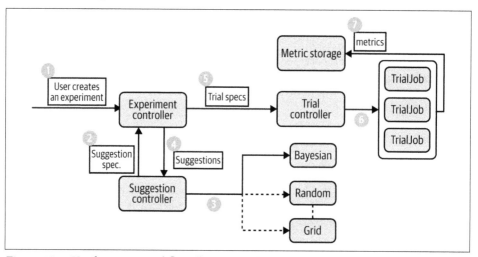

Figure 10-1. Katib system workflow (https://oreil.ly/BW4TM)

In Katib, experiments, suggestions, and trials are all custom resources. This means they are stored in Kubernetes and can be manipulated using standard Kubernetes APIs.

Another important aspect of hyperparameter tuning is how to find the next set of parameters. As of the time of this writing, Katib supports the following search algorithms:

Grid search
Also known as a parameter sweep, grid search is the simplest approach—exhaustively search through possible parameter values in the specified search space. Although resource-intensive, grid search has the advantage of having high parallelism since the tasks are completely independent.

Random search
Similar to grid search, the tasks in random search are completely independent. Instead of enumerating every possible value, random search attempts to generate parameter values through random selection. When there are many hyperparameters to tune (but only a few have significant impact on model performance), random search can vastly outperform grid search. Random search can also be useful when the number of discrete parameters is high, which makes grid search infeasible.

Bayesian optimization
This is a powerful approach that uses probability and statistics to seek better parameters. Bayesian optimization builds a probabilistic model for the objective function, finds parameter values that perform well on the model, and then iteratively updates the model based on metrics collected during trial runs. Intuitively speaking, Bayesian optimization seeks to improve upon a model by making informed guesses. This optimization method relies on previous iterations to find new parameters, and can be parallelized. While trials are not as independent as grid or random search, Bayesian optimization can find results with fewer trials overall.

Hyperband
This is a relatively new approach that selects configuration values randomly. But unlike traditional random search, hyperband only evaluates each trial for a small number of iterations. Then it takes the best-performing configurations and runs them longer, repeating this process until a desired result is reached. Due to its similarity to random search, tasks can be highly parallelized.

Other experimental algorithms
These include the tree of Parzen estimators (TPE) and covariance matrix adaptation evolution strategy (CMA-ES), both implemented by using the Goptuna (*https://oreil.ly/PDGOg*) optimization framework.

One final piece of the puzzle in Katib is the metrics collector. This is the process that collects and parses evaluation metrics after each trial and pushes them into the persistent database. Katib implements metrics collection through a sidecar container, which runs alongside the main container in a pod.

Overall, Katib's design makes it highly scalable, portable, and extensible. Since it is part of the Kubeflow platform, Katib natively supports integration with many of Kubeflow's other training components, like the TFJob and PyTorch operators. Katib is also the first hyperparameter tuning framework that supports multitenancy, making it ideal for a cloud hosted environment.

Installing Katib

Katib is installed by default. To install Katib as a standalone service, you can use the following script in the Kubeflow GitHub repo:

```
git clone https://github.com/kubeflow/katib
bash ./katib/scripts/v1beta1/deploy.sh
```

If your Kubernetes cluster doesn't support dynamic volume provisioning, you would also create a persistent volume:

```
pv_path=https://raw.githubusercontent.com/kubeflow/katib/master/manifests\
/v1beta1/pv/pv.yaml
kubectl apply -f pv_path
```

After installing Katib components, you can navigate to the Katib dashboard to verify that it is running. If you installed Katib through Kubeflow and have an endpoint, simply navigate to the Kubeflow dashboard and select "Katib" in the menu. Otherwise, you can set up port forwarding to test your deployment:

```
kubectl port-forward svc/katib-ui -n kubeflow 8080:80
```

Then navigate to:

```
http://localhost:8080/katib/
```

Running Your First Katib Experiment

Now that Katib is up and running in your cluster, let's take a look at how to run an actual experiment. In this section we will use Katib to tune a simple MNist model. You can find the source code and all configuration files on Katib's GitHub page (*https://oreil.ly/tdSM_*).

Prepping Your Training Code

The first step is to prepare your training code. Since Katib runs training jobs for trial evaluation, each training job needs to be packaged as a Docker container. Katib is language-agnostic, so it does not matter how you write the training code. However, to be compatible with Katib, the training code must satisfy a couple of requirements:

- Hyperparameters must be exposed as command-line arguments. For example:

```
python mnist.py --batch_size=100 --learning_rate=0.1
```

- Metrics must be exposed in a format consistent with the metrics collector. Katib currently supports metrics collection through standard output, file, TensorFlow events, or custom. The simplest option is to use the standard metrics collector, which means the evaluation metrics must be written to stdout, in the following format:

```
metrics_name=metrics_value
```

The example training model code that we will use can be found on this GitHub site (*https://oreil.ly/USb-Y*).

After preparing the training code, simply package it as a Docker image and it is ready to go.

Configuring an Experiment

Once you have the training container, the next step is to write a spec for your experiment. Katib uses Kubernetes custom resources to represent experiments. Example 10-1 can be downloaded from this GitHub page (*https://oreil.ly/nwbbJ*).

Example 10-1. Example experiment spec

```
apiVersion: "kubeflow.org/v1beta1"
kind: Experiment
metadata:
  namespace: kubeflow
  labels:
    controller-tools.k8s.io: "1.0"
  name: random-example
spec:
  objective:                     ❶
    type: maximize
    goal: 0.99
    objectiveMetricName: Validation-accuracy
    additionalMetricNames:
      - Train-accuracy
  algorithm:                     ❷
    algorithmName: random
  parallelTrialCount: 3          ❸
```

```
maxTrialCount: 12
maxFailedTrialCount: 3
parameters:                    ❹
  - name: --lr
    parameterType: double
    feasibleSpace:
      min: "0.01"
      max: "0.03"
  - name: --num-layers
    parameterType: int
    feasibleSpace:
      min: "2"
      max: "5"
  - name: --optimizer
    parameterType: categorical
    feasibleSpace:
      list:
      - sgd
      - adam
      - ftrl
trialTemplate:                 ❺
  goTemplate:
    rawTemplate: |-
      apiVersion: batch/v1
      kind: Job
      metadata:
        name: {{.Trial}}
        namespace: {{.NameSpace}}
      spec:
        template:
          spec:
            containers:
            - name: {{.Trial}}
              image: docker.io/kubeflowkatib/mxnet-mnist
              command:
              - "python3"
              - "/opt/mxnet-mnist/mnist.py"
              - "--batch-size=64"
              {{- with .HyperParameters}}
              {{- range .}}
              - "{{.Name}}={{.Value}}"
              {{- end}}
              {{- end}}
            restartPolicy: Never
```

That's quite a lot to follow. Let's take a closer look at each part of the spec section:

❶ *Objective.* This is where you configure how to measure the performance of your training model, and the goal of the experiment. In this experiment, we are trying to maximize the validation-accuracy metric. We are stopping our experiment if we reach the objective goal of 0.99 (99% accuracy). The additionalMetrics Names represents metrics that are collected from each trial, but aren't used to evaluate the trial.

❷ *Algorithm.* In this experiment we are using random search; some algorithms may require additional configurations.

❸ *Budget configurations.* This is where we configure our experiment budget. In this experiment, we would run 3 trials in parallel, with a total of 12 trials. We would also stop our experiment if we have three failed trials. This last part is also called an *error budget*—an important concept in maintaining production-grade system uptime.

❹ *Parameters.* Here we define which parameters we want to tune and the search space for each. For example, the `learning rate` parameter is exposed in the training code as `--lr`. It is a double, with a contiguous search space between 0.01 and 0.03.

❺ *Trial template.* The last part of the experiment spec is the template from which each trial is configured. For the purpose of this example, the only important parts are:

```
image: docker.io/kubeflowkatib/mxnet-mnist
command:
  - "python3"
  - "/opt/mxnet-mnist/mnist.py"
  - "--batch-size=64"
```

This should point to the Docker image that you built in the previous step, with the command-line entry point to run the code.

Running the Experiment

After everything is configured, apply the resource to start the experiment:

```
kubectl apply -f random-example.yaml
```

You can check the status of the experiment by running the following:

```
kubectl -n kubeflow describe experiment random-example
```

In the output, you should see something like Example 10-2.

Example 10-2. Example experiment output

```
Name:         random-example
Namespace:    kubeflow
Labels:       controller-tools.k8s.io=1.0
Annotations:  <none>
API Version:  kubeflow.org/v1beta1
Kind:         Experiment
Metadata:
  Creation Timestamp:  2019-12-22T22:53:25Z
  Finalizers:
    update-prometheus-metrics
```

```
    Generation:            2
    Resource Version:      720692
    Self Link:             /apis/kubeflow.org/v1beta1/namespaces/kubeflow/experiments/random-example
    UID:                   dc6bc15a-250d-11ea-8cae-42010a80010f
Spec:
  Algorithm:
    Algorithm Name:        random
    Algorithm Settings:    <nil>
  Max Failed Trial Count:  3
  Max Trial Count:         12
  Metrics Collector Spec:
    Collector:
      Kind:  StdOut
  Objective:
    Additional Metric Names:
      accuracy
    Goal:                  0.99
    Objective Metric Name: Validation-accuracy
    Type:                  maximize
  Parallel Trial Count:    3
  Parameters:
    Feasible Space:
      Max:                 0.03
      Min:                 0.01
    Name:                  --lr
    Parameter Type:  double
    Feasible Space:
      Max:                 5
      Min:                 2
    Name:                  --num-layers
    Parameter Type:  int
    Feasible Space:
      List:
        sgd
        adam
        ftrl
    Name:                  --optimizer
    Parameter Type:  categorical
  Trial Template:
    Go Template:
      Raw Template:  apiVersion: batch/v1
kind: Job
metadata:
  name: {{.Trial}}
  namespace: {{.NameSpace}}
spec:
  template:
    spec:
      containers:
      - name: {{.Trial}}
        image: docker.io/kubeflowkatib/mxnet-mnist-example
        command:
        - "python"
        - "/mxnet/example/image-classification/train_mnist.py"
        - "--batch-size=64"
        {{- with .HyperParameters}}
        {{- range .}}
        - "{{.Name}}={{.Value}}"
        {{- end}}
```

```
        {{- end}}
        restartPolicy: Never
Status:                                              ❶
  Conditions:
    Last Transition Time:  2019-12-22T22:53:25Z
    Last Update Time:      2019-12-22T22:53:25Z
    Message:               Experiment is created
    Reason:                ExperimentCreated
    Status:                True
    Type:                  Created
    Last Transition Time:  2019-12-22T22:55:10Z
    Last Update Time:      2019-12-22T22:55:10Z
    Message:               Experiment is running
    Reason:                ExperimentRunning
    Status:                True
    Type:                  Running
  Current Optimal Trial:                             ❷
    Observation:
      Metrics:
        Name:    Validation-accuracy
        Value:   0.981091
    Parameter Assignments:
      Name:            --lr
      Value:           0.025139701133432946
      Name:            --num-layers
      Value:           4
      Name:            --optimizer
      Value:           sgd
    Start Time:        2019-12-22T22:53:25Z
  Trials:              12                             ❸
  Trials Running:      2
  Trials Succeeded:    10
Events:                <none>
```

Some of the interesting parts of the output are:

❶ *Status.* Here you can see the current state of the experiment, as well as its previous states.

❷ *Current Optimal Trial.* This is the "best" trial so far, i.e., the trial that produced the best outcome as determined by our predefined metrics. You can also see this trial's parameters and metrics.

❸ *Trials Succeeded/Running/Failed.* In this section, you can see how your experiment is progressing.

Katib User Interface

Alternatively, you can use Katib's user interface (UI) to submit and monitor your experiments. If you have a Kubeflow deployment, you can navigate to the Katib UI by clicking "Katib" in the navigation panel and then "Hyperparameter Tuning" on the main page, shown in Figure 10-2.

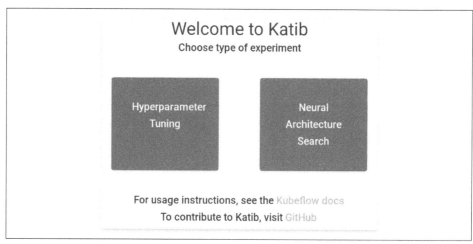

Figure 10-2. Katib UI main page

Let's submit our random search experiment (see Figure 10-3). You can simply paste a YAML in the textbox here, or have one generated for you by following the UI. To do this, click the `Parameters` tab.

Figure 10-3. Configuring a new experiment, part 1

You should see a panel like Figure 10-4. Enter the necessary configuration parameters on this page; define a run budget and the validation metrics.

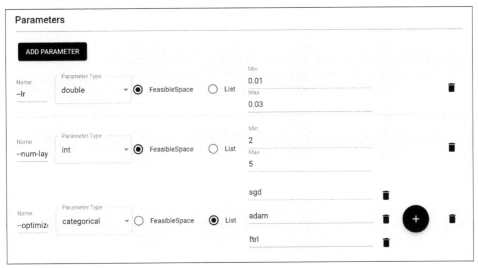

Figure 10-4. Configuring a new experiment, part 2

Then scroll down the page and finish up the rest of the experiment by configuring the search space and the trial template. For the latter, you can just leave it on the default template. When you are done, click "Deploy."

Now that the experiment is running, you can monitor its status and see a visual graph of the progress (see Figure 10-5). You can see your running and completed experiments by navigating to the drop-down menu in the Katib dashboard, and then selecting "UI" and then "Monitor."

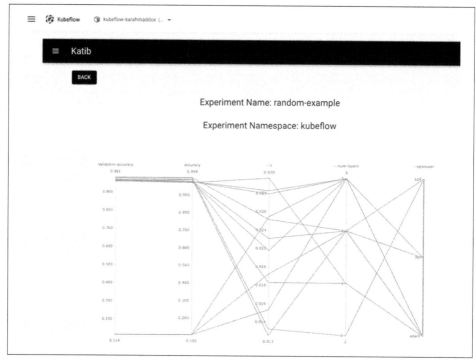

Figure 10-5. Katib UI for an experiment

Below this graph, you will see a detailed breakdown of each trial (shown in Figure 10-6), the values of the hyperparameters for each of the trials, and the final metric values. This is very useful for comparing the effects of certain hyperparameters on the model's performance.

trialName	Status	Validation-accuracy	accuracy	--lr	--num-layers
random-experiment-6r2d69hw	Succeeded	0.945263	0.947092	0.026327465376429264	4
random-experiment-6zc46zs5	Succeeded	0.113854	0.120781	0.011849107354863664	3
random-experiment-9b9tr9kk	Succeeded	0.977010	0.995204	0.01094711184545228	5
random-experiment-b4bqc6jv	Succeeded	0.113854	0.120781	0.028994058992997625	3
random-experiment-dhxd285c	Succeeded	0.113854	0.122370	0.020585920667142765	4
random-experiment-dzgq9qkg	Succeeded	0.113854	0.121719	0.02980842874463672	4
random-experiment-fhmttpc8	Succeeded	0.934216	0.937964	0.029884129440740717	4

Figure 10-6. Katib metrics for an experiment

Since we are also collecting validation metrics along the way, we can actually plot the graph for each trial. Click a row to see how the model performs with the given hyperparameter values across time (as in Figure 10-7).

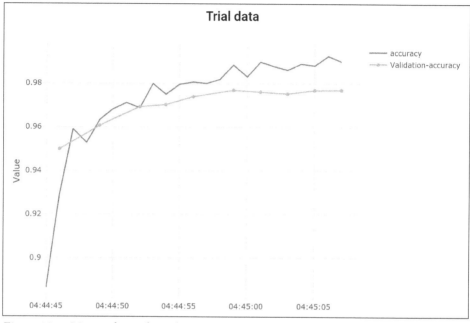

Figure 10-7. Metrics for each trial

Tuning Distributed Training Jobs

In Chapter 7 we saw an example of using Kubeflow to orchestrate distributed training. What if we want to use Katib to tune parameters for a distributed training job?

The good news is that Katib natively supports integration with TensorFlow and PyTorch distributed training. An MNIST example with TensorFlow can be found at this Katib GitHub page (*https://oreil.ly/I3q4x*). This example uses the same MNIST distributed training example we saw in Chapter 7, and directly integrates it into the Katib framework. In Example 10-3, we will launch an experiment to tune hyperparameters (learning rate and batch size) for a distributed TensorFlow job.

Example 10-3. Distributed training example

```
apiVersion: "kubeflow.org/v1beta1"
kind: Experiment
metadata:
  namespace: kubeflow
  name: tfjob-example
spec:
```

```
parallelTrialCount: 3                    ❶
maxTrialCount: 12
maxFailedTrialCount: 3
objective:                               ❷
  type: maximize
  goal: 0.99
  objectiveMetricName: accuracy_1
algorithm:
  algorithmName: random
metricsCollectorSpec:                    ❸
  source:
    fileSystemPath:
      path: /train
      kind: Directory
  collector:
    kind: TensorFlowEvent
parameters:                              ❹
  - name: learning_rate
    parameterType: double
    feasibleSpace:
      min: "0.01"
      max: "0.05"
  - name: batch_size
    parameterType: int
    feasibleSpace:
      min: "100"
      max: "200"
trialTemplate:
  trialParameters:
    - name: learningRate
      description: Learning rate for the training model
      reference: learning_rate
    - name: batchSize
      description: Batch Size
      reference: batch_size
  trialSpec:
    apiVersion: "kubeflow.org/v1"
    kind: TFJob
    spec:
      tfReplicaSpecs:                    ❺
        Worker:
          replicas: 2
          restartPolicy: OnFailure
          template:
            spec:
              containers:
                - name: tensorflow
                  image: gcr.io/kubeflow-ci/tf-mnist-with-summaries:1.0
                  imagePullPolicy: Always
                  command:
                    - "python"
                    - "/var/tf_mnist/mnist_with_summaries.py"
                    - "--log_dir=/train/metrics"
                    - "--learning_rate=${trialParameters.learningRate}"
                    - "--batch_size=${trialParameters.batchSize}"
```

❶ The total and parallel trial counts are similar to the previous experiment. In this case they refer to the total and parallel number of distributed training jobs to run.

❷ The objective specification is also similar—in this case we want to maximize the `accuracy` measurement.

❸ The metrics collector specification looks slightly different. This is because this is a TensorFlow job, and we can use TFEvents outputted by TensorFlow directly. Using the built-in `TensorFlowEvent` collector type, Katib can automatically parse TensorFlow events and populate the metrics database.

❹ The parameter configurations are exactly the same—in this case we are tuning the learning rate and batch size of the model.

❺ The trial template should look familiar to you if you read Chapter 7—it's the same distributed training example spec that we ran before. The imporant difference here is that we've parameterized the input to `learning_rate` and `batch_size`.

So now you have learned how to use Katib to tune hyperparameters. But notice that you still have to select the model yourself. Can we reduce the amount of human work even further? What about other subfields in AutoML? In the next section we will look at how Katib supports the generation of entire artificial neural networks.

Neural Architecture Search

Neural architecture search (NAS) is a growing subfield in automated machine learning. Unlike hyperparameter tuning, where the model is already chosen and our goal is to optimize its performance by turning a few knobs, in NAS we are trying to generate the network architecture itself. Recent research has shown that NAS can outperform handcrafted neural networks on tasks like image classification, object detection, and semantic segmentation.[1]

Most the methodologies for NAS can be categorized as either *generation* methods or *mutation* methods. In *generation* methods, the algorithm will propose one or more candidate architectures in each iteration. These proposed architectures are then evaluated and then refined in the next iteration. In *mutation* methods, an overly complex architecture is proposed first, and subsequent iterations will attempt to prune the model.

---

1 T. Elsken, J. H. Metzen, F. Hutter, "Neural Architecture Search: A Survey," *Journal of Machine Learning Research* 20 (2019), *https://oreil.ly/eO-CV*, pp. 1-21.

Katib currently supports two implementations of NAS: *Differentiable Architecture Search (DARTS)*,[2] and *Efficient Neural Architecture Search (ENAS)*.[3] DARTS achieves scalability of NAS by relaxing the search space to be continuous instead of discrete and utilizes gradient descent to optimize the architecture. ENAS takes a different approach, by observing that in most NAS algorithms the bottleneck occurs during the training of each child model. ENAS forces each child model to share parameters, thus improving the overall efficiency.

The general workflow of NAS in Katib is similar to hyperparameter search, with an additional step for constructing the model architecture. An internal module of Katib, called the *model manager*, is responsible for taking topological configurations and mutation parameters, and constructing new models. Katib then uses the same concepts of trials and metrics to evaluate the model's performance.

As an example, see the spec of a NAS experiment using DARTS in Example 10-4.

Example 10-4. Example NAS experiment spec

```
apiVersion: "kubeflow.org/v1beta1"
kind: Experiment
metadata:
  namespace: kubeflow
  name: darts-example-gpu
spec:
  parallelTrialCount: 1
  maxTrialCount: 1
  maxFailedTrialCount: 1
  objective:
    type: maximize
    objectiveMetricName: Best-Genotype
  metricsCollectorSpec:
    collector:
      kind: StdOut
    source:
      filter:
        metricsFormat:
          - "([\\w-]+)=(Genotype.*)"
  algorithm:
    algorithmName: darts
    algorithmSettings:
      - name: num_epochs
        value: "3"
  nasConfig:                        ❶
    graphConfig:
      numLayers: 3
    operations:
      - operationType: separable_convolution
        parameters:
```

---

2 H. Liu, K. Simonyan, and Y. Tang, "Differentiable Architecture Search (DARTS)," *https://oreil.ly/JSAIX*.

3 H. Pham et al., "Efficient Neural Architecture Search via Parameter Sharing," *https://oreil.ly/SQPxn*.

```
        - name: filter_size
          parameterType: categorical
          feasibleSpace:
            list:
              - "3"
    - operationType: dilated_convolution
      parameters:
        - name: filter_size
          parameterType: categorical
          feasibleSpace:
            list:
              - "3"
              - "5"
    - operationType: avg_pooling
      parameters:
        - name: filter_size
          parameterType: categorical
          feasibleSpace:
            list:
              - "3"
    - operationType: max_pooling
      parameters:
        - name: filter_size
          parameterType: categorical
          feasibleSpace:
            list:
              - "3"
    - operationType: skip_connection
trialTemplate:
  trialParameters:
    - name: algorithmSettings
      description: Algorithm settings of DARTS Experiment
      reference: algorithm-settings
    - name: searchSpace
      description: Search Space of DARTS Experiment
      reference: search-space
    - name: numberLayers
      description: Number of Neural Network layers
      reference: num-layers
  trialSpec:
    apiVersion: batch/v1
    kind: Job
    spec:
      template:
        spec:
          containers:
            - name: training-container
              image: docker.io/kubeflowkatib/darts-cnn-cifar10
              imagePullPolicy: Always
              command:
                - python3
                - run_trial.py
                - --algorithm-settings="${trialParameters.algorithmSettings}"
                - --search-space="${trialParameters.searchSpace}"
                - --num-layers="${trialParameters.numberLayers}"
              resources:
                limits:
                  nvidia.com/gpu: 1
          restartPolicy: Never
```

❶ The general structure of a NAS experiment is similar to that of a hyperparameter search experiment. The majority of the specification should look very familiar; the most important difference is the addition of the `nasConfig`. This is where you can configure the specifications of the neural network that you want to create, such as the number of layers, the inputs and outputs at each layer, and the types of operations.

Advantages of Katib over Other Frameworks

There are many similar open source systems for hyperparameter search, among them NNI (*https://oreil.ly/lDwpN*), Optuna (*https://oreil.ly/gAHgZ*), Ray Tune (*https://oreil.ly/CnNFZ*), and Hyperopt (*https://oreil.ly/jlfoP*). In addition, the original design of Katib was inspired by Google Vizier (*https://oreil.ly/q1xiz*). While these frameworks offer many capabilities similar to Katib's, namely the ability to configure parallel hyperparameter sweeps using a variety of algorithms, there are a few features of Katib that make it unique:

Design catering to both user and admin
Most tuning frameworks are designed to cater to the *user*—the data scientist performing the tuning experiment. Katib is also designed to make life easier for the *system admin*, who is responsible for maintaining the infrastructure, allocating compute resources, and monitoring system health.

Cloud native design
Other frameworks (such as Ray Tune) may support integration with Kubernetes, but often require additional effort to set up a cluster. By contrast, Katib is the first hyperparameter search framework to base its design entirely on Kubernetes; every one of its resources can be accessed and manipulated by Kubernetes APIs.

Scalable and portable
Because Katib uses Kubernetes as its orchestration engine, it is very easy to scale up an experiment. You can run the same experiments on a laptop for prototyping and deploy the job to a production cluster with minimal changes to the spec. By contrast, other frameworks require additional effort to install and configure depending on the hardware availability.

Extensible
Katib offers flexible and pluggable interfaces for its search algorithms and storage systems. Most other frameworks come with a preset list of algorithms and have hardcoded mechanisms for metrics collection. In Katib, the user can easily implement a custom search algorithm and integrate it with the framework.

Native support

Katib natively supports advanced features like distributed training and neural architecture search.

Conclusion

In this chapter we've taken a quick overview of AutoML and learned how it can accelerate the development of machine learning models by automating time-consuming tasks like hyperparameter search. With techniques like automated hyperparameter tuning, you can scale up the development of your models while sustaining high model quality.

We have then used Katib—a Kubernetes-native tuning service from the Kubeflow platform—to configure and execute a hyperparameter search experiment. We have also shown how you can use Katib's dashboard to submit, track, and visualize your experiments.

We've also explored how Katib handles neural architecture search (NAS). Katib currently supports two methods of NAS—DARTS and ENAS, with more development to follow.

Hopefully, this has given you some insights into how Katib can be leveraged to reduce the amount of work in your machine learning workflows. Katib is still an evolving project, and you can follow the latest developments on this Katib GitHub page (*https://oreil.ly/OHFAL*).

Thank you for joining us on your adventures in learning Kubeflow. We hope that Kubeflow meets your needs and helps you deliver on machine learning's ability to bring value to your organization. To keep up to date on the latest changes with Kubeflow, we encourage you to join the Kubeflow Slack workspace and mailing lists (*https://oreil.ly/4fT2i*).

Argo Executor Configurations and Trade-Offs

Until recently, all Kubernetes implementations supported Docker APIs. The initial Argo implementation depended on them. With the introduction of OpenShift 4 (*https://oreil.ly/bIoqk*), which doesn't support the Docker APIs, the situation changed. To support the absence of Docker APIs, Argo introduced several new executors: Docker, Kubelet, and Kubernetes APIs. The `containerRuntimeExecutor` config value in the Argo parameters file controls which executor is used. The pros and cons of each executor (based on the information here) are summarized in Table A-1. This table should help you pick the correct value of the Argo executor.

Table A-1. Argo and Kubernetes APIs

Executor	Docker	Kubelet	Kubernetes API	PNC
Pros	Supports all workflow examples. Most reliable, well tested, very scalable. Communicates with Docker daemon for heavy lifting.	Secure. Can't escape pod's service account privileges. Medium scalability. Log retrieval and container polling are done against Kubelet.	Secure. Can't escape privileges of pod's service account. No extra configuration.	Secure. Can't escape service account privileges. Artifact collection can be done from base image layer. Scalable: process polling is done over procfs, not kubelet/k8s API.
Cons	Least secure. Requires `docker.sock` of host to be mounted (often rejected by OPA).	Additional kubelet configuration may be required. Can only save params/artifacts in volumes (e.g., `empty Dir`), and not the base image layer (e.g., `/tmp`).	Least scalable. Log retrieval and container polling are done against k8s API server. Can only save params/artifacts in volumes (e.g., `empty Dir`), and not the base image layer (e.g., `/tmp`).	Processes no longer run with pid 1. Artifact collection may fail for containers completing too fast. Can't capture artifact directories from base image layer with volume mounted under it. Immature.
Argo Config	docker	kubelet	k8sapi	pns

Cloud-Specific Tools and Configuration

Cloud-specific tools can accelerate your development, but they can also cause vendor lock-in.

Google Cloud

Since Kubeflow originates from Google, it is no surprise that there are some extra features available when running on Google Cloud. We'll quickly point out how to use TPUs and Dataflow to accelerate your machine learning pipelines, and more Google-specific components are available in the Kubeflow GitHub repo (*https://oreil.ly/F7c9l*).

TPU-Accelerated Instances

Different parts of the machine learning process can benefit from not only different numbers of machines, but also different types of machines. The most common example is with model serving: often lots of low-memory machines can perform reasonably well, but for model training, high-memory or TPU accelerated machines can offer greater benefits. While there is a handy built-in shorthand for using GPUs, with TPUs you need to explicitly `import kfp.gcp as gcp`. Once you've imported kfp's gcp you can add TPU resources to any container operation in a similar way to GPUs by adding `.apply(gcp.use_tpu(tpu_cores=cores, tpu_resource=version, tf_version=tf_version))` to your container operation.

> TPU nodes are only available in certain regions. Check this Google Cloud page (*https://oreil.ly/1HAzM*) for a list of supported regions.

Dataflow for TFX

On Google Cloud you can configure Kubeflow's TFX components to use Google's Dataflow for distributed processing. To do this, you will need to specify a distributed output location (since there is not a shared persistent volume between the workers), and configure TFX to use the Dataflow runner. The simplest way to show this is by revisiting Example 5-8; to use Dataflow we would change it to Example B-1.

Example B-1. Changing the pipeline to use Dataflow

```
generated_output_uri = root_output_uri + kfp.dsl.EXECUTION_ID_PLACEHOLDER
beam_pipeline_args = [
    '--runner=DataflowRunner',
    '--project=' + project_id,
    '--temp_location=' + root_output_uri + '/tmp'),
    '--region=' + gcp_region,
    '--disk_size_gb=50', # Adjust as needed
]

records_example = tfx_csv_gen(
    input_uri=fetch.output, # Must be on distributed storage
    beam_pipeline_args=beam_pipeline_args,
    output_examples_uri=generated_output_uri)
```

As you can see, changing the pipeline to use Dataflow is relatively simple and opens up a larger scale of data for processing.

While cloud-specific accelerations can be beneficial, be careful that the trade-off is worth the additional future headache if you ever need to change providers.

Using Model Serving in Applications

In Chapter 8 you learned different approaches for exposing model servers provided by Kubeflow. As described there, Kubeflow provides several ways of deploying trained models and providing both REST and gRPC interfaces for running model inference. However, it falls short in providing support for using these models in custom applications. Here we will present some of the approaches to building applications by leveraging model servers exposed by Kubeflow.

When it comes to applications leveraging model inference, they can be broadly classified into two categories: real time and batch applications. In the real time/stream applications model, inference is done on data directly as it is produced or received. In this case, typically only one request is available at a time and it can be used for inferencing as it arrives. In the batch scenarios all of the data is available up front and can be used for inference either sequentially or in parallel. We will start from the streaming use case and then take a look at possible batch implementations.

Building Streaming Applications Leveraging Model Serving

The majority of today's streaming applications leverage Apache Kafka (*https:// kafka.apache.org*) as the data backbone of a system. The two possible options for implementing streaming applications themselves are: usage of stream processing engines and usage of stream processing libraries.

Stream Processing Engines and Libraries

As defined in the article "Defining the Execution Semantics of Stream Processing Engines,"[1] modern stream processing engines are based on organizing computations into blocks and leveraging cluster architectures.[2] Splitting computations in blocks enables execution parallelism, where different blocks run on different threads on the same machine, or on different machines. It also enables failover by moving execution blocks from failed machines to healthy ones. Additionally, checkpointing supported by modern engines further improves the reliability of cluster-based execution.

Stream processing libraries, on the other hand, are libraries with a domain-specific language providing a set of constructs that simplify building streaming applications. Such libraries typically do not support distribution and/or clustering—this is typically left as an exercise for developers.

Because these options sound similar, they are often used interchangeably. In reality, as Jay Kreps has outlined in his blog (*https://oreil.ly/hzK4d*), stream processing engines and stream processing libraries are two very different approaches to building streaming applications and choosing one of them is a trade-off between power and simplicity. As described previously, stream processing engines provide more functionality, but require a developer to adhere to their programming model and deployment. They also often require a steeper learning curve for mastering their functionality. Stream processing libraries, on another hand, are typically easier to use, providing more flexibility, but require specific implementation of deployment, scalability, and load balancing.

Today's most popular stream processing engines (*https://oreil.ly/h7bKa*) include the following:

- Apache Spark (*https://spark.apache.org*)
- Apache Flink (*https://flink.apache.org*)
- Apache Beam (*https://beam.apache.org*)

The most popular stream libraries are:

- Apache Kafka streams (*https://oreil.ly/phyB-*)
- Akka streams (*https://oreil.ly/-qlfT*)

---

1 L. Affetti et al., "Defining the Execution Semantics of Stream Processing Engines," *Journal of Big Data* 4 (2017), *https://oreil.ly/TcI39*.

2 Compare to MapReduce architecture.

All of these can be used as a platform for building streaming applications including model serving.[3]

A side-by-side comparison (*https://oreil.ly/LehcG*) of stream processing engines (Flink) and stream processing libraries (Kafka streams), done jointly by data Artisans (currently Vervetica) and Confluent teams, also emphasizes yet another difference between stream processing engines and libraries: enterprise ownership. Stream processing engines are typically owned and managed centrally by enterprise-wide units, while stream processing libraries are typically under the purview of individual development teams, which often makes their adoption much simpler. A stream processing engine is a good fit for applications that require features provided out of the box by such engines, including cluster scalability and high throughput through parallelism across a cluster, event-time semantics, checkpointing, built-in support for monitoring and management, and mixing of stream and batch processing. The drawback of using engines is that you are constrained by the programming and deployment models they provide.

In contrast, the stream processing libraries provide a programming model that allows developers to build the applications or microservices the way that fits their precise needs and deploy them as simple standalone Java applications. But in this case they need to roll out their own scalability, high availability, and monitoring solutions (Kafka-based implementations support some of them by leveraging Kafka).

Introducing Cloudflow

In reality, most of the streaming application implementations require usage of multiple engines and libraries for building individual applications, which creates additional integration and maintenance complexities. Many of these can be alleviated by using an open source project, like Cloudflow (*https://cloudflow.io*), which allows you to quickly develop, orchestrate, and operate distributed streaming applications on Kubernetes. Cloudflow supports building streaming applications as a set of small, composable components communicating over Kafka and wired together with schema-based contracts. This approach can significantly improve reuse and allows you to dramatically accelerate streaming application development. At the time of this writing, such components can be implemented using Akka Streams; Flink and Spark streaming with Kafka Streams support is coming soon. The overall architecture of Cloudflow is presented in Figure C-1.

---

3 For implementation details, see the report, *Serving Machine Learning Models* (*https://oreil.ly/UW1KP*), and Kai Waehner's project on GitHub (*https://oreil.ly/8vtK3*).

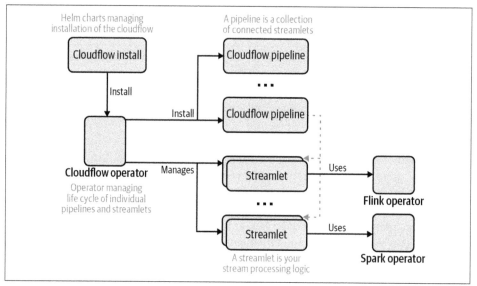

Figure C-1. Cloudflow architecture

In the heart of Cloudflow is a Cloudflow operator, which is responsible for deploying/ undeploying, management, and scaling of pipelines and individual streamlets. The operator also leverages existing Flink (*https://oreil.ly/pg2JL*) and Spark (*https://oreil.ly/ J2umN*) operators to manage Flink and Spark streamlets. A set of provided Helm charts allows for simple installation of the operator and supporting components.

A common challenge when building streaming applications is wiring all of the components together and testing them end-to-end before going into production. Cloudflow addresses this by allowing you to validate the connections between components and to run your application locally during development to avoid surprises during deployment.

Everything in Cloudflow is done in the context of an application, which represents a self-contained distributed system (graph) of data processing services connected together by data streams over Kafka.

Cloudflow supports:

Development

By generating a lot of boilerplate code, it allows developers to focus on business logic.

Build

It provides all the tooling for going from business logic to a deployable Docker image.

Deploy

It provides Kubernetes tooling to deploy your distributed application with a single command.

Operate

It provides all the tools you need to get insights, observability, and life cycle management for your distributed streaming application. Another important operational concern directly supported by Cloudflow is an ability to scale individual components of the stream.

When using Cloudflow for implementing streaming applications, model server invocation is typically implemented by a separate streamlet[4] based on a dynamically controlled stream (*https://oreil.ly/Wijie*) pattern.

In Figure C-2 an implementation contains a state, where a state is a URL to the model serving server, in the case when a model server is used for inference.[5] The actual data processing in this case is done by invoking a model server to get an inference result. This call can be done using either REST or gRPC (or any other interface supported by the model server).

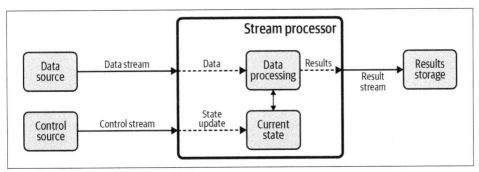

Figure C-2. Dynamically controlled stream pattern

This state can be updated through an additional Kafka topic, which allows for switching the URL (in the case when model server deployment is moved) without redeployment of the applications. The state is used by a data processor for processing incoming data.

Additional streamlets (with the same architecture) can be introduced into the application to get model serving insights, such as explanation and drift detection (see "Model Monitoring" on page 134 for more details).

---

4 Some of the examples of such implementations for TFServing integration can be found in this GitHub repo (*https://oreil.ly/7cJ4O*), and for Seldon integration, in this GitHub repo (*https://oreil.ly/6Sqff*).

5 In the case of embedded model usage, the state is a model itself.

Building Batch Applications Leveraging Model Serving

A typical batch application is implemented by reading a dataset containing all the samples and then processing them, invoking the model server for every one of them. The simplest batch application implementation is doing this sequentially, one data element at a time. Although such implementation will work, it is not very performant, due to the network overhead for processing every element.

One popular way to speed up processing is to use batching. TFServing, for example, supports two batching approaches (*https://oreil.ly/v7LFl*): server-side batching and client-side batching.

Server-side batching is supported out of the box by TFServing.[6] To enable batching, set --enable_batching and --batching_parameters_file flags. To achieve the best trade-offs between latency and throughput, pick appropriate batching parameters.[7] Some of the recommendations for the parameters values for both CPU and GPU usage can be found in this TFServing GitHub repo (*https://oreil.ly/TecPs*).

Upon reaching full batch on the server side, inference requests are merged internally into a single large request (tensor) and a Tensorflow Session is run on the merged request. You need to use asynchronous client requests to populate server-side batches. Running a batch of requests on a single session is where CPU/GPU parallelism can really be leveraged.

Client-side batching is just grouping multiple inputs together on the client to make a single request.

Although batching can significantly improve performance of the batch inference, it's often not sufficient for reaching performance goals. Another popular approach for performance improvement is multithreading.[8] The idea behind this approach is to deploy multiple instances of a model server, split data processing into multiple threads, and allow each thread to do inference for part of the data it is responsible for.

One of the ways to implement multithreading is through a batch implementation via streaming. This can be done by implementing software component[9] reading source data and writing each record to Kafka for processing. This approach effectively turns batch processing into a streaming one to allow for better scalability through an architecture as shown in Figure C-3.

---

6 See this TFServing document (*https://oreil.ly/iXsah*) for more details.

7 For the complete definitions of available parameters, see this TFServing GitHub repo (*https://oreil.ly/FoHx6*).

8 Compare to the MapReduce (*https://oreil.ly/OHV3Q*) programming model.

9 Streamlet, in the case of Cloudflow-based implementation.

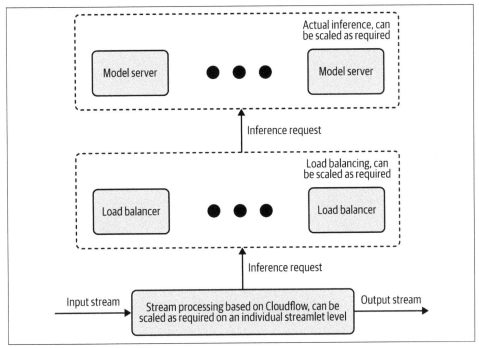

Figure C-3. Using stream processing for batch serving implementation

This deployment includes three layers:

- Cloudflow-based stream processing that invokes model serving for every element of the stream. Every streamlet of this solution can be scaled appropriately to provide required throughput.

- A model server that does the actual model inference. This layer can be independently scaled by changing the amount of model servers.

- Load balancers, for example Istio or Ambassador, that provide load balancing for inference REST/gRPC requests.

Because every layer in this architecture can scale independently, such an architecture can provide a model serving solution that is quite scalable for both streaming and batch use cases.

Index

About the Authors

Trevor Grant is a member of the Apache Software Foundation, and is heavily involved in the Apache Mahout, Apache Streams, and Community Development projects. He often tinkers and occasionally documents his (mis)adventures at *www.rawkintrevo.org*. In the before time, he was an international speaker on technology, but now he focuses mainly on writing. Trevor wishes to thank IBM for their continued patronage of his artistic endeavors. He lives in Chicago because it's the best city on the planet.

Holden Karau is a queer transgender Canadian, Apache Spark committer, Apache Software Foundation member, and an active open source contributor. She also extends her passion for building community with industry projects including Scaling for Python for ML (*http://scalingpythonml.com*) and teaching distributed computing to children (*https://www.distributedcomputing4kids.com*). As a software engineer, she's worked on a variety of distributed compute, search, and classification problems at Google, IBM, Alpine, Databricks, Foursquare, and Amazon. She graduated from the University of Waterloo with a bachelor of mathematics in computer science. Outside of software she enjoys playing with fire, welding, riding scooters, eating poutine, and dancing.

Boris Lublinsky is a principal architect at Lightbend. Boris has over 25 years' experience in enterprise, technical architecture, and software engineering. He is an active member of OASIS SOA RM committee, coauthor of *Applied SOA: Service-Oriented Architecture and Design Strategies* (Wiley), and author of numerous articles on architecture, programming, big data, SOA, and BPM.

Richard Liu is a senior software engineer at Waymo, where he focuses on building a machine learning platform for self-driving cars. Previously he has worked at Microsoft Azure and Google Cloud. He is one of the primary maintainers of the Kubeflow project and has given several talks at KubeCon. He holds a master's degree in computer science from the University of California, San Diego.

Ilan Filonenko is a member of the Data Science Infrastructure team at Bloomberg, where he has designed and implemented distributed systems at both the application and infrastructure level. Previously, Ilan was an engineering consultant and technical lead in various startups and research divisions across multiple industry verticals, including medicine, hospitality, finance, and music. He actively contributes to open source, primarily Apache Spark and Kubeflow's KFServing. He is one of the principal contributors to Spark on Kubernetes—primarily focusing on remote shuffle and HDFS security, and to multi-model serving in KFServing. Ilan's research has been in algorithmic, software, and hardware techniques for high-performance machine learning with a focus on optimizing stochastic algorithms and model management.

Colophon

The animal on the cover of *Kubeflow for Machine Learning* is the Cape Barren goose (*Cereopsis novaehollandiae*). This unusual goose (it is the only member of the genus *Cereopsis*) is found in the southern coastal areas of Australia.

Cape Barren geese are light grey with some darker dappling, and have stocky pink legs and lightly webbed black feet. The small head and large yellow cere, combined with a short black, slightly downturned bill, distinguishes their appearance from other geese. Adults average 35 inches long with a 70-inch wingspan, and weigh about 10 pounds.

These geese feed primarily on grasses and other vegetation. Though this bird does not often swim, it does have the ability to drink salt and brackish water, allowing it to inhabit coastal areas and the many islands off southern Australia.

Cape Barren geese form lifelong pair bonds, and make down-lined nests in the grass. They raise three to six chicks per clutch, and like all geese, they aggressively defend their nest and young against intruders. When chicks hatch, they have black-and-white fuzz, and acquire their grey feathers as they get bigger.

Though Cape Barren geese nearly went extinct in the mid-twentieth century, now that they have protected status, their numbers have recovered. Many of the animals on O'Reilly covers are endangered; all of them are important to the world.

The cover illustration is by Karen Montgomery, based on a black and white engraving from *Meyers Kleines Lexicon* (1908). The cover fonts are Gilroy Semibold and Guardian Sans. The text font is Adobe Minion Pro; the heading font is Adobe Myriad Condensed; and the code font is Dalton Maag's Ubuntu Mono.

O'REILLY®

There's much more where this came from.

Experience books, videos, live online training courses, and more from O'Reilly and our 200+ partners—all in one place.

Learn more at oreilly.com/online-learning

Milton Keynes UK
Ingram Content Group UK Ltd.
UKHW050358030824
446490UK00006B/260